JOURNAL·OF MORAL THEOLOGY

VOLUME 11, SPECIAL ISSUE NUMBER 2
OCTOBER 2022

VOCATION, FRIENDSHIP,
AND THE
CATHOLIC MORAL TRADITION: FURTHER
EXPLORATIONS FROM *NEW WINE, NEW WINESKINS*

EDITED BY
ALESSANDRO ROVATI
AND
MATTHEW PHILIPP WHELAN

JOURNAL · OF MORAL THEOLOGY

Journal of Moral Theology is published semiannually, with regular issues in January and July. Our mission is to publish scholarly articles in the field of Catholic moral theology, as well as theological treatments of related topics in philosophy, economics, political philosophy, and psychology.

Articles published in the *Journal of Moral Theology* undergo at least two double blind peer reviews. To submit an article for the journal, please visit the "For Authors" page on our website at jmt.scholasticahq.com/for-authors.

Journal of Moral Theology is available full text in the *ATLA Religion Database with ATLASerials®* (RDB®), a product of the American Theological Library Association.

Email: atla@atla.com, www.atla.com.
ISSN 2166-2851 (print)
ISSN 2166-2118 (online)

Journal of Moral Theology is published by The Journal of Moral Theology, Inc.

Copyright © 2022 individual authors and The Journal of Moral Theology, Inc. All rights reserved

Pickwick Publications, An Imprint of Wipf and Stock Publishers, 199 W. 8th Ave., Suite 3, Eugene, OR 97401
www.wipfandstock.com. ISBN: 978-1-6667-6385-0

JOURNAL·OF
M·O·R·A·L
THEOLOGY

EDITOR EMERITUS
Jason King, *Saint Vincent College*

EDITOR
M. Therese Lysaught, *Loyola University Chicago Stritch School of Medicine*

SENIOR EDITOR
William J. Collinge, *Mount St. Mary's University*

ASSOCIATE EDITORS
Jean-Pierre Fortin, *St. Michael's College, University of Toronto*
Mari Rapela Heidt, *Notre Dame of Maryland University*
Alexandre A. Martins, *Marquette University*
Christopher McMahon, *Saint Vincent College*
Kate Ward, *Marquette University*

MANAGING EDITOR
Mary Doyle Roche, *College of the Holy Cross*

EDITORIAL ASSISANT
Aaron Weisel, *Ave Maria University*

EDITORIAL BOARD
Christine Astorga, *University of Portland*
Jana M. Bennett, *University of Dayton*
Mara Brecht, *St. Norbert College*
Jim Caccamo, *St. Joseph's University*
Carolyn A. Chau, *King's University College at Western University, Ontario Canada*
Meghan Clark, *St. John's University*
David Cloutier, *The Catholic University of America*
Christopher Denny, *St. John's University*
Julia Fleming, *Creighton University*
Joseph Flipper, *University of Dayton*
Nichole M. Flores, *University of Virginia*
Craig Ford, *St. Norbert College*
Matthew J. Gaudet, *Santa Clara University*
Natalia Imperatori-Lee, *Manhattan College*
Kelly Johnson, *University of Dayton*
Andrew Kim, *Marquette University*
Warren Kinghorn, *Duke University*
Leocadie Lushombo, *Santa Clara University*
Ramon Luzarraga, *St. Martin's University, Lacey, Washington*
William C. Mattison III, *University of Notre Dame*
Christian McRorie, *Creighton University*
Cory D. Mitchell, *Trinity Health Muskegon*
Suzzane Mulligan, *Catholic Theological Ethics in the World Church Liaison, St. Patrick's Pontifical University, Maynooth, Ireland*
Anna Perkins, *University of the West Indies*
Matthew Shadle, *Marymount University*
Joel Shuman, *Kings College*
Christopher P. Vogt, *St. John's College*
Paul Wadell, *St. Norbert College*

Journal of Moral Theology
Volume 11, Special Issue Number 2
July 2022

Contents

Introduction: Vocation, Friendship, and the Catholic Moral Tradition
  Alessandro Rovati and Matthew Philipp Whelan 1

"A Shadowy Sort of Right": The *Ius Necessitatis* and Catholic Moral Theology
  Matthew Philipp Whelan 7

Nurturing Masculinities: Constructing New Narratives of Fatherhood
  Jacob Kohlhaas 33

Theologies of Labor and the Limits of Capital
  Nicholas Norman-Krause 58

Sensus Fideli—Whom? Retrieving Insights from Johann Adam Möhler
  Gina Maria Noia 78

Virtue as Birth Control: An Examination of the Account of Rational Participation as a Component of Natural Law in *Humanae Vitae* and the Documents of the Papal Commission
  Arielle Harms 106

Catholic Social Teaching, Liberalism, and Economic Justice
  Jason A. Heron and Bharat Ranganathan 126

A Good Moral Teacher Must Be a Good Pre-Moral Teacher: On the Pedagogical Limits of US Constitutional Law
  Jason Menno 147

The Healing Power of the Body of Christ: An Ecclesial and Neurological Argument for Social Connection Despite Social Distancing
  Christopher Krall, SJ 180

Looking for Good Work: From Matthew Crawford to Pope Francis via Wittgenstein
  Mark R. Ryan 203

Introduction: Vocation, Friendship, and the Catholic Moral Tradition

Alessandro Rovati and Matthew Philipp Whelan

THIS SPECIAL ISSUE OF THE *Journal of Moral Theology* (*JMT*) collects essays by current or recent members of New Wine New Wineskins (NWNW), an association for early-career Catholic moral theologians.[1] Many *JMT* readers will be familiar with NWNW because this is the second issue dedicated to the work of the association.[2] Furthermore, many former members of the association regularly write on these pages and are part of the journal editorial staff.

NWNW started in 2002 to give moral theologians at the beginning stages of their careers a place to "engage in scholarly activities relevant to the field of moral theology and devote particular attention to the vocational meaning of being a moral theologian in today's Church and academy."[3] Since then, the group has regularly met for a yearly symposium at the University of Notre Dame's Moreau Seminary for a mix of dialogue with established moral theologians, presentations of the members' research, as well as fellowship and common worship.

NWNW is not a unified school of thought.[4] Its current and past members come from various backgrounds, are formed in diverse graduate programs, and have differing ecclesial and theological sensibilities. In fact, from the beginning, the group intentionally strived to establish an environment where diversity of perspective would be cherished, not just tolerated. The cultivation of friendship has been crucial to that endeavor.

There are three main reasons NWNW has striven to establish such

---

[1] Details about the association and its work can be found on its website www.newwinenewwineskins.com/.
[2] *Journal of Moral Theology* 6, no. 1 (2017). NWNW's members have published two other collections of essays: William C. Mattison III, ed., *New Wine, New Wineskins: A Next Generation Reflects on Key Issues in Catholic Moral Theology* (Lanham, MD: Rowman and Littlefield, 2005); David Cloutier, ed., *Leaving and Coming Home: New Wineskins for Catholic Sexual Ethics* (Eugene, OR: Cascade, 2010).
[3] David Cloutier and William C. Mattison III, "Introduction," in *New Wine, New Wineskins*, 12.
[4] Charles Curran reflects on what makes NWNW an identifiable voice in current theological debates in his *Diverse Voices in Modern US Moral Theology* (Washington, DC: Georgetown University Press, 2019), 210–219.

an environment. First, NWNW takes to heart St. Paul's insistence that the Holy Spirit endows people with a diversity of gifts and charisms for the sake of edifying the church (1 Corinthians 12). What is true for the ecclesial community is also true for the moral theological community—or indeed, any community. The other, in her diversity, is always a gift to be welcomed, a companion God gave to enter more deeply into the truth. Second, contestation, debate, and questioning are all part of a healthy living tradition. Consequently, creating intellectual spaces where disagreements may be articulated and discussed constructively is essential.[5] NWNW hopes to be just that: an association where conversations across differences are cultivated, not shut down. Third, in light of the previous two reasons, the polarization that so often determines our society, the church, and even the academy must be resisted. Polarization is like an acid upon genuine theological exploration.[6] Besides leading people to lose sight of the complexity of moral issues, it ends up "othering" those with a different perspective, including those within the same ecclesial body.[7] NWNW, instead, seeks authentic encounters among scholars with differing views.

While it is hard to describe NWNW as a school of thought,[8] the association's work has fostered a distinctive *ethos* among its members. Such *ethos* is constituted by three fundamental commitments.

First, doing moral theology is above all a vocation. NWNW members understand the work of moral theology as an expression of their faith. They think of their scholarship as profoundly connected to both their personal moral formation and call to discipleship. Furthermore, by comprehending the work of moral theology as a vocation, members emphasize the ecclesial location of theology, in

---

[5] For one of the, by now, canonical presentations of such a claim, see Alasdair MacIntyre, *Three Rival Versions of Moral Enquiry: Encyclopedia, Genealogy, and Tradition* (Notre Dame, IN: University of Notre Dame Press, 1990).
[6] For a description of how polarization hurts theological reflection, see David Cloutier, "The Trajectories of Catholic Sexual Ethics," in *Leaving and Coming Home*, 7–10.
[7] For a theoretical and practical description of the phenomenon of polarization among US Catholics, see Mary Ellen Konieczny, Charles C. Camosy, and Tricia C. Bruce, eds., *Polarization in the US Catholic Church: Naming the Wounds, Beginning to Heal* (Collegeville, MN: Liturgical Press, 2015).
[8] Eclecticism in theological methodologies and visions is a foundational feature of NWNW. Still, it is possible to outline some consistent characteristics that mark how NWNW members approach moral theology. Looking back at the four NWNW collections of essays, one notices the following common traits: an emphasis on virtue, character, and moral formation; a focus on practices; an interest in discussing moral norms and exceptions only by inserting them into their broader context; an attempt to find common ground among differing perspectives; and a commitment to cultivating and enriching Christian identity amidst a changing society. On these shared features, see Cloutier and Mattison III, "Introduction," 11–12, and David Cloutier, "The Trajectories of Catholic Sexual Ethics," 10–22.

which scholarship is always ultimately a service to the church and its people. It is no mistake that so many NWNW members couple their individual research and work in the academy with a thick involvement in the life of their local church, be it by teaching seminarians, permanent deacons, and the laity, collaborating with their dioceses, or volunteering in their parishes. Finally, the group has always included space for common prayer and the celebration of the Mass in its gatherings to emphasize that the life of faith must feed theological work and theological work must, in turn, nourish a person's faith journey.

Second, Aristotle famously said in the *Nicomachean Ethics* that friends are integral to the good life, and we believe the same is true of the life of the moral theologian as well. Over the years, NWNW has created an extensive network of friendships that have provided support to its many members and given them occasions for creative projects, theological explorations, and other common undertakings. The annual symposium is characterized by many occasions for informal conversations, a casual ambiance, and uncountable heartfelt exchanges (often accompanied by good drinks and late nights together). Such a context has allowed three generations of moral theologians to enter into intimate relationships that last beyond official membership in the association.[9] It is this climate of friendship that has allowed NWNW to resist polarization, giving space to the bonds of charity that come from common belonging to the church over and above any possible disagreement. The same friendship has allowed constructive dialogues across differences and provided many an opportunity to expand their horizons and add depth and complexity to their theological vision. Finally, the sense of belonging to one another that characterizes NWNW has allowed the association to be especially attentive to and inclusive of those whose academic location makes particularly vulnerable to being excluded from the conversation. NWNW always invites and financially supports contingent faculty, faculty in smaller colleges with little or no institutional support for scholarship, and graduates of PhD programs that do not have the R1 universities' prestige and network.[10]

Third, NWNW members share a profound commitment to the

---

[9] According to NWNW's bylaws, membership concludes either upon reception of tenure or seven years after the completion of a PhD.

[10] On the topic of contingent faculty and university ethics, see *Journal of Moral Theology* 8, Special Issue no. 1 (2019). For an account of the academy's shifting working conditions away from full-time tenure-track opportunities to more precarious forms of employment and the relative pressures they create on NWNW members, see Conor Hill, Kent J. Lasnoski, Matthew Sherman, John Sikorski, and Matthew Whelan, "Is New Wine, New Wineskins Still New? Reflecting on Wineskins after Seventeen Years," *Journal of Moral Theology* 6, no. 1 (2017): 5–9.

Catholic moral tradition and to helping one another find within it lesser-known resources or unexplored paths. Furthermore, they put such a foundational knowledge at the service of today's questions and pressing issues. Finally, they are unafraid to ask questions about and probe the reasons for what the church teaches, knowing that to engage in such work is the way not only to better understand Christian commitments but to live them out more fully as a witness to the world. The result of the NWNW *ethos* is a way of practicing moral theology together with others that seeks to build bridges across theological, ecclesial, and political divides, that draws upon the church's sources creatively to reflect on previously unanswered questions, and that looks for ways to embody the Christian call to holiness today.

The essays contained in this special issue offer a window into the work of early career Catholic moral theologians, embodying the style and sensibility that has characterized the work of NWNW for over two decades now. Several essays in this volume seek to recover parts of the Catholic moral-theological tradition that have been neglected. In "A Shadowy Sort of Right," Matthew Philipp Whelan examines several recent court cases that have appealed to the legal doctrine of necessity in order to reveal how their reasoning is rooted in a much older tradition of moral-theological reflection about the *ius necessitatis* (law of necessity). At the same time, Whelan argues that this tradition, while neglected, has been preserved within Catholic social teaching (CST), and he tries to highlight some of the challenges it poses within a world that not only dismisses but also denies claims of need. Jacob Kohlhaas similarly examines neglected possibilities regarding how CST has envisioned masculinity and fatherhood. His contribution, "Nurturing Masculinities," draws on social scientific research in the field of fatherhood studies to probe different narratives surrounding masculinity and fatherhood, both within CST, as well as within contemporary US society more generally. Kohlhaas attends to diverse expressions of paternal care in order to argue that the realization of authentic personhood and relational potential requires more expansive understandings of male capabilities in caregiving and family life than CST currently envisions.

Other contributions to this volume seek a deeper understanding of what the church teaches on a given topic, as well as to push for greater clarity or development of that teaching. In "Theologies of Labor and the Limits of Capital," Nicholas Norman-Krause turns to CST's conception of work in light of late-capitalist material conditions. In doing so, Norman-Krause uncovers within CST—especially within its US reception—a tension between normative theologies and material realities. Norman-Krause re-reads John Paul II's *Laborem Exercens* in dialogue with the liberationist Gustavo Gutiérrez in order to imagine the underlying material conditions necessary for the encyclical's vision of dignified labor to become a reality. Gina Maria Noia's contribution, "*Sensus Fideli-whom?*," turns to Tübingen scholar Johann Adam Möhler to examine the controverted concept of the *sensus fidei* (sense of the faith) within post-Vatican II theological reflection. Although Möhler himself does not use the term *sensus fidei*, Noia demonstrates how his thought can help us find a way beyond current controversies and unclarities. Finally, the point of departure for Arielle Harms's contribution, "Virtue as Birth Control," is the intra-ecclesial conflict surrounding Pope Paul VI's controversial encyclical *Humanae Vitae* (1968). Harms examines how the competing camps in this conflict assumed and operationalized distinct conceptions of natural law, and she is particularly interested in illuminating the kind of natural law thought embodied in *Humanae Vitae* itself.

The final group of contributions place Catholic moral theology in dialogue with—or seek to clarify its relationship to—non-theological sources. In "Catholic Social Teaching, Liberalism, and Economic Justice," Jason A. Heron and Bharat Ranganathan try to build bridges between Catholic social thought and liberalism, suggesting these two traditions have more to learn from one another than is typically thought. Heron and Ranganathan are especially interested in how the concept of subsidiarity, a key tenet of CST, can benefit from and be deepened by engagement with Rawlsian liberalism. A unique feature of their contribution is that they are two scholars and friends who write together across confessional, moral, and political commitments, embodying the ethos of NWNW. Justin Menno's "A Good Moral Teacher Must Be a Good Pre-Moral Teacher" homes in upon the thought of Cathleen Kaveny, especially her treatment of the virtue of solidarity. Menno is keen to show that, *contra* Kaveny, the underlying contractarian and anthropological assumptions of US constitutional law make it a particularly inhospitable soil for the cultivation of this virtue. Menno also suggests some possible alternative paths forward, which can be found in the work of Carter Snead and Helen Alvaré. In the "Healing Power of the Body of Christ," an article framed against the backdrop of the pandemic, Chris Krall argues that Covid-19 wreaked havoc, not only through the contagion of the virus itself, but also in terms of how it exacerbated pre-existing trends of social disengagement and isolation in the United States. Krall looks to the thought of Yves Congar as a source and guide for reimagining communal life, ecclesial and otherwise, and for offering practical remedies to address and heal social division. Finally, like Krause's contribution, Mark R. Ryan's essay, "Looking for Good Work," examines work from a moral-theological vantage. Ryan relies both on the narrative account—in *Shop Class as Soulcraft*—of Matthew Crawford's experience as an employee, as well as Wittgenstinian "therapy," to help bridge the chasm between Catholic teaching on work and the deformed and deforming reality of work within the contemporary world. Ryan is especially interested in how a ubiquitous technocratic paradigm, along with the confusions about work that arise from it, undermines the skilled, tacit knowledge required for good and dignified work, based upon responsive engagement with creatures and creaturely realities independent of the worker's will. M

Matthew Philipp Whelan, former Board Member of New Wine New Wineskins, is Assistant Professor of Moral Theology at Baylor University in Waco, Texas, where his research centers on Catholic social thought, Latin American and liberation theologies, and ecological theology and ethics. He holds degrees in theology from Duke University (PhD, MTS) and in agriculture from the Centro Agronómico Tropical de Investigación y Enseñanza in Turrialba, Costa Rica.

Dr. Alessandro Rovati is Department Chair and Assistant Professor of Theology at Belmont Abbey College. A graduate of the Università Cattolica in Milan, Italy, Dr. Rovati focuses on Moral Theology, Catholic Social Teaching, and Christian Ethics. He has published his work in peer-reviewed journals and online publications, and is a Board Member of New Wine New Wineskins, an association of early-career Catholic moral theologians.

"A Shadowy Sort of Right":
The *Ius Necessitatis* and Catholic Moral Theology

Matthew Philipp Whelan

For Brian and Elaine

IN 2016, A RULING OF ITALY'S highest court made international news by throwing out the conviction of Roman Ostriakov, a homeless man from Ukraine.¹ Ostriakov's crime was attempting to take approximately five dollars' worth of cheese and sausage from a store in Genoa without paying for it. The court provided the following rationale for its ruling: "The condition of the defendant and the circumstances in which the merchandise theft took place prove that he took possession of that small amount of food in the face of the immediate and essential need for nourishment, acting therefore in a state of need." Therefore the theft, the court concludes, "does not constitute a crime."² According to Massimo Gramellini's explanation of the ruling in an op-ed in *La Stampa*, the court effectively ruled that "the right to survival prevails over that of property"—a view which,

---

¹ "Italian Court Rules Food Theft 'Not a Crime' If Hungry," *BBC*, May 3, 2016, www.bbc.com/news/world-europe-36190557; Nick Squires, "Stealing Food If You Are Poor and Hungry Is Not a Crime, Italy's Highest Court Rules," *The Telegraph*, May 3, 2016, www.telegraph.co.uk/news/2016/05/03/stealing-food-if-you-are-poor-and-hungry-is-not-a-crime-italys-h/; Cristiana Moisescu, "Stealing Food out of Necessity 'Not a Crime,' Italian Court Rules," *CNN*, May 3, 2016, www.cnn.com/2016/05/03/europe/food-theft-italy. Thanks to William Whelan for first alerting me to the Ostriakov case.
² Quoted in Gaia Pianigiani and Sewell Chan, "Can the Homeless and Hungry Steal Food? Maybe, an Italian Court Says," *New York Times*, 3 May 2016, www.nytimes.com/2016/05/04/world/europe/food-theft-in-italy-may-not-be-a-crime-court-rules.html. See Benjamin Soloway, "Stealing Food if You're in Need is Not a Crime, Italian Court Finds," *The Chicago Tribune*, 3 May 2016, www.chicagotribune.com/news/ct-stealing-food-not-a-crime-20160503-story.html; Mary Elizabeth Williams, "Hunger Shouldn't Be a Crime: This is What a Humane Response to Food Insecurity Looks Like," *Salon*, May 4, 2016, www.salon.com/2016/05/04/hunger_shouldnt_be_a_crime_this_is_what_a_humane_response_to_food_insecurity_looks_like/.

he added, in the US would be akin to "blasphemy."[3]

The Ostriakov case is not the only one in which need has been invoked in such a manner. Ostriakov took cheese and sausage. But in recent judgments of the Constitutional Court of Colombia, the defendants' need of land has led to judicial protection of it as a source of livelihood for the community of Las Pavas, whose members occupied unused land beginning in 1997 in order to cultivate it to feed themselves. As a result of their occupation, the community has been repeatedly intimidated and harassed, including by paramilitary groups, and their crops have been destroyed. Two private palm-oil companies claiming ownership of the land sought to evict them forcibly in 2009, relying on the National Police and the mobile riot police squad to do so. Two years later, the Constitutional Court found these actions illegal because they failed to take into account the community's claim on the land—a claim based upon need. The court then ordered the Colombian government to reopen the process begun in 2006 to have that claim acknowledged legally, declaring that the community cannot be evicted until this process has been finalized. Upon returning, one of the community leaders, Misael Payares, said: "We are very happy, because without land we are nothing. It's not just about working on the land; we want to restore our territory, environment, and culture. This is what we are fighting for."[4]

Drawing on cases like those of Ostriakov and Las Pavas, legal scholars Eduardo Peñalver and Sonia Katyal have recently argued not only for recognizing such acquisitive actions as just, but also for broadening the legal doctrine of necessity—a doctrine which permits nonowners to trespass upon and in some cases appropriate the property of others in order to avoid grave harm—beyond the bare minimum to stave off starvation or exposure. In its traditional formulation, this doctrine justifies situations in which someone takes what she needs from another's surplus. In our own day, many of the activities engaged in by the homeless—activities like public camping, sleeping on a blanket or in a vehicle, loitering, and begging, all of which are increasingly criminalized by local governments throughout the US—would also cohere with this broader understanding of necessity.[5]

---

[3] Massimo Gramellini, "Il diritto di avere fame," *La Stampa*, 3 mayo 2016, www.lastampa.it/opinioni/buongiorno/2016/05/03/news/il-diritto-di-avere-fame-1.34996997/.

[4] www.abcolombia.org.uk/constitutional-court-opens-way-restitution-rights-las-pavas-community/. See also Hilal Elver, Report of the Special Rapporteur on the Right to Food, *Access to Justice and the Right to Food: The Way Forward*, submitted to the Twenty-Eighth Session of the Human Rights Council, January 12, 2014, no. 19.

[5] Eduardo Peñalver and Sonia Katyal, *Property Outlaws: How Squatters, Pirates, and Protesters Improve the Law of Property* (New Haven: Yale University Press, 2010), 135–138, 152–156. See also Matt Ford, "Homelessness is Not a Crime," *The New Republic*, May 10, 2019, newrepublic.com/article/153875/homelessness-not-crime.

However, as the case of the homeless makes especially apparent, the doctrine of necessity recognized in US law is so constrained by qualifications and exceptions that it has become functionally inoperative in cases of dire economic necessity. Consequently, while US courts do recognize the necessity defense, they tend to interpret it narrowly, restricting its application to exceptional circumstances such as natural disasters, with several courts categorically rejecting its applicability to cases like those of Ostriakov or Las Pavas, in which defendants act out of economic need. But why, Peñalver and Katyal ask, should cases of economic disaster be treated as different from cases of natural disaster?[6]

What interests me about the Ostriakov and Las Pavas cases is not just the contrast with the US criminal justice system's response to similar cases, but the rationale the Italian and Colombian courts invoked in their rulings—the application of the so-called *ius necessitatis* or law of necessity defense to cases of extreme need. In what follows, my purpose is to show how this rationale draws upon a much older—and admittedly neglected—tradition of moral-theological reflection about need, law, property, and theft, one that is preserved in Catholic social teaching. While it is commonplace, especially in our day, to encounter arguments that Christianity underwrites private property rights and "free" markets,[7] this older tradition understands such defenses as based upon a fundamental misunderstanding of what property is and what it is for, which is to meet the needs of all people, because creation is a common gift from God. On this basis, claims of need take precedence over claims of private property. Rather than threaten property, cases like the above safeguard it by reminding Christians that there is nothing we possess that we did not receive (1 Corinthians 4:7).

The Ostriakov and Las Pavas cases have been hailed as a victory for justice and lauded as a humane response to hunger and need. They have also been derided as a license to thieve, and a threat to property and law. Missing in much of the discussion of these cases and others like these is any recognition of the rulings' relationship to this older tradition of reflection on the *ius necessitatis* within Catholic moral theology and the theological moorings of that law.[8] This essay is therefore an attempt to provide for this lack. Its aim is to resuscitate the *ius necessitatis* by rearticulating its theological rationale, as well

---

[6] Peñalver and Katyal, *Property Outlaws*.
[7] See, for instance, www.acton.org, www.libertarianism.org, and www.tifwe.org.
[8] For an exception in this regard, see Frank Weathers, "Italian Supreme Court Knows When Stealing Food Is Lawful," *Patheos*, May 3, 2016, www.patheos.com/blogs/yimcatholic/2016/05/breaking-italian-supreme-court-knows-when-stealing-food-is-lawful.html.

as to show how it is preserved in Catholic social teaching, especially in relation to what *Gaudium et Spes* calls the common or universal destination of created goods.

What follows consists of three main parts. The first provides a sketch of this tradition of moral-theological reflection as it emerged within early Church and medieval thought, while the second examines its preservation in Catholic social teaching. The third and final part suggests what taking this moral-theological tradition seriously would involve in our own day, when the claim of need not only continues to be minimized and dismissed but is also increasingly criminalized.

IUS NECESSITATIS

The charge of thievery in the cases mentioned above seems straightforward, even commonsensical. A shop owner has items that Ostriakov needs but is unable to purchase, so Ostriakov attempts to take them in secret. The people of Las Pavas begin to settle upon and then cultivate land for which they have no legal title. Many countries, including the US, view these and similar actions as unjustified and respond by punishing what they deem to be transgressions.

As mentioned above, the Italian and Colombian courts did not hold such views. Instead, they invoked an older strand of moral-theological reflection according to which the charge of thievery is more complicated—for at least two reasons. The first is because this older strand privileges the claim of need above all other claims upon created goods. The use of created goods to meet the needs of all takes priority over the private appropriation of those same goods. In Gramellini's words, the right to survival prevails over that of property. What is more, the whole rationale of private appropriation, at least as this tradition understands it, is meant to ensure that the needs of all are met, including the needs of those who privately appropriate goods. Being part of the "all" legitimizes possession. At the same time, as we shall see, that possession is fundamentally shaped by an orientation to the "all." In this view, to return to Gramellini's formulation, the right to survival and the right to property are not mutually exclusive rights. The very articulation of the right to property—at its most fundamental level—aims at ensuring the survival of the many and must therefore bend to that reality.

The second reason the charge of thievery is more complicated relates to the fact that this older strand of moral-theological reflection recognizes two distinct forms of thievery: the unjust taking of created goods (the kind of taking normally criminalized), as well as the unjust retention of created goods. In other words, it is not just those who take sausage and cheese from stores or those who occupy and cultivate land to which they have no legal title who are potentially guilty of theft. For this tradition, those like the owners of shops or landholders who possess the world's goods but fail to share them with the needy are also potentially guilty of theft. Basil the Great memorably articulates this view:

> Who are the robbers? Those who take for themselves what rightfully belongs to everyone. ... Is not the person who strips another of clothing called a thief? And those who do not clothe the naked when they have the power to do so, should they not be called the same? The bread you are holding back is for the hungry, the clothes you keep put away are for the naked, the shoes that are rotting away with disuse are for those who have none, the silver you keep buried in the earth is for the needy. [9]

Informing Basil's understanding of robbery is the theological claim that creation is a gift given by God "for the benefit of all in common." The problem with the rich fool in the Lukan parable (which Basil is commenting in his homily)—whose land produces so abundantly that he decides to tear down his barns and build bigger ones (see Luke 12:16–21)—is not that he possessed land, nor that his land produced a banner harvest. Rather, it is that he failed to acknowledge the commonality of the gift he had been given, a failure that can best be seen in the exclusivity of his possession. "From God comes everything beneficial: fertile soil, temperate weather, plenty of seeds, cooperation of the animals, and whatever else is required for successful cultivation," Basil explains. "But human beings [like the rich fool] respond with bitter disposition, misanthropy, and an unwillingness to share." [10] John Chrysostom therefore gets to the heart of the matter in one of his homilies on Luke 16 (on Dives and Lazarus) when he says, "This is also robbery: not to share one's possessions." [11]

Courts of law might never be able to adjudicate the unjust retention of which Basil and Chrysostom speak. The rich fools of the world might continue to regard their land and its harvests for the benefit of themselves alone, and the Lazaruses might continue to sit and die outside the gates of the rich. But according to this tradition of moral-theological reflection, there is a higher court of law to which human beings are ultimately accountable. "We must obey God rather than any human authority" (Acts 5:29), and obedience to God entails acknowledgement that creation is a common gift.

We can begin to get a handle on this tradition of moral-theological reflection by turning to the emergence of the *ius necessitatis* in the

---

[9] Basil the Great, "I Will Tear Down My Barns," in *On Social Justice*, trans. C. Paul Schroeder (Crestwood, NY: St Vladimir's Seminary Press, 2009), 69–70.
[10] Basil the Great, "I Will Tear Down My Barns," 69, 60.
[11] John Chrysostom, "Second Sermon on Lazarus and the Rich Man," in *On Wealth and Poverty*, trans. Catherine P. Roth (Crestwood, NY: St Vladimir's Seminary Press, 1981), 49.

discussions of medieval canonists and theologians around the twelfth century. For them, the *ius necessitatis* is that law according to which those in extreme need can legitimately take the surplus goods of others to sustain themselves or their dependents—the kind of desperate act famously depicted in Victor Hugo's *Les Misérables*, in which an unemployed Jean Valjean takes a loaf of bread to feed himself, his sister, and her seven children. [12] While *ius necessitatis* explicitly emerges for the first time during these discussions, it is important to observe that this law—or something like it—is implied in the views of Basil and Chrysostom I have just sketched. For instance, Basil is concerned with those who unjustly retain more food, clothing, shoes, and money than they need, labeling them thieves. If, as he says, the goods retained *belong* to those in need, how should we regard the taking of what belongs to them? That is the question of the *ius necessitatis*, raised by the grammar of this moral-theological tradition.

Explicit articulation of the *ius necessitatis* emerged in discussions by medieval canonists and theologians as they considered the issue of property and its relation to natural law. Many of the early Christian sources Gratian gathers for inclusion within the *Decretum*—the great collection of canon law—seem to critique the abuses of the wealthy and the exploitation of the poor, along with the very idea of private property. Consider the following statements, which Gratian attributes respectively to Clement of Rome and Ambrose of Milan, that by natural law: "The use of all things ought to be common to all" and "no one may call his own what is common." [13]

Statements like these seem to provide *prima facie* evidence of the illegitimacy of private property in light of the gift of creation, which God has given for common use. Given the clear imperative of common use, how can anyone claim created goods as their own? At the same time, how do we understand the fact that scripture seems to condone some form of private possession? To return to the examples above, the problem with the rich fool and Dives seems not to be *that* they have possessions. The men are not condemned for possessing created goods but for refusing to share them. Along these same lines, in Gratian's day, both canon law and civil law recognized the legitimacy of private property. [14] These were questions that required resolution.

Setting the problem of the legitimacy of private property aside for a moment, another and closely related difficulty has to do with the

---

[12] Nina Martyris, "Let Them Eat Bread: The Theft that Helped Inspire *Les Misérables*," *NPR*, March 20, 2017, www.npr.org/sections/thesalt/2017/03/20/520459332/let-them-eat-bread-the-theft-that-helped-inspire-les-miserables.

[13] Quoted in Brian Tierney, *The Idea of Natural Rights* (Grand Rapids, MI: Eerdmans, 1997), 71–72.

[14] Tierney, *The Idea of Natural Rights*, 60–61.

multiple senses of the term "natural law" as employed by Gratian throughout the *Decretum*. For instance, does natural law refer to an original condition that was once valid but subsequently passed away and now no longer obtains? Or is it an intrinsic and enduring feature of God's gift of creation for humankind's use? For this reason, it soon became commonplace for Decretists and others to distinguish between multiple senses of natural law. [15]

Various solutions were proposed to the problem of property. For our purposes, the twelfth century canonist Huguccio provided an especially important solution that helped resolve the apparent tension between private property and the claim that creation is a gift God gives to humankind in common. As Brian Tierney observes, prior to Huguccio, the usual response to the problem of property was that common property was an original condition no longer valid after the introduction of human and divine positive law. [16] Despite this, the claims of Basil and Chrysostom, as well as those Gratian attributes in the *Decretum* to Clement of Alexandria and Ambrose of Milan, still persisted and provoked. These voices suggest that common property was not obsolete but an enduring feature of the gift of creation. Huguccio's response to this conundrum is to argue that: "[b]y natural *ius*, that is in accordance with the judgment of reason, all things are common, that is, they are to be shared with the poor in time of need. For reason naturally leads us to suppose that we should keep only what is necessary and distribute what is left to the needy." [17] The phrase that Huguccio uses in this passage—common, that is, to be shared (*communis ... id est communicanda*)—will be reiterated repeatedly in later discussions.

Notice how Huguccio argues for the commonality of property by appeal to natural law, but also how he understands this commonality as a permanent feature binding upon all property. As Tierney explains Huguccio's view, "private property was itself a social institution involving obligations to others. *Property could and should be private and common at the same time.*" [18] It is private in that it belongs to a person, to be possessed and administered by her. Because she is included within the community of common use, she may legitimately take what she needs for herself and her dependents. But property is common because social claims always inhere to it. All that a person possesses is given to her and to humankind as a whole for common use. God gives property not only to meet her own needs but those of

---

[15] Tierney, *The Idea of Natural Rights*, 60; Brian Tierney, *Medieval Poor Law* (Berkeley: University of California Press, 1959), 30–31.
[16] Tierney, *The Idea of Natural Rights*, 71.
[17] Quoted in Tierney, *The Idea of Natural Rights*, 72; see also 139.
[18] Tierney, *The Idea of Natural Rights*, 72, emphasis mine.

everyone—and above all, those who presently lack the world's goods. On this construal, all property—even private property—involves essential social obligations. To anticipate the much later language of Pope Pius XI in *Quadragesimo Anno* (1931), all ownership, as well as all economic activity based upon it, has a "social character" (nos. 49, 101). In the language of Pope John Paul II's address during the Third General Conference of the Latin American Bishops at Puebla, Mexico (1979): "All private property involves a *social mortgage*" (*sobre toda propiedad privada grava una hipoteca social*).[19] In this way, for Huguccio and those who followed him in this line of thought, the claim that all things are common (because creation is a gift meant to benefit all) continued to impinge and place demands upon even personal possession of property.

Notice also that Huguccio's solution relies upon a distinction between ownership and use: *that* a person possesses property must be distinguished from *how* a person possesses it. Created goods belong to a person in the sense that she is in possession of them—she personally holds and administers them. They are, after all, in her hands. But the created goods are not hers in the sense that they are hers alone to use in whatever way she wants; they are meant for common use, and she must help facilitate it. She must open her hands and share what she has, because what she has in her hands is not for her alone. She must, therefore, always look for ways to include others in the use of what she has been given. Huguccio's solution thus coheres with while at the same time develops the view we saw in Basil, for whom those who have the world's goods but fail to share them are like thieves. The basic theological grammar Huguccio assumes is that once a person's needs and the needs of those who depend upon her have been met, her surfeit belongs to others, especially the poor. As Pope Leo XIII later puts the point in his encyclical *Rerum Novarum* (1891): "It is one thing to have a right to the possession of money [and property] and another to have a right to use that money as one wills. ... But, when what necessity demands has been supplied, ... it becomes a duty to give to the indigent out of what remains over" (no. 22).[20]

---

[19] Pope John Paul II, *Address at the Opening of the Third General Conference of the Latin-American Bishops*, Puebla, México, January 28, 1979, www.vatican.va/content/john-paul-ii/en/speeches/1979/january/documents/hf_jp-ii_spe_19790128_messico-puebla-episc-latam.html, III.4, emphasis in original.

[20] In the same passage, Leo does say that "what necessity demands" includes "one's standing," which should be "fairly taken thought for." There are disagreements about this within the moral-theological tradition we are considering. As Catholic social teaching develops, maintenance of social standing drops out of consideration as a legitimate criterion and "the measure of the needs of others," as John XXIII puts it, becomes primary. For more on this topic, see Matthew Philipp Whelan, *Blood in the*

By articulating the relationship between private property and the common gift of creation in this way, Huguccio and those like Thomas Aquinas who followed him not only resolved some of the difficulties surrounding how to understand the relationship between private property and natural law's claim that the use of all things ought to be common to all. They also effectively decoupled the claim of commonality from particular configurations of economic life, for instance, from the communal ownership practiced by those Christians described in the book of Acts and the monastic communities modeled upon them. On Huguccio's terms, even possessors of private property can participate in the common destination of created goods, a view that coheres with scripture's recognition of the legitimacy of some form of private possession. Once again, the problem with the rich fool and Dives is not that they have possessions, but the use they make of them. More precisely, they are condemned for their failure to acknowledge that what they possess also belongs to others, especially those who lack what they need. To be sure, communal ownership remains an important, even preeminent, witness to God's purpose for creation, which is to meet the needs of all. But communal ownership is not the only witness. Holders of private property can also testify to creation's common character. Shop owners and landholders can recognize the injustices of a given property regime and the exclusion of many from what is theirs, responding with justice and mercy to those like Ostriakov and the people of Las Pavas, and working to ensure that they, too, have access to what belongs to them.[21]

Until now, we have been considering the grammar of creation as a common gift from the perspective of those in possession of the world's goods, because this is the context within which discussion of the *ius necessitatis* emerges. We have been examining how, for this moral-theological tradition, it is incumbent upon possessors to learn to see their possessions for what they are, namely, given for common use. Above all, those who have the world's goods must learn to acknowledge the claim of the needy upon those goods as a matter of justice. The obligation to share reflects, strictly speaking, what is *owed* to others, what *belongs* to them. It is not primarily an act of supererogation for wealthy shop-owners to give food to the hungry man or a wealthy landholders to relinquish some of their for land the

---

Fields: Óscar Romero, Catholic Social Teaching, and Land Reform (Washington, DC: Catholic University of America Press, 2020), 85–139.

[21] Along these lines, Peñalaver and Katyal write that property lawbreaking can have a "communicative power," by which they mean that it can help us "to reimagine our relationships with the material world and with each other," while also providing "an informal forum for airing conflicts over resources between owners and nonowners, which the law can eventually shift to accommodate" (*Property Outlaws*, 26).

landless; it is an act of justice. In Pope Pius XII's words in *Sertum Laetitiae* (1939), charity certainly helps, but it is justice that must guide.[22]

But what about the other perspective? Are those without the world's goods to wait patiently to receive what is theirs in justice? What happens when what is their due does not arrive? Might they justifiably take what belongs to them? If so, in the name and under the protection of what law? We saw above that these questions, while not raised explicitly by Basil or Chrysostom, are implied by the grammar of the moral-theological tradition out of which they speak. Basil, for instance, states that the goods retained by the wealthy *belong* to those in need. In what sense—precisely—do they belong to the needy? Tierney reports that twelfth-century Decretists distinguished between duties and rights. While it was certainly recognized that the rich had a duty to those in need, this did not necessarily imply that those in need had a right to the goods in question.[23]

Leo XIII suggests something similar in the passage quoted above from *Rerum Novarum*, in which he distinguishes between possession and use, and says that it is a person's duty to give her surfeit to those in need. Leo goes on to identify the duty in question not with justice ("save in extreme cases") but with charity, which means, he explains, it is "a duty not enforced by human law." In Leo's view, then, the identification of the duty with charity does not lessen its force, for "the laws and judgments of men [sic]," he insists, "must yield place to the laws and judgments of Christ the true God," who exhorts his followers to perform such duties (no. 22). Rather, this identification simply means that the duty in question falls within the purview of a person's conscience and the moral suasion of the Church, and is not a matter of legal enforcement by civil authorities. A person should give what she has in excess, but she cannot be compelled to do so.

One important way these questions were framed in the late twelfth century was in terms of whether those in extreme need who took another's goods were guilty of the sin of theft. As Tierney observes, debates about these matters typically turned to the mind of the agent. By definition, theft requires taking something from an owner who is unwilling to relinquish it. Thus, Huguccio reasons, the poor person is not guilty of theft because "he believes or should believe" in the owner's willingness to relinquish possessions in the face of need. The needy person, then, has a right to such goods, but in Tierney's words, it is still "a shadowy sort of right, based only on an unprovable hypothesis about the state of the mind of the needy person."[24]

Although Huguccio did not argue for a natural right of the needy

---

[22] Pope Pius XII, *Sertum Laetitiae*, no. 34.
[23] Tierney, *The Idea of Natural Rights*, 70–71.
[24] Quoted in Tierney, *The Idea of Natural Rights*, 71.

to the surfeit of the rich, his understanding of the relationship between private property and the common gift of creation certainly pressed that issue. Writing in the late-twelfth century, Ricardus Anglicus advances the discussion considerably when he interrogates the category of thievery in light of cases of extreme need. "Since by natural *ius* all things are common, that is to be shared in times of need," he explains, the person in extreme need who takes what she needs "is not properly said to thieve."[25] To return to the cases of Ostriakov and Las Pavas, Ricardus Anglicus's terms permit us to pose the question: are they even thieves? In the media coverage surrounding Ostriakov, all sides agree that he is. The disagreement concerns whether his thievery is justified. "Can the homeless and hungry steal food?" one prominent headline asks. "Maybe, an Italian Court Says."[26] But notice that Ricardus Anglicus's own position is significantly different. For him, those in need are not properly said to steal because, strictly speaking, they do not take what belongs to *others*; they take what belongs to *them*—what is meant to be shared, especially in times of need.

Above we saw that while the rich had a duty to those in need, questions persisted regarding whether this entailed the needy had a right to the goods in question. Ricardus Anglicus's position suggests that the poor do indeed have a natural right to the goods in question. And circa 1200 CE, this is effectively what Alanus argues: those in need do not steal because they take what is their own *iure naturali*—by "natural right" or "natural law." Others began to adopt this view, increasingly asserting that those in need had an assertible right. Laurentius, for instance, writes that when a person took what he needed, it was "as if he used his own right and his own thing." Soon after, the *ius necessitatis* entered the mainstream of medieval jurisprudence.[27] As Thomas Aquinas will later argue in the *Summa theologiae*: those in need take what "necessity has made common," what has become their own by reason of their need.[28] If the need is manifest and urgent, it is lawful for people to take another's property, either in the open or in secret. Also, like Ricardus Anglicus, Thomas adds that it is inaccurate to describe such actions as theft or robbery.[29] As Marcus Lefébure explains, what Thomas is suggesting is that "a particular human system of distribution [of the world's goods] may be … resolved back into the primitive state of undifferentiated community in the case of blatant and extreme necessity."[30]

---

[25] Quoted in Tierney, *The Idea of Natural Rights*, 73.
[26] Pianigiani and Chan, "Can the Homeless and Hungry Steal Food?"
[27] Quoted in Tierney, *The Idea of Natural Rights*, 73.
[28] ST II-II q. 66, a. 7, sed contra; ad. 2.
[29] ST II-II q. 66, a. 7, resp.
[30] ST II-II q. 66, a. 7, note a.

It is important to stress that for this moral-theological tradition, the commonality in question does not pertain to an original condition that has now been superseded and no longer obtains, nor does commonality mean that all property law is suspended and anarchy reigns. The fundamental point is that this tradition is making a claim about what property is, what possessing it entails, and what law and policy regarding property is meant to do, which is to facilitate common use.[31] In the case of the *ius necessitatis*—perhaps counter-intuitively—it is precisely the *circumvention* of the property arrangements secured by positive or customary law that helps to bring into clear relief the commonality of the gift of creation.

Yet, as Tierney points out, while this moral-theological tradition holds that those in need have a right to the goods of others, in another sense this right remains a shadowy one. As Tierney explains, "The situation is not wholly satisfactory from the point of view of the person in want; the secular judge would probably hang him," because "none of the established forms of legal action covered this kind of case."[32] Huguccio's perspective on this question is similar to Leo XIII's: "Many things are owed that cannot be sought by judicial procedure," Leo writes, "such as dignities and dispensations and alms ... but they can be sought as something due mercifully for the sake of God and piety."[33] In this connection, it is worth noting that alongside the formal judicial procedures, through which, as Huguccio says here, alms cannot be sought, there existed another mechanism known as "evangelical denunciation," in which bishops at that time could hear such cases and provide remedies. Beginning around 1200, canonists argued that those in need could avail themselves of such mechanisms, and that bishops could even compel—by excommunication, if necessary—the wealthy who refused to relinquish their surfeit.[34] Despite these mechanisms, as we will see in the following section, while the *ius necessitatis* continues to be preserved by the Catholic social teaching tradition, the right in question remains shadowy because of its complex and oftentimes fraught relationship to positive law.

CATHOLIC SOCIAL TEACHING

My treatment of the law of necessity has been admittedly cursory, leaving aside many complexities and questions. Moreover, I cannot

---

[31] For insightful discussions of Franciscan approaches to these questions, see Giorgio Agamben, *The Highest Poverty: Monastic Rules and Form-of-Life*, trans. Adam Kotsko (Stanford: Stanford University Press, 2013); Michael F. Cusato, OFM, "Highest Poverty or Lowest Poverty?: The Paradox of the Minorite Charism," *Franciscan Studies* 75 (2017): 275–321.
[32] Tierney, *The Idea of Natural Rights*, 74.
[33] Quoted in Tierney, *The Idea of Natural Rights*, 74.
[34] Tierney, *The Idea of Natural Rights*, 74; Tierney, *Medieval Poor Law*, 67–89.

deal here with the additional complexities and questions related to the transmission of this teaching over the course of subsequent centuries. René Laurentin, for instance, has argued that it gradually grew obscure in modernity, because of the pressures of capitalism and forms of economic life that prioritize individual appropriation, and construe the common good as a secondary effect of that appropriation. "The doctrine on [exclusive] private property," Laurentin writes, "moved into first place and seemed to be basic, primary, and absolute."[35] These developments obscure belief that creation is a common gift and its implications for property, including the *ius necessitatis*.[36] Nevertheless, the moral-theological tradition we have been examining persists. There are legal scholars, such as Peñalver and Katyal, who are trying to resuscitate its legal implications.[37] Yet another place we see the persistence of this tradition is in Catholic social teaching.[38]

Pope Leo XIII draws on this tradition in *Rerum Novarum*—the so-called Magna Carta of Catholic social teaching[39]—when he states near the beginning of the encyclical that "the fact that God has given the earth for the use and enjoyment of the whole human race can in no way be a bar to the owning of private property" (no. 8). While this statement may seem counterintuitive, even contradictory, it is precisely because Leo assumes the moral-theological tradition that we have been examining as axiomatic that he sees no need for further

---

[35] René Laurentin, *Liberation, Development, and Salvation* (Maryknoll, NY: Orbis Books, 1972), 96–101. Laurentin traces this misconception of private property across the encyclical tradition until the "restoration of the obscured message" in Pius XII's 1941 radio address. To my mind, Laurentin misunderstands how the designation "private property" in Catholic social teaching is not univocal, which is why Leo does not see the common gift of creation and private property as incompatible. Additionally, Laurentin's concern is with the reversal in "the normal order of expository thought," which he thinks should first insist upon the common purpose of creation and private ownership as a derivation. However, in Leo's thought, Laurentin discerns the prioritization of private property and the treatment of the common destination "in second place, on a secondary plane," as if it were merely "an invitation to owners to use private property well." Thus, Laurentin writes, "the common purpose doctrine passed from the first to the second rank, and then into the background; and in that way it was devalued, minimized, and distorted." While I disagree with this characterization of Leo's position in *Rerum Novarum*, Laurentin's overarching point is an important one and captures the trajectory of Catholic social teaching.
[36] See Laurentin, *Liberation, Development, and Salvation*, 99–100.
[37] Another is Jeremy Waldron, who writes: "Nobody should be permitted ever to use force to prevent another man [sic] from satisfying his very basic needs in circumstances where there seems to be no other way of satisfying them" (*Liberal Rights: Collected Papers, 1981–1991* [Cambridge: Cambridge University Press, 1993], 240–41).
[38] This point receives fuller treatment in Whelan, *Blood in the Fields*, 85–250.
[39] See Pius XI, *Quadragesimo Anno*, no. 39. Subsequent commentators will speak of *Rerum Novarum* in similar terms as the foundational document of modern Catholic social teaching.

elaboration. What becomes clearer as the encyclical proceeds is that Leo regards the property-related institutions as internal to and derivations of God's giving of the earth for common use. Leo assumes these institutions play an essential role in mediating common access to the gift, and that they must constantly be strengthened in this regard. In this way, God elicits and enables creaturely participation in God's giving of the common gift of creation. As Matthew Habiger convincingly argues, Leo understands property and its associated institutions to be a "derived principle," by which Habiger means that property derives from and is essentially subordinated to God's gift of the earth for the use and enjoyment of the whole human race.[40]

In the much-discussed initial sections of the encyclical, Leo famously argues for property as a natural right, rooting property in human beings' rational nature (no. 6). On this view, access to property is constitutive of human flourishing. However, in considering this right, many commentators fail to see Leo's argument for property in relation to what he calls "the misery and wretchedness pressing so unjustly on the majority of the working class," a misery and wretchedness, it is important to add, clearly tied to the dispossession of the working class (nos. 3–4). For Leo is not just arguing against socialism in *Rerum Novarum*; he is arguing against the exclusivist account of property associated with the emerging capitalist order, which abolished property for many. Indeed, Leo frames the whole encyclical in terms of the injustices of capitalism, the condition of the dispossessed streaming into the cities, and how their lack of property makes them particularly vulnerable to exploitation. When seen from this vantage point, Leo's argument for the natural right to property is an argument for the natural right of *all* people to property, especially those deprived of access to it by the emerging capitalist order. A distributive concern underlies his articulation of the right in question, which is precisely why, as Leo goes on to argue later in the encyclical, "The law should favor ownership, and its policy should be to induce as many as possible of the people to become owners" (no. 46).

That Leo's understanding of property derives from the theological conviction that creation is a common gift emerges with even greater clarity later in the encyclical, in the passage already mentioned, where Leo distinguishes between possession and use.[41] In relation to

---

[40] Admittedly, Habiger thinks Leo is not as clear as he could be on this point, writing that "Leo does not closely differentiate between the principle of private property and the more fundamental principle of the common use of all material goods. The source he draws upon [ST II-II q. 66, aa. 1, 2] is clear about this distinction, but that is not reflected as clearly in *Rerum Novarum*." Habiger, *Papal Teaching on Private Property (1891–1981)* (Lanham, MD: University Press of America, 1990), 32–33.

[41] In distinguishing between possession and use, Leo draws on the passage in the *Summa Theologiae* where Thomas writes of a "twofold competence in relation to material things." The first, which Thomas calls the power to procure and dispense,

humankind's common destiny, the "only important thing" about possessions, Leo writes, "is to use them aright" (no. 21). What does this mean? Leo quotes the passage of the *Summa Theologiae* where Thomas explains right use in this way: people should not consider material possessions as exclusively theirs but "as common to all, so as to share them without hesitation when others are in need" (no. 22). Notice that this understanding of property differs quite strikingly from classic early modern accounts, in which possession of property is understood to be both individual and absolute, with the owner exercising complete control over access, use, and disposal.[42] In contrast, right use of property for Leo always involves acknowledging that possessors are members of a community of common use. The paradigmatic expression of this acknowledgement is returning what they have in surfeit to those who lack what they need.[43]

In articulating his account of property and possession, Leo inherits and works within an older tradition of moral-theological reflection. While it is beyond the scope of the present essay to do justice to this topic, Catholic social teaching as it develops over the course of the twentieth century takes up and preserves this approach. Within this tradition, appeal to the *ius necessitatis* occasionally, but dramatically, rises to the surface.

Perhaps the most important of these appeals can be found in *Gaudium et Spes* (1965), the Second Vatican Council's Pastoral Constitution on the Church in the Modern World, one of the most authoritative documents of the Church's social teaching. The relevant passage reads:

> God intended the earth with everything contained in it for the use of all human beings and peoples. Thus, under the leadership of justice

---

correlates with what Leo has already said about property in the encyclical, which is that it is not only legitimate for people to possess things as their own, but it is even necessary to do so. This is how Thomas explains the second competence, what he calls use: "Now with regard to [use], no man is entitled to manage things merely for himself, but as common, so that he is ready to share them easily with others in the case of necessity" (ST II-II q. 62, a. 1, resp).

[42] Jeremy Waldron, *The Right to Private Property* (Oxford: Oxford University Press 1988), 137–252; Jedediah Purdy, *The Meaning of Property: Freedom, Community, and the Legal Imagination* (New Haven: Yale University Press, 2010), 40–43.

[43] This moral-theological grammar raises many additional questions about what is the "need" beyond which we have a duty to give what remains as a surplus. These questions are beyond the scope of this essay and call for much more extensive reflection. Two important guides in that regard are Charles C. Camosy and David Cloutier. See Camosy, *Peter Singer and Christian Ethics: Beyond Polarization* (Cambridge: Cambridge University Press, 2012) and Cloutier, *The Vice of Luxury: Economic Excess in a Consumer Age* (Washington, DC: Georgetown University Press, 2015).

and in the company of charity, created goods should be in abundance for all in like manner. Whatever the forms of property may be, as adapted to the legitimate institutions of peoples, according to diverse and changeable circumstances, attention must always be paid to this universal destination of earthly goods. In using them, therefore, man [sic] should regard the external things that he legitimately possesses not only as his own but also as common in the sense that they should be able to benefit not only him but also others. On the other hand, the right of having a share of earthly goods sufficient for oneself and one's family belongs to everyone. The Fathers and Doctors of the Church held this opinion, teaching that men are obliged to come to the relief of the poor and to do so not merely out of their superfluous goods. If one is in extreme necessity, he has the right to procure for himself what he needs out of the riches of others. Since there are so many people prostrate with hunger in the world, this sacred council urges all, both individuals and governments, to remember the aphorism of the Fathers, "Feed the man dying of hunger, because if you have not fed him, you have killed him," and really to share and employ their earthly goods, according to the ability of each, especially by supporting individuals or peoples with the aid by which they may be able to help and develop themselves (no. 69).

This passage is a concise articulation of the major claims of the moral-theological tradition we have been considering, both from the perspective of those in possession of the world's goods, as well as from the perspective of those who are not in possession of them. The passage begins with the belief that creation is a common gift, given for the common use of all peoples, and before going on to specify its implications for property and the duties holding it entails. In terms of the formulation that property owners should see their possessions "not only as [their] own but as common," *Gaudium et Spes* cites the passage discussed above from *Summa Theologiae*, as well as Leo's rendering of it in *Rerum Novarum*.

The last part of the passage is particularly pertinent, because it proceeds to argue in unmistakable terms for the enduring moral force of the *ius necessitatis*. To return to the questions I posed above, what happens when those in need do not receive what is theirs? Are they to wait patiently for it? Or might they justifiably take what they need? The answer given by *Gaudium et Spes* is simple and straightforward: in cases of extreme necessity, people can indeed by right secure what they need from the surfeit of others. This is an unambiguous reiteration of Anglicus, Laurentius, and Aquinas's belief that the needy have a natural right to this surfeit, and that those who assert their right do not steal. In such cases, the violation of prevailing property arrangements reveals the character of God's creation, which is too often obscured by sin. Those who assert their right to others' property show what property is *for*, underscoring property's derived status, as well as the primacy of the principle of common use. Moreover, though *Gaudium et Spes* does not say so explicitly, the Pastoral Constitution's moral-theological grammar seems to entail Basil's understanding of a twofold account of thievery: unjust taking and unjust retention of created goods. While *Gaudium et Spes* does not explicitly use the language of thievery, it does use the language of murder, attributing a kind of violence to the failure to attend to those afflicted with hunger. [44]

Above we examined the emergence of the law of necessity in medieval theology, and we see it carried forward into our own day in *Gaudium et Spes*. However, numerous questions remain. While the document invokes the *ius necessitatis*, there is no mention of the perils of its enactment within property regimes that do not recognize—or are even antithetical to it. One reason Peñalver and Katyal argue to extend the necessity defense to cover cases of poverty and economic disaster is precisely because of the marginal status of the moral-theological tradition within which the *ius necessitatis* is intelligible.

Questions remain for still other reasons. Above we also saw Leo argue, as *Gaudium et Spes* does, that it is a person's duty to give her surfeit to those in need. But Leo goes on to say that, except in extreme cases, this duty is not enforceable by law. It is not the normal role of governments to take the excess property from some and redistribute it to others. [45] On Leo's view, the duty to distinguish between what is sufficient and what is superfluous is best left to people themselves. However, it follows from this that the *ius necessitatis* is a law set apart from the actual laws and policies of states, as well as from the actions of civil authorities. All of this raises crucial questions: How best to catechize people to understand and enact this duty? Who is responsible for this catechesis? What happens if the responsible parties fail and the duties are neglected? What counts as extreme cases?

In Catholic social teaching, one important example of such an extreme case is *Gaudium et Spes*'s argument for agrarian reform, which shares the underlying rationale of the *ius necessitatis*. Several paragraphs after the passage just cited, we read of a situation similar to Las Pavas. In many places in the world

> There are large or even extensive rural estates which are only slightly cultivated or lie completely idle for the sake of profit, while the

---

[44] See Matthew Philipp Whelan, "'You Possess the Land that Belongs to All Salvadorans': Óscar Romero and Ordinary Violence," *Modern Theology* 35, no. 4 (2019): 659–661.

[45] To be clear, Leo does think that governments have a role in the proliferation of property through law and policy (no. 47). Therefore, he seems to assume a distinction between facilitating access to property and expropriating/redistributing property. Relatedly, he does not consider what the former looks like in conditions of scarcity.

majority of the people either are without land or have only very small fields, and, on the other hand, it is evidently urgent to increase the productivity of the fields. ... Indeed, insufficiently cultivated estates should be distributed to those who can make these lands fruitful; in this case, the necessary things and means, especially educational aids and the right facilities for cooperative organization, must be supplied. Whenever, nevertheless, the common good requires expropriation, compensation must be reckoned in equity after all the circumstances have been weighed (no. 71).

This is not the first time that the Catholic social teaching tradition calls for agrarian reform, but it is one of the most significant instances of it—a call, I should add, that continues to be reiterated into the present, by Pope Emeritus Benedict XVI[46] and now by Pope Francis.[47]

What is significant for our purposes is that this call is effectively a response to situations like that of Las Pavas, where people who are landless or land-poor need land to farm, while at the same time, there are large tracts only slightly cultivated or left uncultivated. *Gaudium et Spes* does not address specifics, especially cases in which people occupy and use land because of need. But the Pastoral Constitution does clearly address the fact that laws and policies like agrarian reform are one possible response, the underlying rationale of which is to enable people to have the land they need, land that belongs to them. Expropriation of land for the common good shares in the theological grammar of creation as a common gift insofar as law and policy recognize the fact that people's need for land to farm has effectively made the land their own—though admittedly, neither the Pastoral Constitution, nor the laws and policies themselves, use this language.

Notice also how in the case of Las Pavas, there already is what we might call a kind of agrarian reform taking place "from below," enacted through the actions of ordinary people to meet their needs; in this case, by occupying and cultivating unused land titled to others.[48] As Peñalver and Katyal argue, cases like these underscore the "redistributive value" such actions can have. In occupying land only

---

[46] *Caritas in Veritate*, no. 27.
[47] See Whelan, *Blood in the Fields*, 87, 305–312. In his *Address to the Participants in the World Meeting of Popular Movements* (October 28, 2014), www.vatican.va/content/francesco/en/speeches/2014/october/documents/papa-francesco_20141028_incontro-mondiale-movimenti-popolari.html, Pope Francis says, "I know that some of you are calling for agrarian reform in order to solve some of these problems, and let me tell you that in some countries—and here I cite the *Compendium of the Social Doctrine of the Church*—'agrarian reform is, besides a political necessity, a moral obligation' [no. 300]."
[48] The phrase "agrarian reform from below" comes from Peter Rosset, Raj Patel, and Michael Courville, eds., *Promised Land: Competing Visions of Agrarian Reform* (Oakland: Food First, 2006), 9.

slightly cultivated or unused, occupiers are quite literally taking from another's surplus. These actions generate redistributive value by redistributing land from where it is less to more needed. Indeed, Peñalver and Katyal observe that property law often recognizes this redistributive value in doctrines like adverse possession, which permit forced transfers of property under certain circumstances. [49] Relatedly, property lawbreaking can also have what Peñalver and Katyal call crucial "informational value," communicating to a wider public, for instance, that aspects of the extant property regime are obsolete, unjust, or illegitimate—a communication that may in fact lead to calls for change, such as, in this case, by enacting agrarian reform. [50]

Catholic social teaching's support for agrarian reform has been characterized by some as thievery, a characterization that stems from the widespread Christian tendency to defend unrestricted private property rights and capitalism. Along these lines, Walter Block and Guillermo Yeatts have criticized the Pontifical Council for Justice and Peace's *Toward a Better Distribution of Land: The Challenge of Agrarian Reform* (1997) for condoning "theft." "The Ten Commandments," they explain, "prohibit not only robbery, but even coveting the property of others." [51] However, this characterization misconstrues the moral-theological tradition we have been examining, because it overlooks how the belief that creation is a common gift entails unjust retention—to which Catholic social teaching's call for agrarian reform is a response—is itself a form of theft.

Archbishop Óscar Romero of San Salvador gave voice to this view when he said to the oligarchs of El Salvador in 1980 that they "possess the land that belongs to all Salvadorans" (*están poseyendo la tierra que es de todos los salvadoreños*) and himself advocated agrarian reform in order to rectify the situation. [52] Pope John Paul II said something similar in a 1979 address in the Mexican state of Oaxaca. Addressing the "leaders of the peoples" and the "powerful classes," the pope proceeded to tell them that they "keep unproductive lands that hide the bread that so many families lack" (*que tenéis a veces improductivas las tierras que esconden el pan que a tantas familias*

---

[49] Peñalver and Katyal, *Property Outlaws*, 18, 127, 143, 183.
[50] Peñalver and Katyal, *Property Outlaws*, 18, 127, 143, 183.
[51] See for instance Plinio Corrêa de Oliveira, *Reforma agrária: Questão e consciência* (São Paulo: Editora Vera Cruz, 1960). Corrêa de Oliveira founded the Brazilian Society for the Defense of Tradition, Family, and Property (TFP), which continues to be vocal in its defense of private property—a defense which, it claims, is based on Catholic social teaching. See Walter Block and Guillermo Yeatts, "The Economics and Ethics of Land Reform: A Critique of the Pontifical Council for Justice and Peace's *Toward a Better Distribution of Land: The Challenge of Agrarian Reform*," *Journal of Natural Resources and Environmental Law* 15, no. 1 (1999–2000): 41–42.
[52] See Whelan, "'You Possess the Land that Belongs to All Salvadorans.'"

falta).[53] In keeping more land than they could possibly use, they keep what belongs to others—a thievery embedded in the landscape. More recently, in his 2013 apostolic exhortation *Evangelii Gaudium*, Pope Francis cites John Chrysostom's words: "Not to share one's wealth with the poor is to steal from them and to take away their livelihood. It is not our own goods which we hold, but theirs" (no. 57). Earlier that same year, Francis remarked: "Remember well, whenever food is thrown away it is as if it is stolen from the table of the poor, from the hungry!" (*Ricordiamo bene, però, che il cibo che si butta via è come se venisse rubato dalla mensa di chi è povero, di chi ha fame!*)[54]

In critiquing social teaching's support for agrarian reform, Block and Yeatts appeal to the Ten Commandments. However, the actual treatment of the seventh commandment ("Thou Shall Not Steal") in the *Catechism of the Catholic Church* begins not with a defense of property rights as typically understood by property law, but with the common destination of created goods, from which the whole exposition on property and possession follows. "The right to private property, acquired by work or received from others by inheritance or gift," the *Catechism* states, "does not do away with the original gift of the earth to the whole of mankind. The universal destination of goods remains primordial" (no. 2403).[55]

In its treatment of these matters, the *Catechism* even mentions the *ius necessitatis*, stating: "The seventh commandment forbids *theft*, that is, usurping another's property against the reasonable will of the owner. There is no theft if consent can be presumed or if refusal is contrary to reason and the universal destination of goods. This is the case in obvious and urgent necessity when the only way to provide for immediate, essential needs (food, shelter, clothing...) is to put at one's disposal and use the property of others [citing *Gaudium et Spes*, no. 69]" (no. 2408). This point is crucial, and once again, considerably complicates the charge of thievery, because the *Catechism* joins figures like Anglicus, Alanus, and Aquinas in insisting that unjust retention is a form of theft, and that when those in extreme necessity take from the superabundance of others, there is, strictly speaking, no thievery. Those in need have a right to the goods in question; their need has made the goods their own.

---

[53] Pope John Paul II, *Apostolic Journey to the Dominican Republic, Mexico, and the Bahamas*, Cuilapan, Mexico, January 29, 1979, www.vatican.va/content/john-paul-ii/en/speeches/1979/january/documents/hf_jp-ii_spe_19790129_messico-arciv-oaxaca.html.

[54] The spontaneous remark only appears in the Italian. See Papa Francesco, *Udienza Generale*, Piazza San Pietro, 5 giugno 2013, www.vatican.va/content/francesco/it/audiences/2013/documents/papa-francesco_20130605_udienza-generale.html.

[55] The *Compendium of the Social Doctrine of the Church* patterns its own approach accordingly, even explicitly endorsing agrarian reform (nos. 171–184, 300).

Although the *Catechism* only mentions food, shelter, and clothing, the ellipses suggest that those are not the only created goods in view. Returning to the question of agrarian reform, what about land? What is the best way to describe what the landless and land-poor are doing when they occupy and cultivate land that belongs to others?[56] Mario Losano poses this question in his book, *La función social de la propriedad y latifundios ocupados: Los sin tierra de Brazil*, characterizing the Landless Workers Movement (*Movimento dos Trabalhadores Sem Terra*) of Brazil as a contemporary application of the law of necessity. Are these workers occupying land on the basis of a law of need more basic than positive law regarding property, testifying to the primordiality of the common destination of goods?[57] Or are they lawless invaders, robbing property that belongs to others? As Losano notes, the difference between these descriptions, and the possible responses they occasion, is significant.[58]

CONCLUSION

In this essay, I have argued that Catholic social teaching preserves a moral-theological tradition which continues to appeal to the *ius necessitatis*. Yet, while social teaching continues to preserve and appeal to this law, there is still a great deal of circumspection with respect to it—a notable hesitancy, that is, to stand by that articulation, be in solidarity with those who assert it, and assume the risks of so doing. Thus, while the law of necessity endures, the right in question, as I have also argued, continues to be a shadowy one.

We especially see this shadowiness in the case of martyrs like Óscar Romero. In El Salvador, like in many other countries in Latin America and elsewhere during the twentieth century, the *campesinado* or peasantry underwent, in Jeffrey L. Gould and Aldo A. Lauria-Santiago's words, "an agonizing decomposition,"[59] which produced landlessness and migration. Within these countries, people increasingly turned to squatting—settling upon and cultivating land for which they had no legal title. On the basis of the moral-theological

---

[56] See Matthew Philipp Whelan, "*Jesus is the Jubilee*: A Theological Reflection on the Pontifical Council for Justice and Peace's *Toward a Better Distribution of Land*," *Journal of Moral Theology* 6, no. 2 (2017): 224.

[57] Gerald Schlabach raises a similar question in "The Nonviolence of Desperation: Peasant Land Action in Honduras," in *Relentless Persistence: Nonviolent Action in Latin America*, ed. Philip McManus and Gerald Schlabach (Philadelphia: New Society, 1991), 64–77.

[58] Mario Losano, *La función social de la propriedad y latifundios ocupados: Los sin tierra de Brazil* (Madrid: Dykinson, 2006), 137–138.

[59] Jeffrey L. Gould and Aldo A. Lauria-Santiago, *To Rise in Darkness: Revolution, Repression, Memory in El Salvador, 1920–1932* (Durham, NC: Duke University Press, 2008), 3.

tradition we have been examining, Romero defended such actions, but he also advocated that the law and policy of the Salvadoran state ameliorate the situation through agrarian reform. As Romero explained in one homily regarding a standoff between squatters and landowners in Azacualpa, Chalatenango, "I know that those who are occupying lands ... are respecting private property. They only want an agreement that enables them to have a place to plant and give food to their families."[60] They are trying to meet, as he put it in one of his pastoral letters, "the vital necessity of subsistence."[61]

Yet, this defense was an important reason why Romero was—and continues to be—controversial in El Salvador and beyond. Growing up, many in El Salvador heard stories of Romero as a "*guerrillero* [guerilla] dressed as a priest*,*" who sided with criminals and permitted the poor to steal from the hard-earned wealth of the rich [62]—stories repeatedly told by fellow Catholics and even endorsed by bishops. As José Luis Escobar Alas, the archbishop of San Salvador, readily admits in his 2017 pastoral letter, the Church in El Salvador failed to stand in solidarity with Romero and so many others like him. "I want to recognize—as I must out of justice, truth, and charity," Escobar Alas writes, "that we in the Archdiocese have crossed the threshold of the third millennium without having acknowledged all the men and women who were victims of persecution, torture, repression, and who were ultimately martyred for following Christ and incarnating the Gospel in this country," "giv[ing] their lives for the love of Christ personified in the poor," especially the landless.[63]

During the 1980s, the US government justified the extraordinary expansion of its support of the Salvadoran military by depicting El Salvador as the front line of a civilizational war with communism. Against the opposition of the United States Conference of Catholic Bishops, many prominent US Catholics argued in favor of these policies precisely on the basis of anti-communism.[64] They not only disregarded the elasticity of the category of communism and the reasons Romero and others like him might be so accused. These

---

[60] Monseñor Óscar A. Romero, *Homilías*, vol. 1 (San Salvador: UCA, 2005), 408.
[61] Monseñor Óscar A. Romero, "La Iglesia y organizaciones políticas populares," in *La voz de los sin voz: La palabra viva de Monseñor Óscar Arnulfo Romero*, ed. Rodolfo Cardenal, Ignacio Martín-Baró, and Jon Sobrino (San Salvador: UCA, 1986), 99.
[62] Luis López-Portillo, "El Salvador, Divided by Its First Saint," *Public Radio International The World*, May 21, 2015.
[63] José Luis Escobar Alas, *Ustedes también darán testimonio, porque han estado conmigo desde el principio*, II Carta Pastoral (San Salvador: Arzobispado de San Salvador, 2017), nos. 3, 160.
[64] Todd Scribner, *A Partisan Church: American Catholicism and the Rise of Neoconservative Catholics* (Washington, DC: Catholic University of America Press, 2015), 137–92.

prominent Catholic anti-communist voices further reinforced the notion that Christianity underwrites private property and capitalism, casting the moral-theological tradition Romero drew upon even further into the shadows.

Why, then, does the law of necessity remain such a shadowy one, even within a tradition that bears it into the present? One reason is that, while social teaching holds as crucial that people distinguish between what is sufficient and what is superfluous, it also argues that it is not the normal role of governments to take and redistribute people's property—notwithstanding extreme cases like agrarian reform, or more ordinary ones like paying taxes.[65] Consequently, the *ius necessitatis*, in some sense, stands apart from and is not adjudicable by the actual laws and policies of states.

Another reason is that there continues to be a great deal of confusion regarding what Catholic social teaching actually teaches about property and how this teaching stands in considerable tension with commonplace understandings of that term, especially in places like the US, a land which tends to regard unrestricted private property as sacrosanct. Even among Catholics, there remains a truly remarkable failure to see that social teaching's account of property and its associated institutions is shaped, at the most basic level, by the belief that creation is a common gift, given by God for common use, along with the radical implications of that belief for the organization of our social and economic life together.

A final reason the law of necessity remains shadowy brings us into more contested territory. When *Rerum Novarum* and the subsequent social teaching tradition argue for the proliferation of property—the expansion of stable and secure access of the dispossessed, the landless, and the indigent to property, encouraging them, in Leo's words, to hope for "a share in the land" (no. 47)—the preference is clearly for that proliferation to occur by way of the law and policy of states. As Leo says, *laws* should favor ownership and *policies* should help as many as possible to become owners. Later teaching continues to emphasize this point, calling upon law and policymakers to realize it. The teaching on agrarian reform that begins to emerge in the 1940s is an extension of that call.

But what happens in situations in which people increasingly misunderstand their duties to one another and the common destination of creation? What happens when laws and policies do not sufficiently favor ownership or enable sharing in the land but, instead, further undermine it? Since Leo wrote *Rerum Novarum* in 1891, property ownership has clearly not proliferated in our world. One glaring

---

[65] *Compendium of the Social Doctrine of the Church*, no. 355.

symptom of this fact is the enormous growth of informal settlements throughout the world. Known by many names—slums, squatter settlements, *favelas, poblaciones*, shacks, *barrios bajos*, bidonvilles, etc.—they are a global phenomenon. According to one study by the UN, fully a quarter of the world's urban population lives within them—a percentage that is only expected to increase.[66]

For our purposes, these settlements are significant, not only because of their inhabitants' lack of access to basic goods like clean water and sanitation, sufficient space to live, and structurally sound shelters, but also because they are synonymous with the inhabitants' insecure tenure over their homes and the lands on which they are built. To use more loaded language, these settlements are "illegal." As Robert Neuwirth explains in his book *Shadow Cities*, the overwhelming majority of those who live in such places "are simply people who came to the city, needed a place to live that they and their families could afford, and not being able to find it on the private market, built it for themselves on land that wasn't theirs."[67] Inhabitants live outside the protections of the laws and policies of states—part of the informal or shadow economy. As a consequence of that status, inhabitants face the constant threat of eviction or even violence.

Closer to home, as Brian Goldstone has recently argued, in the US there is a growing phenomenon of what he calls the "working homeless."[68] "For a widening swath of the nearly seven million American workers living below the poverty line," he writes, "a combination of skyrocketing rents, stagnant wages, and a lack of tenant protections has proved all but insurmountable. Increasingly, this is the face of homelessness in the US: people whose paychecks are no longer enough to keep a roof over their heads."[69] Notably, this phenomenon often occurs in the wealthiest, fastest growing cities— New York, Washington, DC, Seattle, Los Angeles, Charlotte, San Jose, Nashville, Atlanta, and elsewhere—places where it is precisely those workers helping to generate the wealth and sustain the economic growth who are being expelled from those cities due to the lack of affordable housing. At the same time, the support once offered through the laws and policies of the government—for instance, through public housing, Section 8 vouchers, and other federal programs that invest in low-income housing—is being eroded.

---

[66] United Nations Task Team on Habitat III, *Informal Settlements* (no. 22), Habitat III Issue Papers, 31 May 2015, 2–3.
[67] Robert Neuwirth, *Shadow Cities: A Billion Squatters, a New Urban World* (New York: Routledge, 2005), 256–257.
[68] Brian Goldstone, "The New American Homelessness," *The New Republic*, August 21, 2019.
[69] Goldstone, "The New American Homelessness."

To address this reality, Goldstone notes that groups like the Housing Justice League in Atlanta are working to develop a "new language." "Is safe and stable housing a luxury conferred only on those rich enough to afford it? Or is it a basic right, no less fundamental than literacy or access to food and medicine?" Goldstone asks, echoing the group's concerns.[70] My contention in this essay has been that this new language and its claims of justice can be nourished by a much older one.

One of the hopes of Leo and his successors was that the proliferation of property might begin to address the inequalities of the modern world, and in Leo's words, bridge the "gulf between vast wealth and sheer poverty," bringing "the respective classes ... nearer to one another" (*Rerum Novarum*, no. 47). What happens when inequality only mounts and the gulfs between people only grow wider? What about when the whole problem of how the dispossessed, landless, indigent might have stable and secure access to property is dealt with inadequately by law and policy—or worse, ignored or even exacerbated? As many homeless advocacy groups in this country have been arguing for some time now, the laws and policies of local governments have increasingly responded to the homeless by criminalizing their efforts to survive, as well as initiatives trying to serve them, for instance, by increasing restrictions on food sharing programs.[71]

The focus of Catholic social teaching is especially upon the obligations of those in possession of the world's goods, as well as those who have the power to shape law and policy, which is important and must continue to be insisted upon. However, we must not neglect that the teaching also has important implications for the prerogatives of those deprived of the world's goods. The teaching's moral-theological grammar presses us to ask: Must those deprived of the world's goods wait upon the wealthy to be converted or upon laws and policies to be changed, in order to receive what is theirs? What about when their need makes it impossible to wait and compels them to sleep in public because they have nowhere else to go? When they simply take from a store because they are hungry? When they begin to cultivate an abandoned plot to which they possess no title because they have neither land nor work? When they migrate without the requisite legal documents because changes in the climate have made it impossible to earn a livelihood where they are? In what ways and under which circumstances are these actions defensible? When such actions are criminalized, as they increasingly tend to be, who is willing

---

[70] Goldstone, "The New American Homelessness."
[71] National Coalition for the Homeless, *The Criminalization of Efforts to Feed People in Need,* Washington, DC, October 2014; Ford, "Homelessness is Not a Crime."

to help make them intelligible in light of a higher law? It would seem well past time for Catholic moral theologians, as heirs to this tradition, to take on this responsibility. 🅼

Matthew Philipp Whelan, former Board Member of New Wine New Wineskins, is Assistant Professor of Moral Theology at Baylor University in Waco, Texas, where his research centers on Catholic social thought, Latin American and liberation theologies, and ecological theology and ethics. He holds degrees in theology from Duke University (PhD, MTS) and in agriculture from the Centro Agronómico Tropical de Investigación y Enseñanza in Turrialba, Costa Rica.

Nurturing Masculinities: Constructing New Narratives of Fatherhood

Jacob Kohlhaas

DESPITE CALLS FOR GREATER ATTENTION to the study of fathers since the late 1970s, until recently research on fatherhood was likely to come through research on motherhood; either via direct report or through research tools originally designed to study motherhood.[1] While there are important and significant similarities across parental experiences, patterns in experiences of paternal caregiving retain distinctive features. This essay is not intended to proceed from an essentialist perspective in regards to gender and parenthood, but instead simply recognizes that practices and patterns of parenthood have varied and continue to meaningfully vary by gender.[2] In addition, the use of maternal reports to track paternal practices creates inaccuracies in the research.[3] For example, parents tend to downplay the impact of their own unhealthy ways of managing conflict on their children while believing the same actions in their spouse are more harmful.[4] Finally, past research overrepresented white, middle-class fathers (a demographic relatively adaptable in renegotiating fatherly roles),[5] while too quickly ascribing variances from this norm to racial

---

[1] Lori Roggman, Hiram E. Fitzgerald, Robert H. Bradley, and Helen Raikes, "Methodological, Measurement, and Design Issues in Studying Fathers: An Interdisciplinary Perspective," in *Handbook of Father Involvement: Multidisciplinary Perspectives*, ed. Catherine S. Tamis-LeMonda and Natasha Cabrera (Mahwah, NJ: Lawrence Erlbaum, 2002), 2.
[2] For responses to gender essentialism, see James V. Brownson, *Bible Gender Sexuality: Reframing the Church's Debate on Same-Sex Relationships* (Grand Rapids: Eerdmans, 2013), 22–38; Megan K. DeFranza, *Sex Difference in Christian Theology: Male, Female, and Intersex in the Image of God* (Grand Rapids: Eerdmans, 2015), chapter 4; Mari Mikkola, "Feminist Perspectives on Sex and Gender," *The Stanford Encyclopedia of Philosophy* (Fall 2019 Edition), ed. Edward N. Zalta, plato.stanford.edu/archives/fall2019/entries/feminism-gender/.
[3] V. Jeffery Evans, "Foreword," in *Conceptualizing and Measuring Father Involvement*, ed. Randal D. Day and Michael E. Lamb (Mahwah, NJ: Lawrence Erlbaum, 2004), x.
[4] Marcie C. Geoke-Morey and E. Mark Cummings, "Impact of Father Involvement: A Closer Look at Indirect Effects Models Involving Marriage and Child Adjustment," *Applied Developmental Sciences* 11, no. 4 (2007): 221.
[5] Evans, "Foreword," x.

differences rather than historical and economic factors.[6] The contemporary field of fatherhood studies is more careful in accounting for such biases, yet fatherhood remains a complex and moving target. Experiences and understandings of fatherhood vary both across demographics and across time. Moreover, the personal and social beliefs attached to fatherhood are difficult to untangle from research methodology and interpretation. Consequently, fatherhood research is "inescapably value laden."[7]

The present essay will proceed with its own value-orientation based in the Catholic moral tradition while utilizing social scientific research in fatherhood studies to consider how human relational potentials are encouraged or limited by narratives surrounding fatherhood today. Such narratives will be sketched within both contemporary American society and Catholic magisterial teaching, which are linked by the broader socio-historical backdrop of the modern industrialized West. This context gave rise to the influential differentiation of the father as public-provider and mother as private-nurturer. While both American society and Catholic teaching continue to develop and contain significant diversities in their conceptions and presentations of fatherhood, the narratives they each provide tend to remain similarly limited in important ways regarding diverse expressions of paternal care. This essay contends that contemporary implications of basic Catholic moral commitments suggest an obligation to promote narratives that support more expansive understandings of male capabilities in childcare and domestic life than are presently realized in Catholic teaching.[8] This appraisal roots itself theologically in the dignity of all human persons and the role of

---

[6] Ronald E. Hall and colleagues argue that "a dominant theme in the study of Black family life has been descriptions and analysis of what has been referred to as the 'disorganized' and the 'matricentric' family structures, implying a reduction of the male role." This association with race has been so influential that the same family systems have been largely ignored among similarly economically situated white families. Ronald E. Hall, Jonathan N. Livingston, Valerie V. Henderson, Glenn O. Fisher, and Rebekah Hines, "Post-modern Perspective on the Economics of African American Fatherhood," *Journal of African American Studies* 10, no. 4 (Spring 2007): 113.

[7] Rob Palkovitz, "Involved Fathering and Child Development: Advancing Our Understanding of Good Fathering," in *Handbook of Father Involvement*, 132.

[8] As a Catholic father, educator, and theologian, I have personal and professional interests in how fathers come to understand themselves in changing contexts. Throughout the last decade, my wife and I have traded periods of being the primary caregiver with being the primary income earner and navigated dual full-time employment. The motivation behind this essay comes from this experience of negotiating parental roles and my own limited experience as a primary caregiver. In these times, I became aware of both the remarkably low social expectations placed on paternal caregiving (in sharp contrast to expectations from mothers) as well as the complex social influences surrounding men who undertake traditionally female parental functions.

interpersonal, familial, and communal solidarity as an expression and realization of that dignity. Consequently, safeguarding and encouraging the individual capacity to express love, concern, and care through relationship with others is fundamental to the full realization of personhood and therefore ought to be protected and encouraged as among the most basic of human needs and obligations. In particular, the essay explores this moral theological commitment in light of contemporary experiences of fatherhood. It seeks to identify ways in which male parental experiences are truncated by prevailing narratives and offer pathways to support fuller realization of human capabilities in male caregiving.

FATHERHOOD TODAY

Fathers today, particularly those of the white, heterosexual, middle to upper income ilk (to which the author belongs), are increasingly likely to find themselves occupying social positions related to their parental practices that are simultaneously privileged and restrictive.[9] Such men are heirs to cultural patterns of heterosexual hegemonic masculinity that tend to carry forth social power on their behalf.[10] Yet, those whose experiences deviate from the norm can find themselves trapped within its restrictions.[11] The challenges faced by the central occupants of hegemonic masculinity are not the pressing issues of justice faced by those who do not fit within its norms and influence (i.e., those marginalized by race, class, income, sexuality, etc., and the intersectional identities among these). Nonetheless, felt disruptions in masculine norms are worthy of attention as they have prompted naïve and narrow-minded reactions such as those popularized within the ever-changing men's rights movement. Such views cling to positions

---

[9] "Research indicates that men with higher levels of educational attainment contribute a substantial amount more to childcare than men with lower educational attainment (Sullivan, 2010) and may be best placed to take action towards achievement of 'new' models of fathering (Dermott, 2008), which suggests they may be more likely to experience the demands of intensive parenting" (Fiona Shirani, Karen Henwood, and Carrie Coltart, "Meeting the Challenges of Intensive Parenting Culture: Gender, Risk Management, and the Moral Parent," *Sociology* 46, no. 1 [February 2012]: 28).

[10] Hegemonic masculinity has been an influential concept in social analysis of gender for several decades. More recently, the limitations of the concept itself and the pluralities of gender hegemonies have been emphasized. Although the concept still remains useful and is commonly invoked, emphasis on singular and uniform conceptions of hegemonic masculinity have declined as research has shifted towards the particularities of diverse contexts. See R. W. Connell and James W. Messerschmidt, "Hegemonic Masculinity: Rethinking the Concept," *Gender and Society* 19, no. 6 (December 2005): 829–859.

[11] Hegemonic masculinity is itself propped up by hegemonic femininity which likewise reinforces norms and restrictions for acceptable expression of womanhood. See Mimi Schippers, "Recovering the Feminine Other: Masculinity, Femininity, and Gender Hegemony," *Theory and Society* 36, no. 1 (February 2007): 85–102.

of privilege over and against the equitable inclusion of others and gain traction through the unfounded presumption that threats to "traditional" male scripts constitute threats to men themselves.[12] Present renegotiations of masculine norms create an opportunity for shaping narratives about fathering that are more robust and inclusive. Advocating for this expansion does not require assent to either male normativity or privilege. Rather, it requires concern for diverse expressions of human dignity that allow for rich and rewarding participation in familial and social life.[13]

At present, a small but growing fraction of fathers are primary caregivers for their children, while an increasing share of spouses are negotiating dual full-time employment and confronting an ideal of equitable co-parenting that lags behind in actual practice. American parents generally espouse egalitarian parental ideals but tend to be frustrated with the difficulty of achieving these in reality. Although nearly three quarters of US women are employed outside the home, they retain the majority of domestic duties and frequently report unmet expectations of paternal involvement in childcare.[14] Married women

---

[12] The men's right movement, a subset of the larger men's movement, is a broad, primarily Western, phenomenon that encompasses many concerns but is generally united by a perception of unequal treatment of men in contemporary societies and criticism or outright rejection of feminist social gains. Groups within the movement display varying levels of misogynistic and violent thought. Recently some groups have shifted to presenting men's health as their primary concern, using this focus to advance grievances regarding the social determinants of men's wellbeing while repurposing certain feminist lines of argumentation. See Michael Salter, "Men's Rights or Men's Needs? Anti-Feminism in Australian Men's Health Promotion," *Canadian Journal of Women and the Law* 28, no. 1 (2016): 66–90. Representative websites include A Voice for Men (www.avoiceformen.com), Return of the Kings (www.returnofthekings.com), and the National Center for Men (www.nationalcenterformen.org). Powered largely through the internet, these organizations have recently found convergence with the Alt-Right and other extremist political groups. The predominant influence of white, male, and often Christian identifications further suggests the gravity of the need for rethinking social and religious narratives of masculinity. See "Male Supremacy," The Southern Poverty Law Center, www.splcenter.org/fighting-hate/extremist-files/ideology/male-supremacy.

[13] As a rule, those who occupy the positions of greatest privilege have the least experience contending against the systems that provide that privilege. Marginalized experiences provide key resources for understanding how prevailing social scripts can be rejected, revised, and expanded. For this reason, while neither same-sex nor single parenthood meet the approval of Catholic moral teaching (depending on the originating circumstances of the latter), the experiences of male parents in such contexts provide valuable perspective on how parental capacities are negotiated in the absence of direct female mothering.

[14] Jeffrey Scott Turner, *Families in America* (Santa Barbara: ABC CLIO, 2002), 49. Female income tends to increase women's marital power and equitable division of household labor. However, when women out-earn their husbands the trend in shared labor drops significantly. This suggests that out-earned men devote increased attention to work outside the home. See Rebecca Glauber, "Race and Gender in

are more than ten times as likely to be unemployed outside the home in order to provide care for children than are their male spouses, among whom less than 2% are similarly situated.[15] However, the number of single-parent households headed by fathers has increased from 1% to 8% in the last two generations.[16] Moreover, about half of all US two-parent families are now headed by parents who are both employed full time. Despite similar employment among spouses, the vast majority of these families are split between those with wives providing most of the childcare and domestic labor and those with more equally shared arrangements between partners.[17] Fathers are also significantly more likely to use the plural "we" when describing their parental responsibilities, suggesting a shared parental identity, while mothers favor the singular, suggesting a self-understanding as primary parent.[18] In relationships where mothers are relatively more breadwinning and fathers more caregiving, women also become more likely to represent themselves as co-parents.[19]

Sociologist Andrea Doucet argues that American culture is actually far less welcoming of egalitarian parenthood than opinion polls suggest. Men are much more inhibited and viewed with greater suspicion in communal settings including children or when expressing interest in the children of others.[20] Moreover, widespread belief in "men's incompetence in caregiving" is communicated in a variety of

---

Families and at Work: The Fatherhood Wage Premium," *Gender and Society* 22, no. 1 (February 2008): 11.

[15] The number of stay-at-home fathers more than doubled between 1990 and 2010, but declined again as the unemployment rate fell. See Gretchen Livingston, "Stay-at-Home Moms and Dads Account for One-in-Five US Parents," September 24, 2018, www.pewresearch.org/fact-tank/2018/09/24/stay-at-home-moms-and-dads-account-for-about-one-in-five-u-s-parents/.

[16] Gretchen Livingston, "The Rise of Single Fathers," *Pew Research Center*, July 2, 2013, www.pewsocialtrends.org/2013/07/02/the-rise-of-single-fathers/. This number includes some households with unmarried adult partners.

[17] Pew Research Center, "Raising Kids and Running a Household: How Working Parents Share the Load," November 4, 2015, www.pewsocialtrends.org/2015/11/04/raising-kids-and-running-a-household-how-working-parents-share-the-load/.

[18] "The relative representation of one's parental self and one's partner in arranging and planning narratives may denote the extent to which the parental self, at a superordinate level, is a 'self-as-sole-executive-parent' as compared to a 'self-as-coexecutive-parent'" (Joseph H. Pleck and Jeffrey L. Stueve, "A Narrative Approach to Paternal Identity: The Importance of Parental Identity 'Conjointness,'" in *Conceptualizing and Measuring Father Involvement*, 84).

[19] Pleck and Stueve, "A Narrative Approach to Paternal Identity," 103.

[20] Some evidence suggests that mothers tend to set the course for fathers' involvement. See Brent A. McBride, Sarah J. Schoppe, Moon-Ho Ho, and Thomas R. Rane, "Multiple Determinants of Father Involvement: An Exploratory Analysis Using the PSID-CDS Data Set," in *Conceptualizing and Measuring Father Involvement*, 323.

social contexts.[21] Glenda Wall and Stephanie Arnold similarly contend that more involved fathering is "undermined by images and texts that position fathers as part-time, secondary, less competent parents with fewer parenting responsibilities and greater breadwinning responsibilities than mothers."[22] Many of these social biases flow from models of parenthood that are both inherited from and projected onto past generations. For example, the traditional "Breadwinner" (dependent on industrialization and therefore traditional only in a historically shallow sense) continues to exert significant influence.

The "Breadwinner" model was disrupted repeatedly throughout the twentieth century but ultimately began being dismantled by women's increasing participation in the workforce.[23] Second-wave feminism may have initially led to a reactive "hardening" of masculine concepts (as evidenced by late-twentieth century cinematic artifacts such as *Rambo, Die Hard,* and *Robocop*), but notions of masculinity were relatively quickly renegotiated with a new vision of fatherhood that reworked traditional gender binaries.[24] This "New Man" was tough but sensitive and skilled in both his profession and domestic life.[25] Contemporary fathers influenced by the "New Man" ideal still tend to emphasize the financial support they provide their families but also value their role in childcare and emotional investment in their children's lives.[26] Moreover, such fathers tend to limit investment in work and adult friendships for the sake of relationships with their children. The developmental benefits of this tradeoff for children appear significant. Paternal involvement plays an important role in children's "cognitive competence, school performance, empathy, self-esteem, self-control, well-being, life skills, and social competence."[27]

---

[21] Andrea Doucet, "'It's Just Not Good for a Man to be Interested in Other People's Children': Fathers, Public Displays of Care, and 'Relevant Others,'" in *Displaying Families: A New Concept for the Sociology of Family Life*, ed. Esther Dermott and Julie Seymour (New York: Palgrave Macmillan, 2012), 84, 91.
[22] Glenda Wall and Stephanie Arnold, "How Involved Is Involved Fathering? An Exploration of the Contemporary Culture of Fatherhood," *Gender and Society* 21, no. 4 (August 2007): 511.
[23] Non-white women have a longer history of substantial rates of employment and, in contrast to white women's trends, employment among African American women dropped from the 1960s to 1990s. While necessity remains a significant factor, today education is a strong predictor of female employment. See Paula England, Carmen Garcia Beaulieu, and Mary Ross, "Women's Employment among Blacks, Whites, and Three Groups of Latinas: Do More Privileged Women Have Higher Employment?" *Gender and Society* 18, no. 4 (August 2004): 494–495.
[24] Evans, "Foreword," x.
[25] Angela Smith, "Bulging Biceps and Tender Kisses: The Sexualisation of Fatherhood," *Social Semiotics* 28, no. 3 (2018): 318.
[26] Rachel M. Schmitz, "Constructing Men as Fathers: A Content Analysis of Formulations of Fatherhood in Parenting Magazines," *Journal of Men's Studies* 24, no. 1 (2016): 4.
[27] Rob Palkovitz, "Involved Fathering and Child Development," 131.

Still, adjustment to this vision of fatherhood can be difficult as "many men lack knowledge of child development, developmentally appropriate parenting skills, and sensitivity to children's needs."[28]

At the same time, socially dominant expectations of parenthood itself have become more challenging. Particularly among the upper classes, "intensive parenting" (more widely known as "helicopter" or "bulldozer" parenting) gained influence.[29] This model of parenting tends to emphasize "nurture over nature" and associates parenthood with assuring children's developmental path to success, particularly financial success.[30] The raised stakes of intensive parenting tend to undermine confidence in parents' own capacities and thereby encourage greater reliance on professional support.[31] Thus, the "New Man" fathers are seeking greater parental involvement at a time when parenthood itself is increasingly held to higher expectations and parents are simultaneously undermined as incapable of meeting them. These shifting expectations may have been a factor in the slow growth of male caregiving; however, their differentiated impacts along gendered lines limit any strong claim in this direction.[32]

Perhaps more tellingly, men typically have limited awareness of the actual challenges involved in realizing their ideals of engaged fathering. Many men who expect strong co-parenting relations with their spouse are shocked by the barriers paid employment places on this expectation. These men tend to recast their ideals by turning to less direct parental investment, such as responsibility for their family's long-term financial security. Paradoxically, their drive for greater involvement can reinforce the centrality of financial provision in fatherhood. Not surprisingly, while these men still understand their efforts as expressing involved parenthood, such efforts go largely unrecognized by their spouse unless men also participate in direct care giving and demonstrate awareness of their parental role through their

---

[28] Many new mothers likewise lack these skills despite cultural presumptions of innate female capabilities in caregiving (Turner, *Families in America*, 49).

[29] Annette Lareau has described prominent models of childrearing that differ by social class, namely, "concerted cultivation" and "accomplishment of natural growth." See Annette Lareau, *Unequal Childhoods: Class, Race, and Family Life* (Berkeley: University of California Press, 2011), 2–3.

[30] Shirani, Henwood, and Coltart, "Meeting the Challenges of Intensive Parenting Culture," 29.

[31] Shirani, Henwood, and Coltart, "Meeting the Challenges of Intensive Parenting Culture," 26.

[32] Mothers appear to have borne the brunt of the anxieties associated with intensive parenting, whereas standards for fathers tend to revolve around meeting the minimal expectations of this model (e.g., awareness of food allergies at a child's birthday party). Moreover, men tend to acquiesce more readily to the limits of their parental abilities and appeal to "doing my best" over external measurements of parental performance (Shirani, Henwood, and Coltart, "Meeting the Challenges of Intensive Parenting Culture," 30, 35).

daily lives.[33] As such, it seems the "New Man" model is difficult to translate in practice and susceptible to reverting to a subjectively redefined "Breadwinner" model when faced with barriers.

Despite the rise of more involved ideals, fatherhood remains primarily positioned as a supporting parental role to motherhood.[34] Moreover, not all forms of fatherly involvement are valued equally. While the "New Man" is idealized as both income earner and emotionally invested caregiver, the "Householder" is stigmatized as ineffectual and incapable of either successful employment or fully caring for his children. Conversely, men who are primary income earners tend to be "framed as absent from their children's lives."[35] As such, well-intended fathers are positioned between failing in their parental ideals or failing in their manhood.

Bradford Wilcox presents yet another model of fatherhood that seems to more readily overcome these challenges. Wilcox argues that contemporary conservative Protestant discourse, replete with ideals of male authority in a servant leader model, has made the greatest strides in actualizing increased paternal investment while maintaining clear lines of gender distinction.[36] This "Soft Patriarchs" model of fatherhood has offered men "a 'patriarchal bargain' that accords men symbolic authority in the home in return for their exercise of greater responsibility for the well-being of their families."[37] Despite the clear gains in certain areas relative to other cultural trends, this conservative Christian model of fatherhood still fails to fully realize reflexive adaptability or fully equal co-parenting through negotiated parental roles. For instance, fathers in the "Soft Patriarchs" model are relatively more involved with their children, and happier for it, but they also report some of the lowest levels of sharing in domestic chores.[38] In fact, Wilcox finds, "men who hold profamily attitudes tend to be gender traditionalists" and as such are more likely to live in households where labor is more clearly divided by gender.[39] Expressions of appreciation for women's labor also vary by

---

[33] Shirani, Henwood, and Coltart, "Meeting the Challenges of Intensive Parenting Culture," 35.
[34] Schmitz, "Constructing Men as Fathers," 7.
[35] Schmitz, "Constructing Men as Fathers," 12.
[36] John Wall, "Fatherhood, Childism, and the Creation of Society," *Journal of the American Academy of Religion* 75, no. 1 (March 2007): 53.
[37] W. Bradford Wilcox, *Soft Patriarchs, New Men: How Christianity Shapes Fathers and Husbands* (Chicago: University of Chicago Press, 2004), 9.
[38] Wilcox, *Soft Patriarchs*, 149. Though not statistically significant, Wilcox found religious involvement to have reverse impacts on household labor for conservative and mainline Protestant men. Nominally affiliated conservative men do slightly less household labor than their active coreligionists, while active mainline Protestant men do slightly more than active conservative Protestants, but less than nominally associated mainline Protestants.
[39] Wilcox, *Soft Patriarchs*, 148.

theological commitments and religious involvement. Active mainline and conservative Protestant men tend to show the greatest appreciation for their wives' efforts. Meanwhile, nominally affiliated conservative and mainline Protestant men, respectively the religious affiliations that share domestic labor least and most, show the least appreciation for their wives' labor.[40]

The responses in Wilcox's study do, however, provide compelling grounds for the role of religious messaging in shaping parental practices.[41] The "Soft Patriarchs" model is especially pronounced among conservative Christians who frequently attend church and identify religion as central to their lives.[42] Conversely, conservative Christian fathers who rarely attend church score the lowest in paternal investment among all groups studied. Consequently, even as the "Soft Patriarchs" model raises concern regarding the extent of its adaptability and equitability, it also demonstrates the influence religious narratives about fatherhood can have on men who are exposed to them.

NARRATIVES AND INDIVIDUAL FUNCTIONING

Neuroscientist Antonio Damasio writes: "Consciousness begins when brains acquire the power ... of telling a story."[43] From a functionalist psychological perspective, social and self-narratives help establish self-understanding and interpret individual behavior.[44] For example, men's perception of their role as fathers appears to be a powerful predictor of their involvement with children.[45] Contemporary fathers who appropriate parental functions associated with motherhood may encounter psychological conflicts if resources do not exist for balancing their parental and gendered identities.[46] Highly socially scripted identities (e.g., the "Breadwinner") require integrating fewer conflictual dimensions of the self-concept but can also be devastated by the loss of one important dimension (e.g., unemployment). Conversely, high differentiation creates potential for adaptable identities but requires greater effort to integrate these

---

[40] Wilcox, *Soft Patriarchs*, 152.
[41] Wilcox, *Soft Patriarchs*, 165–176.
[42] Pew Research Center, "Religious Landscape Study," www.pewforum.org/religious-landscape-study/.
[43] Dan P. McAdams, Ruthellen Josselson, Amia Lieblich, "Introduction," in *Identity and Story: Creating Self in Narrative*, ed. Dan P. McAdams, Ruthellen Josselson, and Amia Lieblich (Washington, DC: American Psychological Association, 2006), 3.
[44] Martin Albrow, *Sociology; The Basics* (New York: Routledge, 1999), 110–11. See Peter T. F. Raggatt, "Unity Versus Multiplicity," in *Identity and Story; Creating Self Narrative*, 16.
[45] McBride, Schoppe, Ho, and Rane, "Multiple Determinants of Father Involvement," 334.
[46] Schmitz, "Constructing Men as Fathers," 19.

various dimensions.[47] Integration may be less about constructing a single seamless narrative than an individual's ability to harmonize the interactions of multiple synchronic narratives as circumstances require. This personal positioning takes place alongside social positioning as societal expectations exert influence on the individual's interpretations of self.[48] Low integration carries the risk of experiencing cognitive dissonance caused by conflictual perceptions.[49] Individuals are highly motivated to avoid the discomfort of dissonance, which may be especially pronounced when the concept of self is involved, and will therefore adjust perceptions and behaviors in order to avoid it.[50]

Sociologist Andrea Doucet's extensive research on primary caregiver fathers reveals that these men tend to emphasize their own masculinity and do so according to traditional conceptions of gender.[51] This pattern suggests attempts to overcome dissonance through asserting key aspects of identity (i.e., masculinity) to trump dissonant factors as well as emphasizing more global narratives (i.e., our family works) to overcome inconsistencies in the actual details of their lives.[52] The apparent inability of many men who are primary caregivers to construct new self-affirming narratives without resorting to social stereotypes or factors beyond their control is problematic and may help explain why men so easily resort to subjectively redefined traditional models when challenged. Fulfilling traditional models of

---

[47] Jennifer D. Campbell, Sunaina Assanand, and Adam Di Paula, "Structural Features of the Self-Concept and Adjustment," in *Psychological Perspectives on the Self and Identity*, ed. Abraham Tesser, Richard B. Felson, Jerry M. Suls (Washington, DC: American Psychological Association, 2000), 68.

[48] Raggatt, "Unity versus Multiplicity," 16.

[49] Eddie Harmon-Jones, "An Update on Cognitive Dissonance Theory, with a Focus on the Self," in *Psychological Perspectives on the Self and Identity*, 120.

[50] Individuals experiencing cognitive dissonance may respond by "adding consonant cognitions, subtracting dissonant cognitions, reducing the importance of dissonant cognitions, increasing the importance of consonant cognitions, or by using some combination of these routes" (Harmon-Jones, "An Update on Cognitive Dissonance Theory," 120).

[51] Doucet, "It's Just Not Good for a Man to be Interested in Other People's Children," 88.

[52] "Self-Consistency" theory posits that dissonance involving one's concept of self must be addressed by disproving the threatening cognition or reevaluating the self in order to restore a reliable self-concept. "Self-Affirmation" theory posits that individuals are motivated to maintain the existing integrity of their concepts of self and therefore will respond to dissonance by affirming the "global integrity of the self." This may be done by reaffirming significant but unrelated components of a self-concept. Despite fulfilling "mothering" functions, the men appear determined "to distinguish themselves *as men*, as heterosexual males, and as fathers, *not* as mothers ... they must actively work to dispel the idea that they might be gay, un-masculine, or not men." A similar phenomenon has also been documented among men who work in traditionally female occupations (Doucet, "It's Just Not Good for a Man to be Interested in Other People's Children," 84, 88, 123).

fatherhood offers similar possibilities for adjustment with far less complexity in developing self-identity and conflict in social positioning. Still such reversions do not meet the equitable parental standards to which many couples aspire and may not be possible for men within certain familial circumstances.

Restricted conceptions of maleness may also lead to reduced adaptability and greater stress in encountering changing circumstances and appear to have profound influences on male children.[53] John Cicero argues that children who are raised with rigid concepts of masculinity and femininity are more likely to hold self-constructs that deny specific aspects of their personalities. This is evidenced by men who deny their own needs for "emotional warmth, support, and nurturance on self-report measures" but measure equally with women on "projective measures—where they don't realize what they are endorsing."[54] Many men may lack the individual backgrounds and supportive social narratives to adapt readily to involved caregiving, yet their own failure to do so increases the likelihood that their sons will face the same challenges.

To understand the lack of narrative resources for contemporary shifts in paternal possibilities, brief sketches of developments in American media portrayals of fatherhood and the presentation of fatherhood in magisterial documents follow below. These are at least potentially important sources of narrative formation for Catholic fathers today, although they differ in substantial ways. On the one hand, both American culture and magisterial teaching on the family are largely indebted to the effects of industrialization in shaping homes and conceptions of parental roles. On the other hand, American media is much more diverse and inconsistent in its various portrayals of fatherhood than is magisterial teaching, which attempts a consistent and internally referential vision of the family within which its vision of fatherhood is situated. Moreover, media presentations are delivered directly to consumers whereas knowledge of Catholic magisterial teaching is generally filtered through a process of promulgation to the public through sermons, books, radio, and other media. Along the way, these teachings are made more accessible but also subject to the concerns and contexts of their interpreters. As such, the following sections explore two accessible, but not entirely commensurable, resources for narrative production. These media and magisterial sources are themselves situated within much larger webs of resources and interactions which would require a significantly longer project to

---

[53] David James, "The Integration of Masculine Spirituality," in *Perspectives on Marriage; A Reader,* ed. Kieran Scott and Michael Warren (New York: Oxford University Press, 2001), 290.
[54] John J. Cicero, "Toward Christian Sexual Maturity," in *Human Sexuality in the Catholic Tradition* (New York: Rowman and Littlefield, 2007), 38.

begin to untangle.

Media Portrayals of Fatherhood

Social narratives about fatherhood are reaffirmed through various social artifacts and practices, including popular media. Recent generations of television audiences have witnessed diverse portrayals of fatherhood, from the wisdom of fathers like Mike Brady, Andy Taylor, and Ward Cleaver to the hapless antics of Al Bundy, Homer Simpson, and Tim "The Toolman" Taylor. Present variations range from same-sex dads like Mitchel Pritchett and Cameron Tucker, to firmly committed fathers dealing with complex relationships such as Adam Braverman and Randall Pearson, to television fathers returning as grandfathers in rebooted series, as have Dan Conner and Danny Tanner.[55] Despite these diversities, these men tend to be represented as integral to their children's lives. This is obvious for the firm role models like Danny Tanner, but even a bumbling man-child like Homer Simpson or Tim Taylor always seems to come through in the end. Furthermore, their masculinity is rarely lost even when the characters undertake traditionally feminine roles or otherwise challenge masculine norms. For example, the flamboyantly extroverted, gay adoptive-father Cameron Tucker is revealed to be a former college football lineman and subsequently excels as a football coach.

Beyond television, parenting magazines put many of the contradictions around gender and parenthood on full display. Their titles typically use the gender-neutral "parent" or "parenting" with a relatively small subset appealing to "mother" or "father" directly. Nonetheless, the fact of greater female involvement in caregiving continues to drive content and reinforces the widely held association of mothering with full-time, authentic parenthood.[56] Men are frequently presented through both direct and indirect messaging as secondary parents rather than competent co-parents.[57] When fatherhood is presented directly, masculine identity requires negotiation in relation to parenthood not required of female identity. In this process, men's masculine traits typically overshadow their role

---

[55] The rise of streaming services has disrupted clear lines of generational development in portrayals of fatherhood. For example, in 2020 Netflix offered both *Full House* and *Fuller House*, making it possible to watch Danny Tanner as a father and as a grandfather simultaneously.

[56] Jane Sunderland, "'Parenting' or 'Mothering': The Case of Modern Childcare Magazines," *Discourse & Society* 17, no. 4 (July 2006): 509. A simple perusal of magazine covers gives a quick impression of the same finding. The article also finds that same-sex parents are virtually invisible in these magazines.

[57] Emily Stevens, "Understanding Discursive Barriers to Involved Fatherhood: The Case of Australian Stay-at-Home Fathers," *Journal of Family Studies* 21, no. 1 (2015): 24.

as parents.[58]

In entertainment magazines and websites, successful male celebrities are among the few men who are commonly presented as displaying the full array of desirable masculine and fatherly qualities. Chris Hemsworth, the ultra-masculine star of the *Thor* movies and father of three, is perhaps the clearest example of this sexy "honed and toned" ideal dad. Social media pages across the internet are dedicated to cataloging images of sexy dads that contrast their tender care for children with their muscular physiques.[59] Such image collections can center so much attention on the male body that their children are visually downplayed or obscured from view.[60] Parents around the world lift and carry their children on a daily basis but for these sexualized fathers the disproportionate excess of their bulging biceps to the work of caregiving becomes the center of attention. Because these select few fathers display both superior levels of physical fitness and significant commodities of both disposable income and time to spend with their families, they represent an idealization that lies well beyond most men's reach.

The inability of fathers to be recognized fully for their caregiving potential contrasts markedly with the linkage of motherhood to authentic parenthood itself. Gendered boundaries tend to be policed around concepts of parenthood that relegate men to part-time status while reinforcing mothering as the "gold standard of parenting."[61] Mothering embodies a unity of gender and purpose.[62] Because parenting is not truly a gender-neutral concept, it does not readily admit to greater masculine content. A full incorporation of male caregiving into the concept of parenting requires shifting its meaning beyond this gendered valence. Consequently, terms such as "co-parenting" or "shared-parenting" are more apt for expressing equitable parental roles.

The association of mothering with primary parenting is expressed in a number of ways including, somewhat paradoxically, the "annihilation of the mother" motif in popular fiction. A telling summary of this motif in children's films is presented in the 2018 animated film, "Wreck it Ralph 2: Ralph Breaks the Internet." In an attempt to hide, the protagonist, Princess Vanellope Von Schweetz, finds herself pressed to explain her credentials among thirteen other Disney princesses. As these storied characters interrogate her with plotlines from their own movies, Princess Jasmine asks, "Do you have Daddy issues?" The exasperated misfit responds, "I don't even have a

---

[58] Schmitz, "Constructing Men as Fathers," 11.
[59] Smith, "Bulging Biceps and Tender Kisses," 323.
[60] Smith, "Bulging Biceps and Tender Kisses," 322.
[61] Schmitz, "Constructing Men as Fathers," 14.
[62] Sunderland, "'Parenting' or 'Mothering,'" 524.

mom!" to which eight princesses chime in unison, "Neither do we!"[63] The annihilated mother trope is effective precisely because it removes the central parental figure and thereby opens uncontested dramatic space for narrating children's personal development or exploring male parental experiences.[64]

Although media portrayals of fatherhood are diverse and have developed throughout recent decades, the male parental performances constructed through popular media do not generally encourage individual fathers in developing their full caregiving potentials and therefore remain morally problematic. Fathers, though different, remain largely peripheral to the authentic parenting realized in motherhood. Even in reporting the daily tasks of parenthood, media portrayals tend to emphasize physical actions in fatherhood rather than emotional support and nurturing care.[65] This reinforces the inconsistent social narratives that both encourage involved fathering while also emasculating overly involved fathering and questioning men's capabilities and fitness for caregiving and domestic work more generally. Fathers who are single, same-sex partnered, or primary caregivers obviously must respond to the full range of their children's needs; nonetheless, awareness of the masculine potential to provide this care eludes many social narratives of male parenting.

Fatherhood in Modern Catholic Teaching

Given the conflicting social messages outlined above, it would seem that religious discourse is well positioned to offer a valuable resource in helping contemporary fathers address challenges of identity formation in relation to their evolving roles. The Catholic tradition is committed to the "human person fully alive,"[66] while Catholic moral thought takes authentic human development as its aim.[67] Such aspirations would seem to support a vision of human adaptability and relational fullness that might transcend narrow cultural concerns for properly gendered behavior. Unlike the "Soft Patriarchs" model of fatherhood drawn from conservative Protestantism, Catholicism is theoretically less bound to "biblical models of manhood" in the sense of relying explicitly on scripture as the singular normative source of moral and anthropological

---

[63] *Ralph Breaks the Internet*, directed by Rich Moore and Phil Johnston (Walt Disney Animation Studios, 2018).
[64] Berit Åström, "The Symbolic Annihilation of Mothers in Popular Culture: *Single Father* and the Death of the Mother," *Feminist Media Studies* 15, no. 4 (2015): 594.
[65] Stevens, "Understanding Discursive Barriers to Involved Fatherhood," 28.
[66] This is a common paraphrase of the words of St. Irenaeus. See Irenaeus, *Against Heresies*, Book VI, Chapter XX, Section 7, available online at www.earlychristianwritings.com/text/irenaeus-book4.html. Some translations place the quote at Book 4, Chapter 34, section 7.
[67] *Catechism of the Catholic Church*, 3.1.1, www.vatican.va/archive/ccc_css/archive/catechism/p3s1c1.htm.

understanding. It is, of course, doubtful that any tradition can rely singularly on scripture as a sole normative guide without implicitly importing numerous additional resources as interpretive guides. Catholicism's explicit valuation of tradition as a normative guide to the interpretation of scripture as well as its adoption of critical exegetical methods alleviates that need for such single-minded convictions. While Catholics may still find value in "biblical manhood," Catholic interpretative norms open such readings to explicit recognition of the particularities of our own context as interpreters as well as the broader history of diverse Christian practices of parenthood that have characterized the tradition. Moreover, the natural law tradition provides a theologically defensible position from which observations of the created order can be integrated into an understanding of the creative work of God. In this case, observations of a larger range of masculine parental capabilities than those socially prized in the industrialized West can be embraced as new realizations of the breadth of human potential rather than deviations from a tightly scripted revealed order. Despite these possibilities, existing Catholic narratives of fatherhood within magisterial teaching are strongly implicated in the same Western cultural milieu which has given rise to conflicting and narrow social messages about fatherhood.

From Leo XIII in the late nineteenth century to Pius XII in the mid-twentieth, papal documents describe the family as headed by spouses defined by sexually differentiated parental roles. Parenting is described, at least partially, as an act of caretaking,[68] supervision,[69] and educating,[70] though the details of these functions are generally undeveloped. Pius XII offered high praise for the task of parenting, calling parenthood a "ministry of Christ" and speaking of parents as "priests" of their households.[71] He showed particular concern for instructing fathers and asserted that the entire health and wellbeing of the family, not only physically, but intellectually and spiritually, rested upon the virtue and hard work of the father.[72] He likened fatherhood to God's original act of creation, adding that fatherhood

---

[68] Pius XI, *Divini Illius Magistri*, no. 32, www.vatican.va/holy_father/pius_xi/encyclicals/documents/hf_p-xi_enc_31121929_divini-illius-magistri_en.html.

[69] Pius XI, *Casti Connubii*, no. 15, www.vatican.va/holy_father/pius_xi/encyclicals/documents/hf_p-xi_enc_31121930_casti-connubii_en.html.

[70] Pius XI, *Divini Illius Magistri*, no. 34.

[71] "You are, always under the guidance of the priest, the first and closest educators and teachers of the children of God entrusted and given to you .... You are as it were the spiritual precursors, priests yourselves of the cradle, infancy and childhood, for you must point out to the children the way to heaven" (Pius XII, "Allocution to Newlyweds," in *Matrimony*, trans. Michael J. Byrnes [Boston: Saint Paul, 1963], 318).

[72] Pius XII, "Allocution to Fathers of Families," in *Matrimony*, 398.

communicates "the superior life of intelligence and love."[73] Pius XII suggested that fathers not only fulfill the "priestly" role of parenting, but that they also have an "episcopal" role within the home and, as such, he defended male headship in the familial hierarchy.[74]

Despite this gendered demarcation of the domestic order being clearly articulated in magisterial teaching, by the mid-twentieth century its rigidity began to soften. In 1961, John XXIII's encyclical *Mater et Magistra* assumed an all-male workforce and did not challenge the hierarchical ordering of the family posited by earlier pontiffs.[75] Just two years later, after the opening of Vatican II, John XXIII optimistically reconsidered changes in women's social roles and judged these developments to have stemmed from women's recognition of their own human dignity.[76] This was a remarkable shift as earlier pontiffs had clearly defended women's place in the home as a matter of protecting female dignity.[77] While the justification remained based in the dignity of women, the interpretation of the implications of women's dignity took a notable turn. *Pacem in Terris* began a transition from hierarchical conceptions of female subservience to ideals of both public and private equity.[78] With Vatican II, *Gaudium et Spes* affirmed women's right to take a more active role in cultural life and emphasized equality between spouses.[79]

At the same time, however, there was little reflection on how these changing perceptions of women might also influence the role of men within the domestic sphere. *Gaudium et Spes* encourages fathers to be active in their children's lives, but motherhood remains essential for the care of young children.[80] The newfound recognition of the implications of female dignity did not lead to a similarly concerted

---

[73] Pius XII, "Allocution to Newlyweds," 325.
[74] Pius XII, *Summi Pontificatus*, no. 89, www.vatican.va/holy_father/ pius_xii/encyclicals/documents/hf_p-xii_enc_20101939_summi-pontificatus_en.html.
[75] John XXIII, *Mater et Magistra*, nos. 20, 22, 71 et al., www.vatican.va/holy_father/ john_xxiii/encyclicals/documents/hf_j-xxiii_enc_15051961_mater_en.html.
[76] John XXIII, *Pacem in Terris*, no. 41, www.vatican.va/holy_father/john_xxiii/ encyclicals/documents/hf_j-xxiii_enc_11041963_pacem_en.html.
[77] Leo XIII, *Rerum Novarum*, no. 42, www.vatican.va/holy_father/leo_xiii/ encyclicals/documents/hf_l-xiii_enc_15051891_rerum-novarum_en.html. See Pius XI, *Casti Connubii*, no. 75.
[78] John XXIII, *Pacem in Terris*, no. 12. Even here the transition was not seamless. For example, while women's participation in public life is encouraged, *Gravissimum Educationis* allowed the universal right to education to be conditioned by gender (*Gravissimum Educationis*, no. 1, www.vatican.va/archive/ hist_councils/ii_vatican _council/documents/vat-ii_decl_19651028_gravissimum-educationis_en.html).
[79] *Gaudium et Spes*, nos. 48–52 www.vatican.va/archive/hist_councils/ii_vatican _council/documents/vat-ii_cons_19651207_ gaudium-et-spes_en.html. See Pius XI, *Casti Connubii*, no. 23. *Gaudium et Spes* describes marriage as "covenant founded in mutual love."
[80] *Gaudium et Spes*, no. 52.

effort of rethinking male norms. Instead, magisterial teaching since the mid-century has devoted significant energy towards explaining women's social equality while protecting the private-domestic world of nurture and childrearing as essentially female. Following the council, Paul VI warned against a "false equality" that would deny women's proper roles as "the heart of the family."[81] John Paul II likewise identified the centrality of motherhood in domestic life, clearly differentiated parental gender roles,[82] and once again identified men as the "head" of the household.[83] John Paul II described parents generally as "heralds of the Gospel"[84] who exercise a "true and proper 'ministry.'"[85] Yet, in the daily activities of parenthood, he centralized women's role in nurturing children, and gave little indication that fathers might also fulfill such tasks.[86] John Paul II did emphasize the importance of the father's presence within the home and assistance with caregiving, but fatherhood remained hemmed around the centrality of motherhood.

John Paul II's *Mulieris Dignitatem* presented a conception of womanhood that was tightly bound to motherhood and patterned on the person of Mary.[87] The following year, his apostolic exhortation *Redemptoris Custos* reflected on the life of Joseph, but came nowhere close to the depth of reflection on identity and parenthood presented in the earlier letter. The lack of parity between *Mulieris Dignitatem* and *Redemptoris Custos* is notable. In the former, Mary serves much more directly and explicitly as a model for women, while in the latter, Joseph is generally presented as a paradigm of human virtue while no thick anthropological account of masculinity is attempted. Instead, the description of Joseph's parenthood replicates existing social ideals about fatherhood common throughout the industrialized West, such as support, protection, oversight, and education.[88] Even the silence of Joseph in the Gospels is taken as evidence of his strong and silent,

---

[81] Paul VI, *Octogesima Adveniens*, no. 13, www.vatican.va/holy_father/paul_vi/apost_letters/documents/hf_p-vi_apl_19710514_octogesima-adveniens_en.html.

[82] See Lisa Sowle Cahill, "Notes on Moral Theology: 1989; Feminist Ethics," *Theological Studies* 51 (1990): 58.

[83] John Paul II, *Laborem Exercens*, no. 19, www.vatican.va/holy_father/john_paul_ii/encyclicals/documents/hf_jp-ii_enc_14091981_laborem-exercens_en.html.

[84] John Paul II, *Familiaris Consortio*, no. 39, www.vatican.va/holy_father/john_paul_ii/apost_exhortations/documents/hf_jp-ii_exh_19811122_familiaris-consortio_en.ht ml.

[85] John Paul II, *Familiaris Consortio*, no. 21.

[86] John Paul II, *Familiaris Consortio*, no. 66.

[87] John Paul II, *Mulieris Dignitatem*, no. 3ff, www.vatican.va/content/john-paul-ii/en/apost_letters/1988/documents/hf_jp-ii_apl_19880815_mulieris-dignitatem.html.

[88] John Paul II, *Redemptoris Custos*, no. 8, www.vatican.va/content/john-paul-ii/en/apost_exhortations/documents/hf_jp-ii_exh_15081989_redemptoris-custos.html.

contemplative, and faith-filled way of life. These masculine cultural norms are simply layered into the silence of scripture in order to produce a compelling image of a saint whose actual life and personality remain opaque. Joseph becomes a paradigm for manhood as articulated by the paternal virtues of the modern West, while the lack of scriptural evidence itself is utilized to justify the image being constructed.

Most recently, Pope Francis's 2015 apostolic exhortation *Amoris Laetitia* encourages reciprocity between spouses and urges men to assume greater responsibilities within the home.[89] Despite acknowledging some malleability in the categories of 'masculine' and 'feminine,' the document tends toward the same gender dichotomies that typify John Paul II's writing. For example, while both mothers and fathers are called upon to be involved in the life of the family, only women's role in motherhood is presented as essential to society.[90] Men are to love their wives and are encouraged to take on "some aspects" of childrearing if required for the good of the family.[91] Thus, even as the document pushes towards greater equity and attempts to disrupt rigid gendered categories, it reaffirms the broadly influential assumption that women are essential to parenthood while men play a supporting role.

Throughout recent magisterial teachings, women and motherhood dominate considerations of social change in relation to gender and the family while fathers receive disproportionately little attention characterized by vague references to greater involvement and support of mothers. There are few indications that men may be responsible for, or even capable of, performing a significant set of domestic tasks, particularly those related to the nurture of young children and direct caregiving.

As acknowledged above, the reality of certain patterns of presenting fatherhood within magisterial thought does not necessarily bear directly on the narrative formation of all lay faithful. At a popular level, Catholic organizations commonly support more involved fathering for Catholic men willing to seek out these resources. Numerous websites are dedicated to Catholic parenting and fatherhood in particular, and many Catholic fathers find support through local and national groups and retreats.[92] These instantiations of Catholic belief are shaped by magisterial thought in significant

---

[89] Francis, *Amoris Laetitia*, nos. 55, 286, w2.vatican.va/content/dam/francesco/pdf/apost_exhortations/documents/papa-francesco_esortazione-ap_20160319_amoris-laetitia_en.pdf.
[90] Francis, *Amoris Laetitia*, no. 173.
[91] Francis, *Amoris Laetitia*, no. 286.
[92] *That Man is You* is one such program offered through parishes. Information is available at the *Paradisus Dei* website, www.paradisusdei.org/that-man-is-you/#program-content.

ways, even if indirectly.

John Paul II's thought, including his "theology of the body," has been acutely influential in shaping many such resources. The late pope's vaunted appreciation for gendered difference has provided the foundation for many popular Catholic efforts seeking to recover authentic expressions of masculinity.[93] In some ways this movement mirrors aspects of conservative Protestant thought and aspects of the men's movement; however, its sources and representatives are diffuse as it has not yet given rise to a significant online community. Instead, the movement relies on speakers, authors, and the parishes and dioceses that promote similar causes.[94] The movement itself is largely held together by a perceived need for spiritual revival in the social and religious understanding of masculinity. Additionally, John Paul II's tendencies toward culture war thinking help to link the Catholic movement to broader Christian and social movements similarly invested in high contrast socio-religious identities appealing to gender role distinctions, traditional models of manhood, and hostility towards the progress of the larger culture.[95]

The combination of gender essentialism and a confrontational stance toward secular culture informs a religious construction of fatherhood rooted in socially conservative ideals that replicates the "Soft Patriarchs" model identified among conservative Protestants.[96] This construction of masculinity appeals to a particular segment of American Catholics and is amply supported by magisterial portrayals of fatherhood, which likewise rely on socially conservative norms. Unfortunately, such religious messaging generally works against a concerted commitment to exploring the full diversity of male parental capabilities and experiences by fitting fatherhood into a particular social framework positioned in contrast to motherhood.

---

[93] For a critical assessment of John Paul II's gendered anthropology and its motivations, see Todd Salzman and Michael Lawler, *The Sexual Person: Toward a Renewed Catholic Anthropology* (Washington, DC: Georgetown University Press, 2008), 84–91.

[94] Some representative websites include The Catholic Gentleman's Guide, www.catholicgentlemansguide.com/, The Catholic Gentleman, catholicgentleman.net/, and The New Emangelization, www.newemangelization.com/.

[95] John Paul II's own high contrast orientation towards Western culture is evident in his multiple critiques of consumerism and materialism, but was perhaps more influentially expressed in his identification and rejection of the "culture of death." Notably, this phrase occurs twelve times throughout his 1995 encyclical *Evangelium Vitae* (John Paul II, *Evangelium Vitae*, www.vatican.va/content/john-paul-ii/en/encyclicals/documents/hf_jp-ii_enc_25031995_evangelium-vitae.html).

[96] While there is not room in this essay to explore the connections between violence and traditional constructions of masculinity, it is notable that several online resources for Catholic men openly embrace an overtly militant framing of masculinity. For example, see www.thekingsmen.org and www.romancatholicman.com.

SUPPORTING AND EXPANDING NARRATIVES OF PATERNAL CARE

To support more expansive developments in Catholic narratives of fatherhood based in human dignity, male participation in adaptive parental functions must be understood as advancing the breadth of human potential rather than corrupting some normative model of masculinity. The latter misplaces priority in the construction of gendered norms rather than in the realization of fully human capacities and relational potentials. Not all expressions of diverse human capacities are, in fact, expressions of human dignity. Dignity is tied to moral goodness and therefore only realized in those expressions of human capacities that contribute to—or at the very least do not contradict—the fuller realization of authentic personhood. Because involved fatherhood concerns relational capacities, it is already favorably weighted towards dignity's corollary good—solidarity—which aims precisely at the realization of human relational potentials. Nonetheless, additional resources exist for founding a thicker theological defense of expanded narratives of fatherhood. To conclude, this essay explores two such possibilities in dynamic interpretations of the natural law tradition and child-centered accounts of parenthood.

Natural Law

Natural law has a long history within Catholic moral theology and admits significant diversity in methodological interpretations. While some applications of natural law are certainly culpable for constraining the moral imagination and enforcing unnecessary behavioral boundaries, many contemporary advocates of the tradition promote methodological commitments that open natural law reasoning to more expansive possibilities. Stephen Pope has provided one helpful analysis of variations among distinct strands of natural law reasoning within contemporary Catholic moral thought.[97] In his typology, each form of natural law recognizes a similar set of sources but differs in the importance ascribed to each source. The methodology endemic to magisterial teaching, which he terms "revealed natural law," advances a descriptive account of human nature primarily informed by revelation and its interpretation within the tradition.[98] The strength of this approach is also its weakness; while it can clearly assert strong moral norms deduced from an *a priori* understanding of the human person, it is also prone to underestimating the significance of changing experiences, knowledge, and

---

[97] See Stephen Pope, "Scientific and Natural Law Analysis of Homosexuality: A Methodological Study," *Journal of Religious Ethics* 25, no. 1 (Spring 1997): 89–126.
[98] Pope, "Scientific and Natural Law Analysis of Homosexuality," 104.

conditions.[99] Inattention to these factors also tends to exacerbate unrecognized cultural influences within its application. This tendency plays out quite clearly in the conceptions of motherhood and fatherhood articulated in magisterial documents where socially conservative norms have influenced normative descriptions. Even as the accounts of motherhood and female dignity offered by popes of the late nineteenth and early twentieth century have not worn well with age,[100] having had their cultural presumptions exposed through changing cultural norms and social realities, this general methodological pattern persists into the present through ongoing limited recognition of diversity in male parental experiences.[101]

Despite such trends in authoritative Catholic teaching, natural law can equally be employed with methodological commitments to cultural awareness and the adaptability of human persons creating conditions for a more dynamic vision of the human person and human capabilities. For example, Cristina Traina has made a compelling case for a revised natural law methodology recognizing that the common physical reality of human existence binds moral reflection in significant ways and remaining open to the diversity of human experience in a way that can advance feminist ethical concerns.[102] Despite the tradition's association with absolutizing claims, Traina offers an interpretation of natural law that values cultural plurality and is adaptive to changing social conditions. Consequently, absolutism is not endemic to the natural law tradition even as it does pervade certain foundationalist interpretations of natural law methodology, which

---

[99] Pope, "Scientific and Natural Law Analysis of Homosexuality," 109. This weakness is identified more sharply by Ann Patrick Ware, who points to docetic tendencies in magisterial moral teaching in which "the Church" is presented "as a disembodied concept, speaking an eternal truth arrived at in some mysterious and infallible way" (Ann Patrick Ware, "The Vatican Letter, Presuppositions and Objections," in *The Vatican and Homosexuality: Reactions to the 'Letter to the Bishops of the Catholic Church on the Pastoral Care of Homosexual Persons,'* ed. Jeannine Gramick and Pat Furey [New York: Crossroad, 1988], 29).

[100] For a fuller account of the shifting patterns of conceptualizing parenthood in magisterial thought, see Jacob Kohlhaas, "Constructing Parenthood: Catholic Teaching 1880 to the Present," *Theological Studies* 79 no. 3 (2018): 610–633.

[101] See also Lisa Sowle Cahill, *Family: A Christian Social Perspective* (Minneapolis: Fortress, 2000), 91–92.

[102] See Cristina L. H. Traina, *Feminist Ethics and the Natural Law: The End of the Anathema* (Washington, DC: Georgetown University Press, 1999). James Alison likewise defends natural law for upholding the essential continuity between creation and creator such that "there is not an absolute rupture between that which we see here and now and that which is the divine plan for the fullness of creation." Like Traina, Alison views natural law as a way of grounding human goods in the realities of human existence. See James Alison, *On Being Liked* (New York: Crossroad, 2003).

many magisterial documents might be deemed to promote.[103]

In overcoming this limitation, the moral goods of dignity and solidarity can remain rooted in a methodological commitment to common human realities, while anticipating further disclosures of more robust possibilities for expression through moral evaluation of diverse experiences. Such applications of Catholic moral principles could help map the way to more expansive accounts of paternal capabilities than present resources provide. The Catholic commitment to human dignity implies just such an obligation to develop more robust narratives for supporting greater paternal investment in children and the home inasmuch as these are expressions of authentic human potentials. Advancements in male parental experiences, including equitable co-parenting and nurturing direct care, accord with the Catholic vision of authentic personhood inasmuch as they lead men into deeper relationships of solidarity and, in so doing, allow for the expression and realization of human dignity. When the concerns of natural law reasoning are shifted from preserving a particular normative vision of the person toward attentive evaluation of diverse human capacities, such paternal experiences become revelatory moments that attest to fuller possibilities for expressing dignity and solidarity than dominant gendered scripts have allowed.

Child-Centered Conceptions of Parenthood

John Wall's advocacy of "Childism" provides a further resource for a more reflexive model of parenthood freed from concerns of policing gendered boundaries.[104] Wall decouples parenthood from adult gender roles by centering parenthood squarely on the needs of children. In doing so, Wall gestures to a key aspect of Catholic moral theology by suggesting that his view participates in an "innovative traditionalism"[105] recognizing the need to both restructure narratives in the light of present realities and remain meaningfully connected to

---

[103] Cristina L. H. Traina, "Oh, Susanna: The New Absolutism and Natural Law," *Journal of the American Academy of Religion* 65, no. 2 (Summer 1997): 373. Traina later explains how John Paul II's sympathy towards a "faithful remnant" ecclesiological vision conflicts with the basic assertion of the universality of reason within the natural law tradition. The pervasive corrupting force of sin outside the church becomes the contextual position from which natural law norms can be envisioned as the products of common human reason while also being exclusively promulgated by a particular group, that is, the uncorrupted teachers of the Church within a world otherwise damaged deeply by sin. This "vision of radical separatist witness" was a tenuous interpretation of natural law when utilized by John Paul II and appears even more questionable on this side of the clerical abuse scandal (Traina, "Oh, Susanna," 389).
[104] John Wall, "Fatherhood, Childism, and the Creation of Society," 52–76. For a fuller explanation of Wall's "childist" ethic, see John Wall, *Ethics in Light of Childhood* (Washington, DC: Georgetown University Press, 2010).
[105] Wall, "Fatherhood, Childism, and the Creation of Society," 55.

existing tradition. As Wall rightly identifies, given the breadth and complexity of the Christian biblical and historical tradition, the questions hinge not so much on who is being traditional, but on how we choose to be traditional in response to the needs of the present. [106]

Conceptually centering parenthood on children may also aid in the formation of parents themselves. Parenthood fundamentally responsive to children teaches "one's children to grow in taking on loving responsibility themselves. Between servant leadership and moral permissiveness lies the more dynamic and dialogical possibility for cultivating children's own growing moral capabilities."[107] Wall continues: "Understood in this child-centered way, parents' emotion work and equal household labor are both vitally important. Emotion work increases children's capabilities for attachment with others, both close to and far from the home. Parental equality increases children's senses and capabilities for human justice, both at large and in intimate relations."[108]

Experiences of parental equality already demonstrate that gender is a poor predictor of parental capabilities, as men who are primary caregivers for their children tend to confess that their experiences of actual parental practices reveal few necessarily gendered differences.[109] Moreover, equitable sharing of domestic labor and childcare between partners coincides with reduced behavioral distinctions between motherhood and fatherhood. Sociologist Michael Lamb argues that, functionally, maternal and paternal influences on children are more similar than distinctive.[110] All of this suggests that the actual practices of parenthood, not innately gendered qualities, shape the expression of parental capabilities.[111] Interestingly, John Paul II himself, who held clear ideals of essential gendered traits, nonetheless asserted that motherly nurture grows out of women's *experience* of bearing children.[112]

CONCLUSION

Present social renegotiations of masculinity and fatherhood provide opportunities for encouraging narratives of male fitness for equitable co-parenting, nurture, caregiving, and domestic life which

---

[106] Wall, "Fatherhood, Childism, and the Creation of Society," 57.
[107] Wall, "Fatherhood, Childism, and the Creation of Society," 68.
[108] Wall, "Fatherhood, Childism, and the Creation of Society," 69.
[109] Stevens, "Understanding Discursive Barriers to Involved Fatherhood," 31.
[110] Julie Hanlon Rubio, *A Christian Theology of Marriage and Family* (New York: Paulist, 2003), 135.
[111] Judy Root Aulette, *Changing American Families* (Boston: Pearson, 2007), 328.
[112] John Paul II quite clearly sees the capabilities that grow out of these experiences as related to an innate disposition towards motherhood within women. Nonetheless, they come to expression in response to human experience (*Mulieris Dignitatem*, no. 18).

can take root in the parental experiences of a growing number of fathers. Stephen Williams argues that fathers today are engaged in a "detraditionalization" of fatherhood through actively negotiating their largely unscripted self-identities in increasingly individualized ways.[113] This reflexivity to the demands of actual caregiving is precisely what popular social and religious narratives appear to lack. Concern for fatherhood guided by dignity and solidarity rooted in a dynamic natural law methodology and centered on children themselves could help shift Catholicism from discourse rooted in essentialist constructions of gender towards greater attention to observations of actual parental realities and diverse expressions of human capabilities.

While a more robust account of male parental capacities may well challenge the long-held centrality of motherhood to parental experiences, the displacement of motherhood from its singular association with primary parenthood does not imply a similar challenge to the dignity of women as does inattention to fuller male parental experiences. Building co-parental ideals may also create space for greater exploration of human capacities and capabilities that both expand conceptions of fatherhood and free motherhood from the singular obligation to conceptually uphold authentic parenthood.

Contemporary experience suggests parental traits may be developed from more fundamentally human capabilities. As men increasingly partake in primary and co-parental experiences, emphasis on gendered characterizations of parental aptitudes dismiss the very human adaptability they may be experiencing in their own development of parental capacities. More robust narratives will prize differentiation, complexity, and adaptability over static and restrictive visions of parenthood.

Parenthood is a negotiated and interactive process of discovery. Gender does not make parents, rather parents are made through the responsive care given to children, and this is increasingly being learned as both mothers and fathers engage new parental realities. Given current realities, greater attention to human adaptability in fulfilling parental roles is warranted and can be supported through principled Catholic moral commitments. Such attention should lead to more comprehensive narrative resources for both men and women. Promoting men's abilities to recognize and claim dimensions of their parental experiences traditionally demarcated as feminine is important for the support of involved fathering and the fuller recognition of human adaptability, diversity, and relational potential; each of which can authentically realize human dignity and lead to greater relational fullness. M

---

[113] Stephen Williams, "What is Fatherhood?: Searching for the Reflexive Father," *Sociology* 42, no. 3 (June 2008): 488.

Jacob M. Kohlhaas, PhD, is Associate Professor of Moral Theology at Loras College in Dubuque, Iowa, where he teaches a range of courses in theology, ethics, and general education. His research centers on theological anthropology and relationships. His work has been published in *Theological Studies, Journal of Religious Ethics, Religious Studies Review, America,* and *US Catholic.* He is author of *Beyond Biology: Rethinking Parenthood in the Catholic Tradition,* Georgetown University Press, 2021.

Theologies of Labor and the Limits of Capital

Nicholas Norman-Krause

THIS ESSAY FOCUSES ON HOW theological conceptions of the nature of human work relate to the material conditions of labor in late-capitalist economies. One might expect this relation to feature prominently in Catholic theologies of labor. Yet Catholic thinking about the meaning of labor, particularly in the reception of papal social teaching in North America, has insufficiently examined the ways in which the structure of work and property relations within capitalist production put pressure on and even undermine a theology of dignified labor. In other words, there is significant tension between normative theologies of labor in Catholic social thinking and the material conditions of labor under capitalism.

A most illustrative instance of this tension, and the subject of this essay, is John Paul II's 1981 encyclical *Laborem Exercens* on human work. In what follows, I delineate the encyclical's theology of labor and its complex relationship to capitalist property forms and social relations of production. After a brief review of the reception of *Laborem Exercens* within generally pro-capitalist circles, especially in the United States, I turn to the encyclical itself to sketch the contours of its theological vision of labor within the order of creation. Here, I aim to probe a set of tensions between John Paul's personalist account of the dignity of work and the shape and structure of work in capitalist modes of production, as it concerns the ownership of productive property, the alienation of labor, and the social relations between those who work and those who own. These tensions are immensely important and productive; while *Laborem Exercens* makes no attempt to resolve them systematically, the encyclical invites further reflection on which social, political, and economic conditions are necessary for its vision of dignified labor to be realized. More to the point, *Laborem Exercens* prompts consideration of whether capitalist production systematically inhibits such flourishing. I argue it does. In the latter part of the essay, then, I turn to a rather neglected reading of John Paul II's theology of labor—more radical, social, and explicitly anticapitalist than its North American reception—which pivots on this contradiction between the goodness of labor as a gift of creation and the dehumanizing forces of capitalism. Consideration of Peruvian theologian Gustavo Gutiérrez's development of John Paul's theology of labor reveals possibilities for extending the chief insights of *Laborem Exercens* in more liberating directions than those offered by the encyclical's pro-capitalist interpreters.

My argument is that Gutiérrez's reading and creative expansion of the chief insights of *Laborem Exercens*, especially his joining of John Paul's account of labor in the order of creation to a vision of the redemption and liberation of labor from capitalism, is at the same time more theologically precise and politically ambitious than the dominant stream of the encyclical's reception in North America. In this way, Gutiérrez offers an important vision of just and dignified labor for our contemporary moment in which the viability and moral status of capitalism is undergoing great scrutiny in Catholic theological discourse.

THE RECEPTION OF *LABOREM EXERCENS* IN NORTH AMERICA

The response to the publication of *Laborem Exercens* comprises a wide range of interpretations of the encyclical throughout global Catholicism.[1] In North America, the reception of and commentary on the encyclical has seen the predominance of those who explicitly advocate for the compatibility of the Pope's teaching with capitalist political economy[2] and readers who, assuming capitalist forms of production as given, see the encyclical as calling for reformist measures within them.[3] Figures like Michael Novak understand the encyclical's praise of markets, defense of private property, and acknowledgement of the virtues of entrepreneurialism to demonstrate a clear embrace of American-style democratic capitalism.[4] Others

---

[1] For a summary of the reception of *Laborem Exercens*, see Patricia A. Lamoureux, "Commentary on *Laborem Exercens* (On Human Work)," in *Modern Catholic Social Teaching: Commentaries and Interpretations*, ed. Kenneth R. Himes, OFM (Washington, DC: Georgetown University Press, 2005), 408–410.

[2] See, for example, the essays in *Co-Creation and Capitalism: John Paul II's* Laborem Exercens, ed. John W. Houck and Oliver F. Williams, CSC (Washington, DC: University Press of America, 1983); *Papal Economics*, Heritage Lectures no. 6, ed. Philip F. Lawler (Washington, DC: Heritage Foundation, 1982); Robert A. Destro, "Work: The Human Environment: *Laborem Exercens* (1981)," in *Building the Free Society: Democracy, Capitalism, and Catholic Social Teaching*, ed. George Weigel and Robert Royal (Grand Rapids: Eerdmans, 1993), 163–186; Maciej Zieba, *Papal Economics: The Catholic Church on Democratic Capitalism, from* Rerum Novarum *to* Caritas in Veritate (Wilmington: ISI, 2013), 42–46; Michael Novak, "The Pope's Brilliant Encyclical," *National Review*, October 16, 1981, 1210.

[3] See, for instance, Ikiene Sentime, "*Laborem Exercens* as a Critical Notion of Workplace Spirituality," *Journal of Catholic Social Thought* 12, no. 1 (2015): 143–156; Thomas Kohler, "The Fragile Relevance of *Laborem Exercens*," *Journal of Catholic Social Thought* 6, no. 1 (2009): 185–207; and Gerald Beyer, "Freedom as a Challenge to an Ethic of Solidarity in a Neoliberal Capitalist World: Lessons from Post-1989 Poland," *Journal of Catholic Social Thought* 6, no. 1 (2009): 133–167.

[4] Michael Novak, "Creation Theology," in *Co-Creation and Capitalism*, 17–18.

argue that the Pope's direct criticisms of capitalism reveal a failure to comprehend the nature of capitalist economies, even as the rest of the encyclical is taken generally to affirm the tenets of free-market capitalism.[5] In short, aside from a few early reactions to the encyclical which acknowledged its potential radicality,[6] *Laborem Exercens* has seen a decisively pro-capitalist reception in North America, aided by a close association, in the minds of many US observers, of the Pope with Ronald Reagan's crusade against communism. This reception has entailed eclipsing divergent readings of the encyclical, especially in Latin America, which interrogate the alleged congruity of capitalism and papal teaching.[7]

Debates about *Laborem Exercens* have been occasioned, in part, by uncertainty around some of the encyclical's key terms. In one of the most analytically rigorous commentaries on the encyclical, Daniel Finn examines the ambiguity of the terms "labor" and "capital," arguing that John Paul uses "capital" to refer on the one hand to "the small but highly influential group of entrepreneurs, owners, or holders of the means of production" and on the other to the machines, natural resources, and properties used in the processes of production.[8] The former is a class of persons, while the latter refers to the material means of production. Finn rightly notes that conflicting interpretations of *Laborem Exercens* often come down to differing understandings of the terms "capital" and "labor," especially as they regard the Pope's main argument for the "priority of labor over capital" (no. 12). Left-wing commentators interpret the maxim in more traditionally Marxian

---

[5] Maryann O. Keating and Barry P. Keating, "Economics as a Discipline: The Crossroads between John Paul II's Social Vision and Conservative Economic Thought," *International Journal of Social Economics* 25, nos. 11–12 (1998): 1790–1802.

[6] For instance, Gregory Baum, "John Paul II's Encyclical on Labor," *Ecumenist* 20 (1981): 1–4. For a summary of the range of early responses to the encyclical, see Richard McCormick, "*Laborem Exercens* and Social Morality," in *Official Catholic Social Teaching, Readings in Moral Theology, No. 5*, ed. Charles E. Curran and Richard A. McCormick (New York: Paulist, 1986), 219–232.

[7] In addition to Gutiérrez, whose perspective is considered below, see also Ricardo Antoncich, *Christians in the Face of Injustice: A Latin American Reading of Catholic Social Teaching*, trans. Matthew J. O'Connell (Maryknoll: Orbis Books, 1987), 84–143; Juan Luis Scannone, *Teología de la liberación y doctrina social de la Iglesia* (Buenos Aires: Docencia, 2011); and the essays in *Sobre el trabajo humano: Comentarios a la encíclica "Laborem Exercens*," ed. Gustavo Gutiérrez, Rolando Ames, Javier Iguíñiz, and Carlos Chipoco (Lima: Centro de Estudios y Publicaciones, 1982). The dissimilarity of interpretation between the encyclical's reception in the United States and Latin America itself poses questions about the meaning of social location, particularly within the structures of global capitalism, for thinking about the relationship of Catholic social teaching to capitalist economy.

[8] Daniel Finn, "The Priority of Labor over Capital: Some Needed Extensions," *Journal of Catholic Social Thought* 6, no. 1 (2009): 19–20.

class-analytical terms, seeing in it a preferential option for the propertyless proletariat over the capitalist owning class.[9] Neoconservative and other capitalist-friendly commentators understand "labor" and "capital" not in class terms, but as referring to the activity of work and the property forms of production, respectively. Thus, perspectives on the meaning of John Paul's teaching about labor's priority over capital range from seeing in it a simple moral teaching regarding the responsibility of owners of capital to their workers to a more radical questioning of the legitimacy of forms of private ownership not directly accountable to workers.

While critical of both left and right interpretations of the Pope's teaching, Finn himself favors the latter's eschewal of class terms, arguing that "John Paul does not directly relate the priority of labor over capital" to a conception of capital construed in terms of "those who own the means of production."[10] The teaching is concerned more with the moral responsibility of owners of capital to workers than with any sort of direct contestation of the right of a capitalist class to ownership of production. In Finn's view, John Paul does not see the private ownership of production and its attendant class relations as inherently problematic. Antagonisms and inequalities between those who work and those who own can be justly adjudicated within the structures of capitalist property ownership. Production need not be owned or directed by workers themselves to ensure the priority of labor, Finn believes, as long as those who do own the means of production value and "respect the priority of labor over those instruments which they own."[11] As he puts it elsewhere, John Paul agrees "with capitalists against socialists in the right of persons to own the means of production," believing "private ownership of the means of production can be a service to workers" when it "serves the cause of work and workers."[12] The problem of labor exploitation and inequality is thus registered as a moral problem, not a structural feature of capitalism inherent to the private control of the means of production. In reading *Laborem Exercens* this way, Finn endeavors to disentangle the private ownership of productive property, the utility of markets, and the legitimate place of self-interest in a free economy from neoconservative and neoliberal versions of capitalism which fail

---

[9] See, for instance, Gregory Baum, *The Priority of Labor: A Commentary on* Laborem Exercens, *Encyclical Letter of Pope John Paul II* (New York: Paulist, 1982).
[10] Finn, "Priority of Labor over Capital," 22.
[11] Finn, "Priority of Labor over Capital," 31.
[12] Daniel Finn, "Commentary on *Centesimus Annus* (*On the Hundredth Anniversary of* Rerum Novarum)," in *Modern Catholic Social Teaching*, 437, 448. This responsibility of owners of capital to workers is detailed further in *Centesimus Annus*, no. 43, which Finn sees as "a far better explanation than 'the priority of labor over capital' that played so central a role in *Laborem Exercens*" (448).

to account for the priority of labor and the common good.[13] The class division between those who work and those who own, Finn believes, can be justly ordered to the benefit of workers with the help of the state, civil society, and a robust juridical framework within which economic relations can be managed.[14] Finn, then, agrees with neoconservative and neoliberal readings of the encyclical on at least this point, even as he dissents from their larger claims: dignified labor, of the kind John Paul describes, can be realized within capitalism's social relations of production and structures of property ownership. The problem with capitalism as it regards the priority of labor is not the private ownership of production but the moral failure of the owners of capital to be fully responsible to their workers.[15]

My analysis of *Laborem Exercens* questions this shared assumption and probes the pressures capitalist forms of production and property ownership put on John Paul's theology of labor. I argue the encyclical generates substantial tension between its normative theology of labor and the limits of capital, and so invites further reflection on that tension. This creative tension is, I suggest, inherent to the nature of papal social teaching itself which, as John Paul understands it, is primarily concerned with the ethical dimensions of economic life, not comprehensive economic theories. Papal teaching

---

[13] See also Daniel K. Finn, "John Paul II and the Moral Ecology of Markets," *Theological Studies* 59, no. 4 (1998): 662–679.

[14] Finn takes up one problem this defense of private ownership generates, namely, the question of how it might be morally permissible for owners of capital to "act in their own interest when that will cause direct harm to their employees" (Finn, "Priority of Labor over Capital," 24). How, in other words, can labor be given priority over capital when the owners' ability to terminate workers' employment at will plays such a central role in capitalist production? While he admits that it sits uncomfortably with John Paul's writings on the social obligations of owners, Finn defends the owners' need to dismiss employees in the interest of profitability because of its necessity for capitalist growth. For more on this debate, see Mark Repenshek and Becket Gremmels, "A Catholic Theology of Employment-at-Will," *Health Progress*, January-February 2015, www.chausa.org/publications/health-progress/article/january-february-2015/a-catholic-theology-of-employment-at-will.

[15] To be sure, John Paul does see the affirmation of a right to private ownership of productive property entailed in the right to private property as such. *Rerum Novarum* and *Mater et Magistra*, he says, both affirm "the right to private property even when it is a question of the means of production" (*Laborem Exercens*, no. 14). Such would seem to suggest the Pope's endorsement of capitalist property relations. Yet, as I hope to make clear in what follows, what John Paul has in mind here is not so much the right of a class of owners to hold a claim to production in place of workers, but rather the right to non-state ownership of production. John Paul's affirmation of the latter, I suggest, permits and even encourages collective, shared, and democratic ownership and management of production, even as it opposes the collectivization of the means of production by the State. The principal matter, for John Paul, is that workers have a share in productive property, a right threatened by both capitalist class relations *and* overly Statist forms of collectivization.

offers moral insight and instruction applicable to a wide range of economic forms and philosophies. As John Paul writes in *Sollicitudo Rei Socialis*: "The Church does not propose economic and political systems or programs, nor does she show preference for one or the other, provided that human dignity is properly respected and promoted" (no. 41). Rather, the insight the Church offers in her social teaching is a "category of its own," belonging not to the field "of ideology, but of theology and particularly moral theology" (no. 41). Thus, in *Laborem Exercens* and other encyclicals, John Paul's criticism of liberal capitalism is a moral one, concerned with addressing its excesses and vices rather than affirming or rejecting it as a comprehensive ideology. Indeed, this is why the Pope praises certain aspects of Western capitalism (open markets, the value of entrepreneurialism, freedom of trade) as consistent with a moral economy.[16] Nevertheless, it is capitalism's relations of production and property ownership—the class division between those who work and those who own—that haunts the Pope's account of dignified labor. For if labor is truly a *creative* act, as John Paul says, then to alienate workers from the objects of their labor by denying them ownership and direction of the means of production threatens to corrupt the very nature of work as a created good. What *Laborem Exercens* affirms in its careful theological description of work is that labor is an inherently social and participatory act of creative agency. But this is precisely what capitalist production undermines and systematically so.[17] The encyclical's theology of labor, I argue, has significant implications for thinking about political economy and property ownership, ones which the encyclical only gestures toward, inviting further reflection. My attention in what follows is directed, then, not so much to John Paul's comments regarding the tendencies and dangers of various economic theories and ideologies, even as I reference these at times. Instead, I focus more narrowly on John Paul's theology of labor itself and then take up the encyclical's invitation to consider what kinds of political

---

[16] See also *Centesimus Annus*, no. 42.
[17] I should note at the outset that John Paul's criticism of "capitalism" has in view a much larger reality than simply Western liberal capitalism. For him, capitalism is defined essentially by the denial of ownership and control of production to those who labor. "Capitalism" in this sense characterizes also forms of communism wherein ownership and control of production is entirely given over to the state. Call this "state capitalism." My focus in this essay is primarily on the reception of the encyclical in North America, and the US in particular, and so considers capitalism primarily as a matter of private, non-state ownership of production. I do not directly consider John Paul's critique of "state capitalism" (i.e., communism), as I take his rejection of this form of political economy, in line with the long tradition of papal Catholic social teaching, to be quite well known.

economic conditions would enable such a vision of labor to flourish.[18]

LABOR, CREATION, AND ALIENATION IN *LABOREM EXERCENS*

The central feature and chief contribution of *Laborem Exercens* to Catholic social teaching is doubtless John Paul's extensive delineation of the theological nature of human labor. Several dimensions of that theology are relevant for my concerns here: its grounding in a biblical theological anthropology and doctrine of creation, its personalist dimensions, and its relationship to forms of alienation, property ownership, and the material conditions of capitalist production. My aim is to disclose the tension between John Paul's eloquent theological vision of the goodness of labor and the lived reality of work under capitalism.

Recall that *Laborem Exercens* opens with a recounting of the Genesis creation narrative with a particular eye toward the place of labor in the original creation. In these paragraphs of detailed exegesis, John Paul locates his theology of labor primarily within the doctrine of creation, the centerpiece of which is his argument that the mandate to "fill the earth and subdue it" (Genesis 1:28) by means of human labor is intrinsic to human persons being created in the image of the Creator (no. 4). Labor is a creative human act whereby persons participate in the divine labor of God's primal and ongoing creation. "Man is the image of God," John Paul writes, "among other things because he is charged by his Creator with subjecting and dominating the earth. In carrying out that mandate, man—every human being—reflects the very action of the Creator of the universe" (no. 4).[19] As John Paul says at the end of the encyclical, "Man, created in the image of God, shares by his work in the activity of the Creator" (no. 25). This participatory quality of human labor is given not only in the goodness of creation but also in the Christological reality that God in Christ took the form of a Nazarene carpenter (Mark 6:3) and thus "belongs to the

---

[18] While I occasionally make reference to John Paul's 1987 encyclical *Sollicitudo Rei Socialis* and his 1991 encyclical *Centesimus Annus*, both of which concern questions of economy, labor relations, and property, it is *Laborem Exercens* that will be the main object of my analysis because of its extended and careful treatment of the nature of work and the theological dimensions of labor.

[19] On John Paul's participatory account of labor and the "sacramental meaning of work," see Gerard Beigel, *Faith and Social Justice in the Teaching of Pope John Paul II* (New York: Peter Lang, 1997), 92–94; and Lamoureux, "Commentary on *Laborem Exercens*," 394–398. John Paul uses the language of "subjection" and "domination" in *Laborem Exercens* without the sensitivity to the abuses of human labor upon the earth that he exhibits in later encyclicals. In *Sollicitudo Rei Socialis*, for example, he develops the notion of "dominion" in more helpful directions tying it to the human vocation of "cultivation" (no. 30). For an interpretation of the Genesis mandate along these lines, see Daniel P. Castillo, *An Ecological Theology of Liberation: Salvation and Political Ecology* (Maryknoll, NY: Orbis Books, 2019), 68–72.

'working world'" (no. 26). The "Gospel of work" spoken of throughout the encyclical is good news because "he who proclaimed it was himself a man of work" (no. 26). Labor belongs to the identity of Christ as his earthly trade, but also because the activity of the Logos in the work of creation is the first and preeminent instance of labor.

Insofar as labor belongs to humankind by virtue of its creation in the divine image, the encyclical argues, the goodness of labor is found in its capacity for cooperation and communion with others, first with the Creator, but also with fellow laborers. As a "mark" of humanity, work is an aspect of the social nature of the *imago dei*. It is "the mark of a person operating within a community of persons," the Pope announces in the encyclical's opening paragraph. This sociality of labor "constitutes its very nature," he goes on to say, for work is an activity of participation and communion. John Paul then develops the implications of this critical insight throughout the encyclical. The inherent sociality of work is the theological basis for the right to labor unions (no. 20) and the right to employment (no. 18), the heart of the Pope's theology of solidarity (no. 8), and the backdrop to the encyclical's condemnation of conceptions of labor as a depersonalized commodity to be exchanged on markets or "sold" to employers (no. 7). The social nature of labor also frames the meaning of alienation in John Paul's theology. For labor to humanize, rather than dehumanize, it must be a site of genuine participation in common action, decision-making, and determination with others in the processes of production and work. This cooperative dimension of labor was given in humanity's vocation in the garden of creation, which was "shared from the beginning by a couple" and "therefore fundamentally social" in nature (*Sollicitudo Rei Socialis*, no. 29). Thus, just as John Paul commends democratic political formations for their ability to broaden the arena of political participation and allow for persons to cultivate their capacities for civic engagement and accountability,[20] so too does he extol participatory forms of labor which allow workers to exercise agency, creativity, and cooperation with others in common activity (no. 14). In John Paul's theological construal, work is a form of social activity ordered to communion with others (no. 20). The Pope's insistence on the social nature of work is the basis of his advocacy for forms of worker control and economic democracy, the "joint

---

[20] In *Centesimus Annus*, John Paul continues the affirmation of democratic participation articulated in Pius XII's 1944 Christmas radio message. With reference to that address, John Paul writes: "The Church values the democratic system inasmuch as it ensures the participation of citizens in making political choices, guarantees to the governed the possibility both of electing and holding accountable those who govern them, and of replacing them through peaceful means when appropriate." He advocates for what he terms "the 'subjectivity' of society" through "the creation of structures of participation and shared responsibility" (no. 46).

ownership of the means of work," "associating labor with the ownership of capital," and other aspects of worker self-directed forms of production which ensure that "each person is fully entitled to consider himself a part-owner of the great workbench at which he is working with everyone else" (no. 14).[21] Informed by the same traditions of workplace democracy and worker self-determination that inspired the Solidarity movement in Poland, which burst onto the world stage the year prior to the publication of *Laborem Exercens* and whose successes John Paul celebrates in *Centesimus Annus* (no. 23), the encyclical envisions participatory forms of labor as manifesting the ends and purposes of work given by God in creation.

Grounding the activity of labor in the human person's constitution as *imago dei* is also the basis of John Paul's delineation of the "objective" and "subjective" dimensions of labor (no. 6). Regarding the former, labor's "object" is the created world which, when subjected to human labor, manifests goods, services, art, etc. Yet, it is the subjective dimension of labor that is the encyclical's chief concern—the laboring subject and her or his personhood. Only the *human*, John Paul writes, can properly be said to labor, for the human person is "a subjective being capable of acting in a planned and rational way, capable of deciding about himself, and with a tendency toward self-realization" (no. 6). This is the personalist quality of the Pope's theology of labor. Because labor is a means of cultivating one's humanity, John Paul considers freedom, agency, and the authentic exercise of control over one's laboring activities to be the most important qualities of dignified work. The moral nature of labor is "linked to the fact that the one who carries it out is a person, a conscious and free subject, that is to say a subject that decides about himself" (no. 6). The priority of this subjective dimension of labor over the objective dimension "conditions the very ethical nature of work" (no. 6). Thus, "the basis for determining the value of human work is not primarily the kind of work being done but the fact that the one doing it is a person" (no. 6).

The criteria distinguishing dignified from dehumanizing labor thus refer primarily to the subjective rather than objective dimensions of work. While some critics have seen this turn toward the subjectivity of labor to entail a neglect of the objective conditions of work and prioritizing of an "inner" experience of labor,[22] this is a misunderstanding of John Paul's personalism. The subjective dimension of labor concerns not interiority or private feelings of

---

[21] See also *Centesimus Annus*, no. 43.
[22] See, for instance, Stanley Hauerwas, "Work as Co-Creation: A Critique of a Remarkably Bad Idea," in *Co-Creation and Capitalism*, 49–50; and John Hughes, *The End of Work: Theological Critiques of Capitalism* (Malden, MA: Blackwell, 2007), 18–23.

fulfillment but the very public realities of freedom and participation in the activity of work. Does a person's work enable self-realization and perfection or inhibit it?[23] To inquire into the subjective dimensions of labor is to interrogate the nature of persons' relationships to the objects of labor, the social relations of production, and the material conditions under which persons labor. Do these facilitate or undermine workers' capacities for freedom, agency, and self-determination in their laboring activity? Put theologically, following John Paul, do the conditions and structures of production allow for labor to be a truly *creative* activity? Creativity does not here refer to a quality of artistic or craft work as opposed to, say, manual labor or service work. Rather, creativity is the fundamental structure of all labor that is free and personal, in which one is an authentic agent with respect to deciding about the objects and conditions of one's labor, and in which one exercises direction and determination of productive activities with others. In short, labor manifested in its intended creative form allows the worker to be "a true subject of work with an initiative of his own" (no. 15). According to John Paul, the worker longs for this kind of self-directive power and creative agency in labor: "Using all the means of production, he also wishes the fruit of this work to be used by himself and others, and he wishes to be able to take part in the very work process as a sharer in responsibility and creativity at the workbench to which he applies himself" (no. 15). To participate in dignified, creative work leads the worker to desire "not only due remuneration" for labor, but, even more, that "within the production process, provision be made for him to be able to know that in his work, even on something that is owned in common, he is working 'for himself'" (no. 15).[24] For work to be humanizing, it must be creative in this sense. One must be able to truly recognize one's work as one's own and oneself as possessing authority, agency, and real determination over production. To reflect the divine activity of labor, one must be a true *subject* of work.

Careful thinking about this appeal to the structure of labor as creative action has been lacking in the encyclical's reception and commentary, as has serious reflection upon the forms of participatory, worker-owned, and self-directed productive enterprises correlated to it. For John Paul, however, a theology of labor in the order of creation

---

[23] "Work is a good thing for man—a good thing for his humanity—because through work man *not only transforms nature*, adapting it to his own needs, but he also *achieves fulfillment* as a human being and indeed, in a sense, becomes 'more a human being'" (*Laborem Exercens*, no. 9).

[24] Note that, throughout this section of the encyclical, authentic ownership and direction of productive property are not associated with individualist forms of private ownership but with social and democratic ones, what might be called social ownership or worker ownership.

is directly tied to these questions of property ownership and the social relations of production. Pro-capitalist readers far too often extract the encyclical's affirmation of the right to private property from its larger argument about worker power and shared action. In *Laborem Exercens*, the right to property is directed not toward a defense of capitalist ownership but rather to the socialization of production in which workers direct and control the means of production "in common" (no. 15). To be sure, the Pope's argument for private ownership is set against the collectivization of all industry in the State, but it by no means affirms liberal capitalist property forms. When John Paul appeals to Aquinas's defense of private property, it is for the purposes of advocating for laborer *access* to ownership of productive property against excessive bureaucratic centralization—a reality embodied in our day by neoliberalism just as much as, if not more than, communist states.[25] That workers are due rightful ownership of and directive power over the property they labor upon is the reason for widely dispersing ownership of the means of production into the hands of workers. Rather than being a matter of the moral responsibility of owners of capital to their workers, then, the "priority of labor over capital" concerns the very structure of the social relations and property forms of production, signaling a clear preference for democratic and worker-owned forms of production.[26] For John Paul, the dignity of labor consists in the capacity of workers to act creatively in it, to possess real agency in and power over their labor. Because dignified labor entails such a relationship to the object of one's labor, the encyclical defends the right of workers to own the properties on which they labor. Yet, because dignified labor is also inherently social, ownership of production and productive property is most fully possessed when owned, shared, and directed *with others*. For this reason, John Paul's comments about the superiority of cooperative ownership of the means of work, the need for socialization of certain industries, and the importance of "associating labor with the ownership of capital, as far as possible" (no. 14), are not inconsequential suggestions but clear applications of the heart of his theology of labor, which is cooperative activity, common agency, and

---

[25] On neoliberalism's anti-democratic nature, see Wendy Brown, *Undoing the Demos: Neoliberalism's Stealth Revolution* (Brooklyn: Zone, 2015); and David Harvey, *A Brief History of Neoliberalism* (New York: Oxford University Press, 2005).
[26] In my view, Gregory Baum is right to suggest that the central concern of the encyclical on this point is not so much *ownership* of capital but its *use*. For Baum, the Pope's concern for capital to serve labor is a preference for labor and the laboring class, rather than the managerial or owning class, to exercise power over the use of capital (Baum, *The Priority of Labor*, 24–25). See also the discussion of worker-owned and worker self-directed enterprises in Richard Wolff, *Democracy at Work: A Cure for Capitalism* (Chicago: Haymarket, 2012), 117–122.

shared action.[27]

Within this construal of labor indexed to the doctrine of creation, the Pope also considers labor's distortion and degradation. Throughout John Paul's social encyclicals, the consistent way of naming the disfiguration of labor is "alienation,"[28] which includes two basic dimensions. First, alienation entails a separation of the person from the fruits of her or his labor. The worker desires the "fruit" of work "to be used by himself and others" (no. 15). Already in *Redemptor Hominis*, John Paul had written of the experience of alienated labor, wherein the product of one's laboring activity is "not only subjected to 'alienation,' in the sense that it is simply taken away from the person who produces it," but also "turn[ed] against man himself, at least in part, through the indirect consequences of its effects returning on himself. It is or can be directed against him" (no. 15). Gustavo Gutiérrez comments on this passage in an essay considered below, referring to alienation as a reversal of labor as "dominion" over the earth. Whereas genuine dominion *joins* the laborer and object of labor in a more profound unity, he writes, "'alienation,' the worker's loss of the fruits of his work, leads to the subjection of the human person to the things produced by that person."[29] In *Laborem Exercens*, John Paul speaks of this alienation of the laborer from the fruit of her or his labor as the transformation of labor into "merchandise" (no. 7), what might be called the "commodification" of labor. Later, in *Centesimus Annus*, he refers to Leo XIII's and John XXIII's similar concerns about those who labor on land from whose ownership they "are excluded" and thus "reduced to a state of quasi-servitude," subjected to "inhuman exploitation" (no. 33). In these forms of alienated work, labor is transformed from an authentic act of the person—an "*actus personae*" (no. 24)—to a marketable commodity. As a commodity, labor is extracted from the laborer in exchange for a wage, rendering labor into depersonalized "labor-power" to be sold on a market to owners of capital.

This inversion of primacy, setting "things" over "persons," as John Paul puts it, is the second important aspect of alienation and follows from the first. *Laborem Exercens* refers to this as a "reversal" of the

---

[27] In this, John Paul is following a theme of papal social thought reaching back at least to Pius XI's *Quadragesimo Anno* (1931) which recognizes cooperative and social forms of labor as most conducive to the dignity of work.
[28] On the notion of alienation in John Paul's writings and his understanding of "participation" as the key antidote to alienation, see Dean Edward A. Mejos, "Against Alienation: Karol Wojtyla's Theory of Participation," *Kritike* 1, no. 1 (2007): 71–85.
[29] Gustavo Gutiérrez, "The Gospel of Work: Reflections on *Laborem Exercens*," in *The Density of the Present: Selected Writings* (Maryknoll, NY: Orbis Books, 1999), 15.

"order of work,"[30] wherein labor becomes simply "an impersonal 'force' needed for production" (no. 7). The reversal is, more specifically, a reversal of labor's normative structure as defined in the order of creation: "Man is treated as an instrument of production," rather than its "effective subject" and "true maker and creator" (no. 7). If these latter descriptions name the participatory nature of labor in its created structure, wherein persons reflect and join in divine labor by being proper creators and makers themselves, then alienated labor names the inverse of this. The human person not only loses her or his status as *subject* over the processes and products of labor; the person actually becomes an *object* in labor, a mechanism within the processes of production. Alienation is the loss of creative capacity, dispossessing the worker of meaningful agency, self-determination, and control over the means and activities of production. Theologically construed, this kind of commodified labor is an instance of de-creation rather than co-creation.

Finally, and crucially important for the purposes of this essay, John Paul gives material and historical specification to this notion of alienated labor as a deformation and "reversal" of labor's created structure. "Precisely this reversal of order," he says, "whatever the program or name under which it occurs, should rightly be called 'capitalism'" (no. 7).[31] This is, in my reading, the most radical statement the encyclical makes, and it is important to delineate what exactly the Pope means by it. Importantly, the encyclical does not take capitalism to be essentially defined by the use of markets, the legitimate pursuit of profit, or non-State ownership of the means of production. All of these the encyclical affirms as political economic realities distinguishable from capitalism *per se*, and John Paul elaborates further their significance for a "market," "business," or "free" economy in *Centesimus Annus*. Rather, capitalism names a particular form of *production*, an arrangement of labor and the property forms structuring that labor which denies workers ownership of and control over the means of production. The capitalist property form, as the Pope understands it, is defined by its denial of ownership and direction of production to those who labor, a feature belonging to both capitalism and Statist collectivism alike (no. 7). The Pope understands liberal capitalism's assigning of ownership to a minority

---

[30] Later, John Paul reformulates this as alienation's "reversal of means and ends" (*Centesimus Annus*, no. 41).
[31] Novak argues that the encyclical is mistaken on this point, "accepting a Marxist view of early capitalism" and thus failing to understand the substantial difference between "slave labor" and "free labor" ("Creation Theology," 20–22). Novak's criticism entirely misses that John Paul's condemnation of capitalist production is a direct outworking of his personalist theology of labor, creation, and freedom, as I have been detailing, rather than the adoption of a Marxian definition.

capitalist class and communism's preference for the bureaucratic State's ownership of production to both be manifestations of the basic error of capitalism, for they both deny workers their right to ownership and direction of production. The theological problem of capitalism, whether manifested in liberal or collectivist forms, is that in it the worker "is not treated as subject and maker" of work (no. 7), the condition of which, I have been arguing, is participation in direction and ownership. The important point here is that the encyclical understands capitalism, in its essential structure, to entail a separation or alienation between laborer and the fruits of her or his labor, as well as the absence of meaningful self-determination over the conditions, nature, and ends of such labor. Capitalist production, in the terms delineated above, is *de*-creative, alienated labor. Its essential character is a reversal of labor's normative structure as determined in creation.

My purpose in detailing this theology of labor in *Laborem Exercens* is to disclose the basic tension at the heart of the encyclical between labor as a creative act of free persons and the systematic alienation of labor under capitalism, as well as to identify the places where John Paul gestures toward forms of labor beyond the limits of capital. What the Pope defines as labor alienation is, in fact, the essential form of capitalist production. Thus, while John Paul refuses to condemn certain ancillary features of capitalist political economy, such as markets, his theology of labor leads the reader to see alienation and exploitation at the very heart of capitalist production. To be sure, John Paul does not develop the implications of this seeming incompatibility between a theology of dignified labor and capitalist production within the encyclical. Instead, his advocacy for just wages, incorporation of labor into management, profit-sharing, and other moral admonitions are offered as ways of humanizing a fundamentally distorted labor relation. *Laborem Exercens* does invite further reflection upon what kinds of property forms and social relations of production might facilitate the vision of labor it proposes. Moreover, it opens up space for imagining the overcoming of labor's systematic disfiguration by capitalist production—what we might call labor's *redemption*. To pursue this, I turn now to Gustavo Gutiérrez, who joins the encyclical's creation theology to an account of labor's liberation through anticapitalist struggle.

LIBERATION AND THE REDEMPTION OF LABOR

One of the important gifts of Gutiérrez's reading of John Paul II is his attention to and acute understanding of the constraints placed upon labor by capitalist production, what Gutiérrez understands to be the corruption of the created goodness of labor by sin. In contrast to much of the reception of *Laborem Exercens* in the United States, Gutiérrez grasps the essential tension I have been disclosing between the Pope's theology of labor and the limits of capital. Because of this tension, he deems it necessary to join John Paul's vision of labor in the order of creation to an account of the redemption and liberation of labor from sin, an account he had already been developing in the 1971 first edition of *A Theology of Liberation*, enabling him to receive *Laborem Exercens* within a liberationist framework and supplement the Pope's teaching with a vision of participation in God's redemption of work through anticapitalist struggle. Gutiérrez develops this account of labor in the order of creation and redemption in several key sections of *A Theology of Liberation* [32] and two important, though often neglected, essays on John Paul's social encyclicals. [33] His account of anticapitalist class struggle appears in an important section at the end of *A Theology of Liberation*, which Gutiérrez redrafted in the revised edition of the book after the publication of *Laborem Exercens*.

A central theme running throughout *A Theology of Liberation*, which the book shares with *Laborem Exercens*, is the dignity of labor. Like the encyclical, Gutiérrez develops a theology of the goodness of human work in personalist terms, identifying labor as the social activity wherein persons realize their human capacities through shared productive activity with others. "Only in this way," he writes, "do persons come to a full consciousness of themselves as subjects of creative freedom which is realized through work."[34] Like John Paul, Gutiérrez grounds his vision of labor in the doctrine of the *imago dei* and the Genesis mandate to "subdue the earth," and he emphasizes the centrality of freedom for the right exercise of one's laboring capacities.[35] Labor is a participation in God's creative work, as humans steward and make use of the goods of the earth.[36] However, Gutiérrez writes, labor is a genuine participation in the creative work of God "only if it is a human act, that is to say, if it is not alienated by unjust socio-economic structures."[37] This point, implicit in John Paul's writing, was sometimes obscured by the Pope's desire to affirm all forms of labor, even the most mundane or onerous, as dignified. One must be careful, Gutiérrez insists, not to name labor good and dignified when it is deformed and degraded by alienation and oppression. Doing so risks sanctifying forms of exploitation.

---

[32] Gustavo Gutiérrez, *A Theology of Liberation: History, Politics, and Salvation*, revised ed. (Maryknoll, NY: Orbis Books, 1988).
[33] The essays are "The Gospel of Work: Reflections on *Laborem Exercens*" and "New Things Today: A Rereading of *Rerum Novarum*," in Gustavo Gutiérrez, *The Density of the Present*, 3–38; 39–56.
[34] Gutiérrez, *Theology of Liberation*, 168.
[35] Gutiérrez, "The Gospel of Work," 13–15.
[36] Gutiérrez, *Theology of Liberation*, 158.
[37] Gutiérrez, *Theology of Liberation*, 101. See also Gutiérrez, "The Gospel of Work," 6–7.

Moreover, while Gutiérrez affirms the Pope's principle that capital cannot be opposed to labor (*Laborem Exercens*, no. 13), he nevertheless points to the plain fact that, within capitalism, capital *is* opposed to labor, and structurally so, insofar as labor is instrumentalized in production processes directed by and benefitting the owners of capital.[38]

Likewise, alienation is the central concept Gutiérrez uses to describe the disfigurement of labor's created structure under sin. He construes alienation in scriptural terms as the undoing of creation, a dehumanizing estrangement from one's laboring activity. Gutiérrez refers to the prophet Isaiah's announcement of Israel's future redemption from the oppression of Babylon to describe this undoing of alienation: "They shall build houses and live to inhabit them, plant vineyards and eat their fruit; they shall not build for others to inhabit nor plant for others to eat ... My chosen shall enjoy the fruit of their labor" (65:21).[39] For Gutiérrez, alienated labor is characterized chiefly by the inability to exercise control and self-determination over one's labor, the demand to give one's labor to another as a commodity.[40] Alienation in this sense, he writes, is a "perversion" of labor's created structure, "and usually a structural one."[41] He thus refers to Israel's slavery in Egypt as "alienated labor," the systematic restructuring of labor under bondage to become an instrument of oppression rather than freedom.[42] For this reason, Israel's liberation from Egypt is not only a political act of God's salvation but an economic redemption as well. God rescues Israel from alienated labor in order to gift God's people with dignified and socialized forms of labor ordered to the building up of their common life. Exodus is the redemption of Israel's labor.

This complex thematizing of labor in the orders of creation, sin, and redemption provides an important development of *Laborem Exercens*'s theology of labor, which was indexed primarily to the doctrine of creation. For Gutiérrez, creation and redemption, though conceptually distinct, must always be held together so that liberation is seen as intrinsic to creation, lest one naturalize forms of unfreedom in the created order.[43] For Israel, "liberation from Egypt" was always

---

[38] Gutiérrez, "The Gospel of Work," 31–33.
[39] Gutiérrez, *Theology of Liberation*, 97.
[40] Gutiérrez, "New Things Today," 54.
[41] Gutiérrez, "The Gospel of Work," 16.
[42] Gutiérrez, *Theology of Liberation*, 88.
[43] A similar point has been made by Stanley Hauerwas in his criticism of *Laborem Exercens*, arguing that the encyclical "reflects an implicit but continuing reliance upon the natural law presumption that creation *itself* furnishes sufficient grounds for universally relevant moral assessment," and thus neglects the importance of Christology, ecclesiology, and eschatology for ethical reflection. See Hauerwas, "Work as Co-Creation," 43–44. See also Hughes, *The End of Work*, 18–23.

"linked to" and seen as "coinciding with creation."[44] Redemption is an act of "re-creation," directed to the restoration of the created structure of human life from its effacement and disfiguration by sin.[45] Israel's liberation from Egypt is thus ordered to the re-creation of a flourishing community through labor: "The Exodus is the long march towards the promised land in which Israel can establish a society free from misery and alienation."[46]

Moreover, God's action of liberation is—importantly—a participatory activity. In the Exodus event, Gutiérrez maintains, salvation, "totally and freely given by God," incorporates the human activity of self-liberation into the divine action of redemption.[47] The Exodus experience is "paradigmatic" of human salvation in exactly this way.[48] Just as labor participates in the divine activity of creation, so the struggle for liberation is a participation in the divine activity of redemption in which God re-creates the conditions for just and flourishing forms of work, life, and community. In light of this, liberative struggle must make certain decisive and "historical judgements" regarding where and how God's redemption is taking concrete manifestation, which Gutiérrez sees *Laborem Exercens* as inviting.[49] In the current world order, Gutiérrez argues, the redemption of labor must entail the overcoming of capitalist structures of production. "One cannot support just any solution to the problem," he writes. "Every effort to resolve it must begin at that root"—the "real conflict" between labor and capital existent in "their relationship to the productive process and specifically to the ownership of the means of production."[50] In the language of *Laborem Exercens*, capitalism is the "reversal" of creation's order of work, the "most gigantic and systematic perversion of the values of work."[51] God's liberative redemption of work is a reversal of this reversal, a liberation from capitalism.[52]

The implications of Gutiérrez's joining John Paul II's creation theology to an account of liberation can hardly be overstated in terms

---

[44] Gutiérrez, *Theology of Liberation*, 90. Earlier, Gutiérrez writes of the Bible establishing a "close link between creation and salvation," one "based on the historical and liberating experience of the Exodus" (86). Eschatology also figures in this relation, distinguishing the kind of salvation realizable in history from the full consummation of redemption manifest only in the eschatological kingdom of God. See Gutiérrez, *Theology of Liberation*, 121–139.
[45] Gutiérrez, *Theology of Liberation*, 89.
[46] Gutiérrez, *Theology of Liberation*, 89.
[47] Gutiérrez, *Theology of Liberation*, 91.
[48] Gutiérrez, *Theology of Liberation*, 90.
[49] Gutiérrez, "The Gospel of Work," 22.
[50] Gutiérrez, "The Gospel of Work," 32.
[51] Gutiérrez, "The Gospel of Work," 22.
[52] Gutiérrez, *Theology of Liberation*, 55–56, 65–67.

of their impact on a theology of labor. Exactly where *Laborem Exercens* manifests the greatest tension, Gutiérrez redirects the encyclical's theology of labor toward liberative ends. To labor with God, "to continue creation" through work, Gutiérrez writes, "is worth nothing ... if it does not contribute to human liberation."[53] Moreover, by thematizing God's redemption of labor in terms of anticapitalist struggle, Gutiérrez concretizes John Paul's own acknowledgement of the need for a "struggle against an economic system" bent on "upholding the absolute predominance of capital, the possession of the means of production and of the land, in contrast to the free and personal nature of human work" (*Centesimus Annus*, no. 35).[54]

To close, then, I wish to consider Gutiérrez's reflections on the nature of the struggle of labor for liberation, the redemption of labor. In the fifteenth-year revised edition of *A Theology of Liberation*, Gutiérrez made a significant revision of an important section near the end of the book. Originally titled "Christian Fellowship and the Class Struggle" in the book's first English edition published in 1973, Gutiérrez redrafted this controversial section under the title "Faith and Social Conflict." While the first edition "gave rise to misunderstandings" concerning Gutiérrez's conception of class conflict, antagonism, and the meaning of Christian love, in this 1988 revision he claims to have "rewritten the text in the light of new documents of the magisterium and by taking other aspects of the subject into account."[55] The result is a theological construal of anticapitalist struggle articulated through the language and theology of *Laborem Exercens*, particularly its section on the conflict between labor and capital. In Gutiérrez's reading of the encyclical, conflict is not a historical or ontological necessity but a "social fact" generated by the structures of capitalist property ownership.[56] Because of the contingent, material basis of this conflict—the real "opposition of persons," embodied in the class structuring of labor and capital—its resolution entails a restructuring of the capitalist property relation.[57] To make concrete the "priority of labor over capital," then, entails not a moral reform of the relationship of owners of capital to their workers, but rather a structural transformation of the social relations

---

[53] Gutiérrez, *Theology of Liberation*, 90; see also Gutiérrez, "The Gospel of Work," 29–30.
[54] While *Laborem Exercens* expresses disapproval for a form of class struggle overdetermined by ideology and commending the use of violence (no. 11), John Paul does not dismiss labor struggle as such, even when it "takes on a character of opposition towards others" and a highly conflictual form (no. 20). It is this kind of "struggle for social justice" and "the just good" (no. 20) that Gutiérrez develops in anticapitalist terms.
[55] Gutiérrez, *Theology of Liberation*, 156.
[56] Gutiérrez, *Theology of Liberation*, 157–158; Gutiérrez, "The Gospel of Work," 32.
[57] Gutiérrez, *Theology of Liberation*, 158–159.

of production. In short, the "priority of labor over capital," in Gutiérrez's reading, demands the abolition of capital as a privileged owning class. Where John Paul II commended enterprises of joint ownership between labor and capital and worker involvement in management and decision-making regarding the use of capital, Gutiérrez goes a step further. In order for capitalism's alienations to be overcome, the class structure of capitalism must be abolished. For work to be a creative act of the person, workers must be able to call the fruit of their labor their own, to own and direct the productive property upon which they labor in cooperation with one another. Indeed, Gutiérrez sees that participation in the direction and use of capital absent real ownership does not fully overcome capitalist alienation. Use *and* ownership of capital, in Gutiérrez's view, belong together in the hands of labor.

Such a restructuring of labor relations and property ownership, however, is clearly at odds with the interests of the current owners of capital. The owning class will not voluntarily abolish itself or relinquish its absolute hold on capital, and so workers must engage in contestation. Gutiérrez proposes, then, a theological account of conflict and class struggle, ordered to the common good and motivated by love, which sees the abolition of the class structure as participation in God's redemption of labor.[58] Capitalism, Gutiérrez maintains, makes enemies, antagonistic social relations embodied in and perpetuated by persons' "relation to the ownership of the means of production" and the conflicting interests they generate.[59] To love one's enemies under capitalism, then, means "taking a position, opposing certain groups of persons"—namely those who possess capital against labor—in order to seek their "conversion."[60] The conversion of capital to the common good, on Gutiérrez's terms, entails the concrete restructuring of property ownership and the transfer of the means of production into the hands of workers. Such is the redemption of labor *and capital*. The class struggle of workers against the capitalist class—even one, as John Paul II said, which entails "an aspect of opposition"—does not intend to "eliminate the opponent," but rather to seek their conversion to the common good (*Laborem Exercens*, no. 20).[61] For Gutiérrez, anticapitalist struggle is an expression of "evangelical charity"—the universal love Christians are called to extend even to class-enemies, in order to seek their

---

[58] I develop a theological account of conflict along these lines in Nicholas Norman-Krause, "Political Theology and the Conflicts of Democracy," (PhD Thesis, Baylor University, 2021).
[59] Gutiérrez, "The Gospel of Work," 31–32.
[60] Gutiérrez, *Theology of Liberation*, 159–160.
[61] See Gutiérrez's comments in *Theology of Liberation*, 250–251, n. 62.

reconciliation.[62]

CONCLUSION

I have argued that *Laborem Exercens* develops a theology of labor within which the contradictions and alienation of capitalist production come into view as a moral and theological problem. Whereas the encyclical simply dramatizes the tension between a theology of dignified, creative labor and the limits of capital, Gutiérrez theologizes a way beyond it, imagining the redemption of labor from the sins of capital. For Gutiérrez, labor's redemption is wrought by God's saving action, manifested in the historical struggle of labor to seek the conversion of capital to the common good. The struggle for liberation, even in its most contentious moments, is ordered to the realization of dignified, social, and just forms of work and production, a practice of labor not determined by the limits of capital.[63]

Nicholas Norman-Krause is Postdoctoral Research Associate at the Institute for Studies of Religion at Baylor University. His research examines the relationship between theology, politics, and economy. His current writing project, *Political Theology and the Conflicts of Democracy*, develops a theological account of conflict, pluralism, and moral disagreement in democratic politics.

---

[62] Gutiérrez, *Theology of Liberation*, 156, 159.
[63] Many thanks to Matthew Whelan, Alessandro Rovati, the two anonymous reviewers of this article, and the community of scholars that is *New Wine, New Wineskins*, for their invaluable comments on this essay.

Sensus Fideli—Whom? Retrieving Insights from Johann Adam Möhler

Gina Maria Noia

IN MICHAEL SEAN WINTERS'S JUDGMENT, "The *sensus fidei* may be the single most misunderstood and abused concept in the post-Vatican II era."[1] Specifically, Winters elaborates, "The sense of the faithful has been conflated with public opinion, repeatedly, and used to undermine Church teaching. It has been used to justify a stance of dissent."[2] Others agree that the term is misused in this way.[3] Indeed, the magisterial tradition is clear that one should not equate the *sensus fidei* with public opinion, and such misuse is found in the literature.[4]

Theologians who stress the importance of the *sensus fidei* as a *locus theologicus* and who disagree with Church teaching on controversial issues, typically are careful to qualify their appeals to popular opinion, e.g., they state that popular opinion "may indicate" the *sensus fidei*.[5] Still, to other theologians, any appeal to popular opinion is

---

[1] Michael Sean Winters, "The *Sensus Fidei*," *National Catholic Reporter* 2014, www.ncronline.org/blogs/distinctly-catholic/sensus-fidei.
[2] Winters, "The *Sensus Fidei*."
[3] See, for instance, David A. Tamisiea, "Vatican II, St. Thomas Aquinas, and the *Sensus Fidelium*," in *Wisdom and the Renewal of Catholic Theology: Essays in Honor of Matthew L. Lamb*, ed. Thomas P. Harmon and Roger W. Nutt (Eugene, OR: Pickwick, 2016), 100.
[4] As Winters specifies, "the commentariat" (Winters, "The *Sensus Fidei*"), at least, have misused the term. For instance, the National Catholic Reporter Editorial Staff write: "Our message is that we believe the *sensus fidelium* is that the exclusion of women from the priesthood has no strong basis in Scripture or any other compelling rationale; therefore, women should be ordained" (NCR Editorial Staff, "Editorial: Ordination of Women Would Correct an Injustice," *National Catholic Reporter* 2012, www.ncronline.org/ news/parish/editorial-ordination-women-would-correct-injustice).
[5] For instance, Lawler and Salzman write, "John Paul II teaches that 'the church values sociological and statistical research,' but immediately adds the proviso that 'such research alone is not to be considered in itself an expression of the *sensus fidei*.' The pope is correct. Neither empirical research nor public opinion polls are necessarily expressions of *sensus fidei*, but each may contribute to the illumination of *sensus fidei* and may manifest both *fides qua creditur* and *fides quae creditur*" (Michael G. Lawler and Todd A. Salzman, "Human Experience and Catholic Moral Theology," *Irish Theological Quarterly* 76, no. 1 [2011]: 17).

problematic, given that the *sensus fidei* is only found,[6] or at least only reliably found,[7] among practicing Christians. In turn, this view is critiqued for wrongfully excluding persons from the *sensus fidei*.[8] Thus, the literature on the *sensus fidei* is replete with disagreements regarding, inter alia, who are "the faithful," the relationship between the *sensus fidei* and the Magisterium, and the role of public opinion with respect to the *sensus fidei*. Nonetheless, there are also important points of consensus among theologians.

To help illuminate points of consensus and offer balanced responses to points of dissensus, I would like to turn to Tübingen scholar Johann Adam Möhler. While Johann Adam Möhler's work is mentioned in histories of the concept of the *sensus fidei*,[9] the mention is brief and often suggests that Möhler is too vague to offer a substantive contribution to the post-Vatican II Roman Catholic debate on the topic.[10] However, though Möhler does not treat systematically the topic of the *sensus fidei*, nor indeed even use the term *sensus fidei*,[11] I will demonstrate how his relevant insights can contribute substantively to theological discussion.

I begin this paper by summarizing and commenting regarding magisterial and other theological treatment of the *sensus fidei*, noting both points of consensus and disagreement among authors, as well as the lack of clarity in the literature regarding what the *sensus fidei* is metaphysically. In an effort to clarify the concept, I propose that the *sensus fidei* is best understood as referring to the connatural aspect of

---

[6] See, for instance, E. Christian Brugger, "*Sensus Fidei*, the Magisterium, and the Formation of Conscience," in *Christianity and the Laws of Conscience: An Introduction*, ed. Jeffrey B. Hammond and Helen M. Alvaré, Cambridge Studies in Law and Christianity (Cambridge: Cambridge University Press, 2021), 82.
[7] See, for instance, Tamisiea, "Vatican II, St. Thomas Aquinas, and the *Sensus Fidelium*," 105.
[8] See, for instance, John J. Burkhard, "*Sensus Fidei*: Recent Theological Reflection (1990–2001). Part I," *Heythrop Journal* 46 (2005): 452; Thomas Knieps-Port le Roi, "Church Teaching on Marriage and Family—a Matter of *Sensus Fidelium*?," in *The Sensus Fidelium and Moral Theology*, ed. Charles E. Curran and Lisa A. Fullam, Readings in Moral Theology (New York: Paulist Press, 2017), 289.
[9] Daniel J. Finucane, *Sensus Fidelium: The Use of a Concept in the Post-Vatican II Era* (Bethesda, MD: International Scholars, 1996), 137–141; Peter Hünermann, "*Sensus Fidei*," in *Lexikon für Theologie und Kirche*, ed. Walter Kasper (3rd ed., Freiburg: Herder, 2000), 466; International Theological Commission, Sensus Fidei *in the Life of the Church* (2014), no. 34, www.vatican.va/roman_curia/congregations/cfaith/cti_documents/rc_cti_201406 10_sensus-fidei_en.html.
[10] Owen Chadwick, *From Bossuet to Newman*, 2nd ed. (New York: Cambridge University Press, 1987); Paul Schrodt, *The Problem of the Beginning of Dogma in Recent Theology* (Frankfurt: Peter Lang, 1978).
[11] Note that both the concept and term are found in the writings of theologians who predate Möhler. See Finucane, *Sensus Fidelium*, 18.

the theological virtue of faith along with the connected gifts of understanding and knowledge. In addition to proposing this understanding of the *sensus fidei* as a contribution to the broader literature on the *sensus fidei*, this understanding will also guide my retrieval of Möhler's relevant insights.

With this understanding of the *sensus fidei* in mind, I present four ways in which Möhler can contribute to contemporary discussion on the *sensus fidei*: First, Möhler's insistence that "God can be known by the individual only through the whole"[12] supports a via media between individualistic and authoritarian understandings of the *sensus fidei*. Second, Möhler's attention to living faith's preceding and exceeding doctrinal formulations helps to flesh out the *sensus fidei*'s role in the development of doctrine. Third, Möhler's positive appraisal of the role of heresy in the clarification and purification of doctrine helps to underscore the benefit of public opinion, even while the *sensus fidei* is not the same as public opinion. Fourth, Möhler's distinction between antithesis and contradiction can serve as a principle of discerning the *sensus fidei*.

MAGISTERIAL TRADITION ON THE *SENSUS FIDEI*[13]

In this section I summarize explicit magisterial[14] statements on the

---

[12] Johann Adam Möhler, *Unity in the Church, or, the Principle of Catholicism. Presented in the Spirit of the Church Fathers of the First Three Centuries.*, ed. and trans. Peter C. Erb (Washington, DC: Catholic University of America Press, 1996), 153.

[13] In contemporary literature, the terms *sensus fidelium* ("sense of the faithful"), *sensus fidei* ("sense of faith"), *sensus fidei fidelium* ("sense of faith of the faithful"), and *sensus fidei fidelis* ("sense of faith of the faithful one") all appear. Authors use these terms variously to emphasize the objective versus subjective *sensus*, the individual versus communal *sensus*, or the commonality versus difference between these senses. However, authors do not seem to agree on which term emphasizes what. For analysis of these terms (though they seem to take different positions on which terms emphasize which aspect of the *sensus fidei*), see: John J. Burkhard, "*Sensus Fidei*: Recent Theological Reflection since Vatican II: I. 1965–1984," *Heythrop Journal* 34 (1993): 41–59; Ormond Rush, "*Sensus Fidei*: Faith 'Making Sense' of Revelation," *Theological Studies* 62 (2001): 232; International Theological Commission, Sensus Fidei *in the Life of the Church*, no. 3. I will use *sensus fidei* to refer to both the individual and communal senses, in order to emphasize that both the individual and the Church are the subjects of the same *sensus fidei*, as I will elaborate on later. However, the term *sensus fidelium* features in this paper's title, since it is more conducive to puns.

[14] I use "magisterial" in a semi-broad sense to include conciliar teaching and statements made or approved by the pope.

sensus fidei.[15] The first explicit magisterial statement on the *sensus fidei* is found in the Second Vatican Council's *Lumen Gentium*:

> The entire body of the faithful, anointed as they are by the Holy One, cannot err in matters of belief. They manifest this special property by means of the whole people's supernatural discernment in matters of faith[16] when "from the Bishops down to the last of the lay faithful" they show universal agreement in matters of faith and morals. That discernment in matters of faith is aroused and sustained by the Spirit of truth. It is exercised under the guidance of the sacred teaching authority, in faithful and respectful obedience to which the people of God accepts that which is not just the word of men but truly the word of God. Through it, the people of God adheres unwaveringly to the faith given once and for all to the saints, penetrates it more deeply with right thinking, and applies it more fully in its life (no. 12).

Here *Lumen Gentium* outlines the subjects of the *sensus fidei* ("the entire body of the faithful," the whole "people of God"), from where the *sensus fidei* comes (the Holy Spirit), when it is manifest (in "universal agreement"), what falls within its purview ("matters of faith and morals"), what assists it (the teaching of the Church), and what it enables (infallibility in belief, "supernatural discernment," unwavering adherence to "the faith given once and for all to the saints," the penetration of this faith "more deeply with right thinking," and the application of this faith "more fully in ... life").

Where *Lumen Gentium* notes that the *sensus fidei* comes from the Holy Spirit, Pope John Paul II (*Familiaris Consortio*, no. 5) and Pope Francis[17] specify that the *sensus fidei* is a "gift" of the Holy Spirit. The CDF explicitly connects the *sensus fidei* to the theological virtue of faith, explaining that the *sensus fidei* is "a property of theological faith" (*Donum Veritatis*, no. 35). Pope Benedict XVI characterizes the *sensus fidei* as "a sort of supernatural instinct which has a vital co-naturality with the object of faith itself,"[18] thus suggesting the sort of "property of theological faith" (*Donum Veritatis*, no. 35) the *sensus fidei* is; viz., "a vital co-naturality."

---

[15] In so doing, I do not by any means reject the opinion of many theologians that implicit reference to the *sensus fidei* is found throughout the magisterial tradition. Rather, I limit this section due to space constraints.

[16] "Supernaturali sensu fidei" in the official Latin text.

[17] Francis, "Address to Members of the International Theological Commission," December 6, 2013, www.vatican.va/content/francesco/en/speeches/2013/december/documents/papa-francesco_20131206_commissione-teologica.html.

[18] Benedict XVI, "Address to the International Theological Commission on the Occasion of Its Annual Plenary Assembly," December 7, 2012, www.vatican.va/content/benedict-xvi/en/speeches/2012/december/documents/hf_ben-xvi_spe_20121207_cti.html.

Statements by Pope Paul VI,[19] Pope John Paul II (*Familiaris Consortio*, nos. 5 and 73; *Ut Unum Sint*, no. 80), and Pope Benedict[20] follow *Lumen Gentium* in recognizing that the whole "people of God" are the subjects of the *sensus fidei*. Moreover, Pope Benedict emphasizes that the *sensus fidei* may manifest in the practice and belief of the people of God even before the belief is worked out theologically. "Thanks to that supernatural *sensus fidei*,"[21] Pope Benedict writes, Marian doctrine was "already present in the People of God, while theology had not yet found the key to interpreting it in the totality of the doctrine of the faith."[22] However, Pope John Paul II (*Familiaris Consortio*, no. 5),[23] the CDF (*Donum Veritatis*, no. 35), Pope Benedict,[24] and Pope Francis[25] caution against equating the *sensus fidei* with public opinion. Pope Benedict[26] and Pope Francis[27] add that criteria are needed to discern authentic manifestations of the *sensus fidei*. In this vein, Pope Paul VI,[28] Pope John Paul II (*Familiaris Consortio*, no. 73), the CDF (*Donum Veritatis*, no. 35), and Pope Benedict[29] follow *Lumen Gentium* in affirming that the *sensus fidei* is assisted by the teaching of the Church. Furthermore, Pope Benedict avers that "the *sensus fidei* cannot be authentically developed in believers, except to the extent in which they fully participate in the life of the Church."[30] Yet, bringing together the role of the whole people of God and the role of the Magisterium, Pope Francis speaks of the Magisterium's duty to attend to the *sensus fidei*.[31]

Magisterial statements after *Lumen Gentium* also expand upon what the *sensus fidei* enables. Pope Paul VI adds: deciphering "the signs of the times" and "wise insight";[32] Pope John Paul II adds: "a more profound understanding and activation of the word of God" and a shining forth in the laity of "the power of the Gospel ... in their daily

---

[19] Paul VI, "General Audience: Signs of the Times," *L'Osservatore Romano* (1969): 1.
[20] Benedict XVI, "General Audience: John Duns Scotus," July 7, 2010, www.vatican.va/content/benedict-xvi/en/audiences/2010/documents/hf_ben-xvi_aud_20100707.html.
[21] Benedict XVI, "General Audience."
[22] Benedict XVI, "General Audience."
[23] See also John Paul II, "Letter to Cardinal Roger Etchegaray."
[24] Benedict XVI, "Address to the International Theological Commission."
[25] Francis, "Address to Members."
[26] Benedict XVI, "Address to the International Theological Commission."
[27] Francis, "Address to Members."
[28] Paul VI, "General Audience: Signs of the Times."
[29] Benedict XVI, "Address to the International Theological Commission."
[30] Benedict XVI, "Address to the International Theological Commission."
[31] Francis, "Address to Members."
[32] Paul VI, "General Audience: Signs of the Times."

social and family life" (*Familiaris Consortio*, no. 5); Pope Benedict adds: discernment of "whether or not a truth belongs to the living deposit of the Apostolic Tradition";[33] and Pope Francis adds: discernment of "what is truly of God" (*Evangelii Gaudium*, no. 119).

CONTEMPORARY THEOLOGICAL DISCUSSION ON THE *SENSUS FIDEI*

While theological discussion regarding the *sensus fidei* is extensive and includes many fascinating points, I will mostly limit my summary and remarks here to points of consensus and dissensus in contemporary literature.[34] John J. Burkhard, who provides four helpful summaries of theological discussion of the *sensus fidei* from 1965 to 2001,[35] proposes five points of agreement among theologians: (1) Vatican II understood the *sensus fidei* as pertaining to "the infallibility of the whole Church,"[36] that is, the *sensus fidei* is received by the Church and by each believer, "in the context of the community of all believers."[37] (2) The *sensus fidei* is a "'sense' of the faith,"[38] and a gift of the Holy Spirit. (3) While not irrational, the *sensus fidei* indicates a "realm of knowledge, but where knowledge is understood to be a form other than discursive reasoning."[39] (4) For the Magisterium as much as for the laity, the *sensus fidei* has an "active"[40] character. (5) There are "limitations, dangers, and temptations"[41] related to the *sensus fidei*. To these five points of consensus, I would add a sixth: (6) The *sensus fidei* has a role in the development of

---

[33] Benedict XVI, "Address to the International Theological Commission."
[34] For the historical context, see Hünermann, "*Sensus Fidei*"; International Theological Commission, Sensus Fidei *in the Life of the Church*.
[35] Burkhard, "*Sensus Fidei*: Recent Theological Reflection since Vatican II: I. 1965–1984," 41–59; John J. Burkhard, "*Sensus Fidei*: Recent Theological Reflection since Vatican II: II. 1985–1989," *Heythrop Journal* 34 (1993): 123–136; Burkhard, "*Sensus Fidei*: Recent Theological Reflection (1990–2001). Part I," 450–475; John J. Burkhard, "*Sensus Fidei*: Recent Theological Reflection (1990–2001). Part II," *Heythrop Journal* 47 (2006): 38–54.
[36] Burkhard, "*Sensus Fidei*: Recent Theological Reflection since Vatican II: II. 1985–1989," 133.
[37] Burkhard, "*Sensus Fidei*: Recent Theological Reflection since Vatican II: II. 1985–1989," 133.
[38] Burkhard, "*Sensus Fidei*: Recent Theological Reflection since Vatican II: II. 1985–1989," 133.
[39] Burkhard, "*Sensus Fidei*: Recent Theological Reflection since Vatican II: II. 1985–1989," 133.
[40] Burkhard, "*Sensus Fidei*: Recent Theological Reflection since Vatican II: II. 1985–1989," 133.
[41] Burkhard, "*Sensus Fidei*: Recent Theological Reflection since Vatican II: II. 1985–1989," 133.

doctrine.[42] Arguably consensus point 6 is contained within, or implied by, Burkhard's points of consensus, but it seems important enough to name independently.

The magisterial tradition, which I have summarized above, seems to fall within all six points of theological consensus. Regarding consensus point 1, the magisterial tradition seems to follow Vatican II's understanding of the *sensus fidei* as pertaining to the infallibility of the whole people of God. Consensus point 2, the *sensus fidei* is a "'sense' of the faith" and a gift of the Holy Spirit, is explicit in magisterial statements. Pope Benedict XVI's reference to the *sensus fidei* as a "a sort of supernatural instinct which has a vital co-naturality with the object of faith itself"[43] and Pope Francis' very similar reference to the *sensus fidei* as "a kind of 'spiritual instinct'"[44] align with consensus point 3 (the *sensus fidei*'s indicating a "realm of knowledge, but where knowledge is understood to be a form other than discursive reasoning"[45]). Much of what the Magisterium attests that the *sensus fidei* enables in the lives of all believers[46] has an active character (consensus point 4) and plausibly underlies the development of doctrine (consensus point 6).[47] Pope John Paul II (*Familiaris Consortio*, no. 5), the CDF (*Donum Veritatis*, no. 35), Pope Benedict XVI,[48] and Pope Francis's[49] caution, as summarized above, regarding the equating of public opinion with the *sensus fidei* all point toward

---

[42] Due to space constraints and my belief that this is not a contentious point, I will not present a detailed argument for this consensus point in this paper. See Finucane, *Sensus Fidelium*; International Theological Commission, Sensus Fidei *in the Life of the Church*, no. 74.

[43] Benedict XVI, "Address to the International Theological Commission."

[44] Francis, "Address to Members."

[45] Burkhard, "*Sensus Fidei*: Recent Theological Reflection since Vatican II: II. 1985–1989," 133.

[46] Viz., penetration of faith "more deeply with right thinking" (*Lumen Gentium*, no. 12), the application of this faith "more fully in … life" (*Lumen Gentium*, no. 12), deciphering the signs of the times (Paul VI, "General Audience: Signs of the Times"), "wise insight" (Paul VI, "General Audience: Signs of the Times"), "a more profound understanding and activation of the word of God" (*Familiaris Consortio*, no. 5), a shining forth in the laity of "the power of the Gospel … in their daily social and family life" (*Familiaris Consortio*, no. 5), discernment of "whether or not a truth belongs to the living deposit of the Apostolic Tradition" (Benedict XVI, "Address to the International Theological Commission"), and discernment of "what is truly of God" (*Evangelii Gaudium*, no. 119).

[47] The ITC document also points to the Second Vatican Council's *Dei Verbum* as implicitly acknowledging the *sensus fidei*'s role in the development of doctrine. International Theological Commission, Sensus Fidei *in the Life of the Church*, no. 46.

[48] Benedict XVI, "Address to the International Theological Commission."

[49] Francis, "Address to Members."

"limitations, dangers, and temptations,"[50] related to the *sensus fidei* (consensus point 5).

At the same time, at least four points of dissensus emerge in the contemporary theological literature on the *sensus fidei*: (1) Who, more precisely, are the whole people of God? Only practicing Christians?[51] All baptized Christians?[52] (2) What precisely is the relationship of the Magisterium to the *sensus fidei*?[53] (3) What, if anything, is the role for public opinion in the *sensus fidei*?[54] (4) What ought to be the criteria for discerning the *sensus fidei*?[55]

---

[50] Burkhard, "*Sensus Fidei*: Recent Theological Reflection since Vatican II: II. 1985–1989," 133.

[51] See, for example, Thomas Dubay, "The State of Moral Theology: A Critical Appraisal," in *The Magisterium and Morality*, ed. Charles E. Curran and Richard A. McCormick, Readings in Moral Theology (New York: Paulist, 1982), 352. Wolfgang Beinert recommends that the more one is committed to Christian practices, the more credibility he/she has regarding the *sensus fidei*. Burkhard, "*Sensus Fidei*: Recent Theological Reflection (1990–2001). Part I," 468. David Tamisiea likewise holds that only practicing Christians "can be trusted to express an authentic *sensus fidelium*" (Tamisiea, "Vatican II, St. Thomas Aquinas, and the *Sensus Fidelium*," 103).

[52] See Burkhard, "*Sensus Fidei*: Recent Theological Reflection (1990–2001). Part I," 450–475; Burkhard, "*Sensus Fidei*: Recent Theological Reflection (1990–2001). Part II," 38–54; Patrick J. Hartin, "*Sensus Fidelium*: A Roman Catholic Reflection on Its Significance for Ecumenical Thought," *Journal of Ecumenical Studies* 28 (1991): 74–87.

[53] For discussion, see, for example, Anglican-Roman Catholic Dialogue (ARCIC-II), "The Gift of Authority," *Origins* 29, no. 2 (1999): 17–29; Finucane, *Sensus Fidelium*; Knieps-Port le Roi, "Church Teaching on Marriage and Family—a Matter of *Sensus Fidelium*?"; Brian N. Massingale, "Beyond 'Who Am I to Judge?' The *Sensus Fidelium*, LGBT Experience, and Truth-Telling in the Church," in *Learning from All the Faithful: A Contemporary Theology of the* Sensus Fidei, ed. Peter C. Phan and Bradford E. Hinze (Eugene, OR: Pickwick Publications, 2016); Leo Scheffczyk, "*Sensus Fidelium*-Witness on the Part of the Community," *Communio* 15 (1988): 182–198; Paul Valadier, "Has the Concept of *Sensus Fidelium* Fallen into Desuetude?," in *Catholic Theological Ethics in the World Church: The Plenary Papers from the First Cross-Cultural Conference on Catholic Theological Ethics*, ed. James Keenan (New York: Continuum, 2007).

[54] For discussion, see, for example, Christian Duquoc, "An Active Role for the People of God in Defining the Church's Faith," in *The Teaching Authority of Believers*, ed. J. B. Metz and E. Schillebeeckx, Concilium (Edinburgh: T. & T. Clark, 1985); Abraham Peter Kustermann, "Observations Concerning the Tübingen 'Axiom' Then and Now," in *The Legacy of the Tübingen School: The Relevance of Nineteenth-Century Theology for the Twenty-First Century*, ed. Donald J. Dietrich and Michael J. Himes (New York: Crossroad, 1997); Lawler and Salzman, "Human Experience and Catholic Moral Theology"; Hervé Legrand, "Reception, *Sensus Fidelium*, and Synodal Life: An Effort at Articulation," in *Reception and Communion among Churches*, ed. Julio Manzanares, Hervé Legrand, and Antonio García (Washington, DC: Canon Law Department of the Catholic University of America, 1997).

[55] For proposed criteria, see International Theological Commission, Sensus Fidei *in the Life of the Church*, nos. 88–105; Tamisiea, "Vatican II, St. Thomas Aquinas, and the *Sensus Fidelium*," 104–106.

A Proposal: The Sensus Fidei as the Connatural Aspect of Theological Faith plus the Gifts of Understanding and Knowledge

Having summarized the magisterial tradition as well as points of theological consensus and dissensus regarding the *sensus fidei*, I would like to turn to the work of Tübingen scholar Johann Adam Möhler, to retrieve his relevant insights. While Möhler is one of the few pre-Vatican II theologians mentioned in histories of the concept of *sensus fidei*,[56] Möhler does not treat systematically the topic, nor indeed even use the term *sensus fidei*. Thus, there is some question regarding how I or others can retrieve Möhler's thinking related to the *sensus fidei*. Certainly, theologians could have a clear understanding of what the *sensus fidei* is, even if they disagree on certain aspects of it, and so could recognize in Möhler's writing when he has something in mind like the *sensus fidei*. But do theologians have a clear understanding of the *sensus fidei*? Despite the points of consensus he identifies, Burkhard concludes his *New Catholic Encyclopedia* entry with the admission that "the term has no commonly agreed meaning among theologians."[57] A sketch of the *sensus fidei* emerges from the theological consensus: its subjects are the whole people of God, it is a gift of the Holy Spirit pertaining to faith, it has an active quality, it plays a role in the development of doctrine. But still, what precisely, or one might say, metaphysically, is the *sensus fidei*? Again, consensus point 2 is that the *sensus fidei* is a gift of the Holy Spirit pertaining to faith. But, more specifically, is the *sensus fidei* one or more traditional gifts of the Holy Spirit, is it simply an aspect of the theological virtue of faith, is it a more newly identified gift of the Holy Spirit annexed to theological faith, or is it something else? Clarity regarding the metaphysical referent of the *sensus fidei* is important. Such clarity not only aids retrieval of insights from theologians who do not use the term, but also helps, inter alia, to delineate proper use of the term, to add depth to points of consensus, and resolve points of disagreement.

As I noted earlier, the CDF states that the *sensus fidei* is "a property of theological faith" (*Donum Veritatis*, no. 35). An International Theological Commission (ITC) document on the *sensus fidei* likewise submits that the *sensus fidei* "is intrinsically linked to the virtue of

---

[56] See Finucane, *Sensus Fidelium*, 137–141; Hünermann, "*Sensus Fidei*," 466; International Theological Commission, Sensus Fidei *in the Life of the Church*, no. 34.
[57] John J. Burkhard, "*Sensus Fidelium*," in *New Catholic Encyclopedia* (Detroit: Gale, 2003).

faith itself; it flows from, and is a property of, faith."[58] The ITC proceeds helpfully to specify the sort of property of faith that the *sensus fidei* is: "The *sensus fidei* is the form that the instinct which accompanies every virtue takes in the case of the virtue of faith."[59] Pope Benedict XVI seems to say something similar when, as I indicated above, he characterizes the *sensus fidei* as "a sort of supernatural instinct which has a vital co-naturality with the object of faith itself."[60] I will follow the ITC in accepting that the *sensus fidei* metaphysically refers to the intuitive aspect of faith, or to use Pope Benedict's (and Thomas Aquinas's[61]) language, the "connatural" aspect of faith.

However, it seems that the connatural aspect of theological faith does not capture all of what the Magisterium and other theologians mean by *sensus fidei*. Rather, when the Magisterium and other theologians speak of the *sensus fidei*, they seem implicitly to refer to the gift cluster of theological faith *and* the gifts of understanding and knowledge. Thus, I would like to propose that the *sensus fidei* is best understood as referring to the connatural aspect of the theological virtue of faith along with the gifts of understanding and knowledge. For ease of reference, I will refer to this understanding of the *sensus fidei* by "*sensus fidei cluster*." In the rest of this section, I will first establish the plausibility of this understanding of the *sensus fidei* as a development of consensus point 2, and as an aid to retrieving Möhler's insights on the *sensus fidei*. Next, I will provide evidence that the Magisterium and other theologians implicitly assume the understanding of the *sensus fidei* that I am proposing. Lastly, I will outline some ways in which this clear metaphysical referent benefits theological discussion of the *sensus fidei*.

Thomas Aquinas' account of theological faith,[62] the gifts of understanding and knowledge, and their connection, is foundational for demonstrating that the *sensus fidei* plausibly refers to this gift cluster, as well as for showing that when the Magisterium and other theologians speak of the *sensus fidei*, they seem implicitly to refer to this gift cluster. Aquinas distinguishes between "lifeless," "dead," or

---

[58] International Theological Commission, Sensus Fidei *in the Life of the Church*, no. 49.
[59] International Theological Commission, Sensus Fidei *in the Life of the Church*, no. 53.
[60] Benedict XVI, "Address to the International Theological Commission."
[61] See ST II-II q. 45, a. 2. All translations of the *Summa Theologiae* in this paper are by the Fathers of the English Dominican Province.
[62] Of course, in his account of faith, Aquinas draws from Scripture and other theologians. Stephen F. Brown, "The Theological Virtue of Faith: An Invitation to an Ecclesial Life of Truth (IIa IIae, qq. 1–16)," in *The Ethics of Aquinas*, ed. Stephen J. Pope (Washington, DC: Georgetown University Press, 2002).

"imperfect" faith, and "living" faith (ST II-II q. 4, a. 4), the latter of which is a *theological* virtue, rather than a mere acquired virtue, because it is "infused" into us by God (ST II-II q. 6, a. 1).[63] By the virtue of faith, one believes in God and His revelation (ST II-II q. 2, a. 5 and II-II q. 5, a. 3). God's revelation is not evidently true to the intellect (ST II-II q. 1, a. 4 and II-II q. 4, a. 2). As a result, the human intellect cannot assent to God's revelation on its own, but must remain undecided as to its truth. For Aquinas, the undecided intellect can be moved by the will (ST I q. 82, a. 4 and I-II q. 17, a. 6), which can desire only some true or apparent good (ST I-II q. 8, a. 1). In the case of dead faith, the mere acquired virtue, the will commands the intellect to assent to God's revelation[64] (ST II-II q. 4, a. 7) insofar as it sees it as good.[65] At this point, however, faith is not living faith—faith sufficient for salvation (ST II-II q. 2, a. 5)—though it "is a perfection of the intellect" (ST II-II q. 4, a. 4).

Dead faith is imperfect faith, as it is not yet moved by the perfection of the will (ST II-II q. 4, a. 2). God perfects the will through a separate theological virtue, charity. Charity requires imperfect faith, "because the will cannot tend to God with perfect love, unless the intellect possesses right faith about Him" (ST II-II q. 4, a. 7). Charity, then, directs the will no longer merely towards the willer's good, but towards God as the willer's good (ST II-II q. 23, a. 7). With the theological virtue of charity now perfecting the will, the will can command the intellect to assent to God's revelation as "the Divine Good" (ST II-II q. 4, a. 3). In this way, charity "quickens the act of faith" (ST II-II q. 4, a. 3) to conceive living faith. Importantly, human freedom is preserved, but the command of the will and subsequent assent of the intellect are accomplished by God working in us;[66] God is the cause of one's assent to God's revelation (ST II-II q. 6, a. 1 and II-II q. 23, a. 2). The theological virtue of faith has God and His revelation as both its material object (what is known) and its formal object (means by which it is known) (ST II-II q. 1, a. 1). Thus, Aquinas

---

[63] Aquinas defines infused virtue thusly: "a good quality of mind, by which we live righteously, of which no one can make bad use, which God works in us, without us" (ST I-II q. 55, a. 4).

[64] It is important to note here that Aquinas thinks that whenever we will any good, even if it is not salvific, God has to help us in some way (ST I-II q. 109, a. 2). It follows from this that for the will to move the undecided intellect to assent to God's revelation, some grace must be at work. See ST II-II q. 5, a. 2 and II-II q. 6, a. 2.

[65] Because the will can desire only some true or apparent good, one whose will commands his intellect to assent to God's revelation must perceive that assenting to God's revelation is good; see Eleonore Stump, *Aquinas* (London: Routledge, 2003), 364.

[66] For Aquinas, our will must be moved internally, to preserve human freedom, and by the movement of God, to preserve our *inability* to do anything good without God's grace. See ST I q. 105, a. 4 and I-II q. 9, a. 6.

affirms the definition of faith in Hebrews 11:1: "Faith is the substance of things to be hoped for" (what is known), and the evidence of things that appear not" (means by which it is known) (ST II-II q. 4, a. 1). Accordingly, by the theological virtue of faith the intellect will "infallibly tend towards its object, which is the true ... since nothing false can be the object of faith" (ST II-II q. 4, a. 5).

The theological virtues, like all of the infused virtues, are aided by the gifts of the Holy Spirit. While the infused virtues grant to man the "supernatural perfection" (ST I-II q. 68, a. 2) of his reason, the gifts of the Holy Spirit make man "amenable to the promptings of God" (ST I-II q. 68, a. 2). In so doing, the gifts of the Holy Spirit perfect even the infused virtues, for "the motion of reason does not suffice, unless it receive in addition the prompting or motion of the Holy Ghost" (ST I-II q. 68, a. 2). For Aquinas, the gifts of understanding and knowledge are the gifts that perfect the virtue of faith. The gift of understanding, "denotes a certain excellence of a knowledge that penetrates into the heart of things" (ST II-II q. 8, a. 1); it is an intuitional grasp of things. The gift of knowledge is knowledge of human affairs that is likened to God's knowledge; God's knowledge involves "a sure judgment of truth, without any discursive process, by simple intuition" (ST II-II q. 9, a. 1). The gift of knowledge grants, "a sure and right judgment on [things proposed to be believed], so as to discern what is to be believed from what is not to be believed" (ST II-II q. 9, a. 1).

Thus, one can see the intimate connection between the theological virtue of faith and the gifts of understanding and knowledge: the gifts of understanding and knowledge directly help to perfect the theological virtue of faith. It is this intimate connection between theological faith and the gifts of understanding and knowledge that I believe makes it plausible that the *sensus fidei* refers to them together; that the *sensus fidei* refers to connaturality with God and His revelation arising both from the perfected intellect (theological faith) and from certain promptings of the Holy Spirit (the gifts of understanding and knowledge). Importantly for this paper, I also think that it is reasonable to use a Thomistic understanding of faith and the gifts of understanding and knowledge to aid retrieval of Möhler's insights relevant to the *sensus fidei*. Arguably, Möhler's understanding of faith has enough inheritance from Aquinas to allow a Thomistic understanding to guide retrieval of Möhler's insights. Consider Möhler's description of faith:

> The word faith signifies not so much the act of thinking, or opining, but it has the sense of a firm obligation (contracted in virtue of a free act of submission) whereby the mind decisively and permanently assents to the mysteries revealed by God. Catholics consider faith as the reunion with God in Christ, especially by means of the faculties of

knowledge, illuminated and confirmed by grace, with which the excitement of various feelings is more or less connected. It is in their estimation, a divine light, whereby man discerns, as well as recognizes, the decrees of God, and comprehends not only what God is to man, but also what man should be to God.... But if faith passes from the understanding, and the feelings, excited through the understanding, to the will; if it pervades, vivifies, and fructifies the will ... if love is enkindled out of faith, as fire out of brimstone, then, only after faith and love doth regeneration or justification ensue. Hence, the schools of the middle-age recognised, likewise, a faith, whereof they said, that it alone justified; it is known by the designation of the *fides formata*, under which the school-men understood a faith, that had love itself as its vivifying, its plastic principle (*forma*); and on this account it was called *fides charitate formata, animate, fides viva, vivida.*[67]

Möhler, like Aquinas, suggests: the object of faith as "the mysteries revealed by God," the necessity of grace, and that love requires a type of faith, though faith is not living faith until it is vivified by love. Möhler also assigns to faith functions that sound quite similar to the functions of the gifts of knowledge and understanding, which Aquinas says perfect the theological virtue of faith. Möhler writes that, by faith, "man discerns, as well as recognizes, the decrees of God," suggestive of knowledge, "and comprehends not only what God is to man, but also what man should be to God," suggestive of understanding. Although Möhler does not specify these functions as the gifts of knowledge and understanding, he certainly sees these functions as closely connected to faith, as does Aquinas. Möhler plausibly has Aquinas in mind when he refers to "the school-men" of the middle-

---

[67] Johann Adam Möhler, *Symbolism. Exposition of the Doctrinal Differences between Catholics and Protestants as Evidenced by Their Symbolical Writings*, trans. James Burton Robertson (New York: Crossroad Herder, 1997), 120–121. Consider also, Möhler, *Symbolism*, xxvii: "The very essence of faith ... its nature consists in embracing, with undoubting certainty, the revealed truth, which can be only one ... For with belief in Christ, as a true envoy of the Father of light, it is by no means consistent, that those who have been taught by him, should be unable to define in what his revelations on divine things consist, and what, on the other hand, is in contradiction with his word and ordinances" and Möhler, *Symbolism*, 150: "But the Catholics say, if this adherence be a mere connection of ideas—an empty union of feeling or phantasy with Christ—a mere theoretic faith in him—a mere recognition of Christian truths, in opposition to works wrought in the vital communion of the will with Christ, as well as to the love engendered by faith, and to all other virtues; then this faith is in itself by no means sufficient to render men acceptable to God, or to justify. But if faith, on the other hand, be understood as a new divine sentiment, regulating the whole man—as the new living spirit (*fides formata*); then to this alone, even according to the Catholic system, is the power given to make us the children heirs of eternal happiness."

ages. Indeed, on the page following the above passage, Möhler directly appeals to Aquinas on faith.[68]

Having presented a fairly detailed Thomistic account in order to establish the plausibility of understanding the *sensus fidei* as the gift cluster of theological faith plus the gifts of understanding and knowledge, I now provide evidence that when the Magisterium and other theologians speak of the *sensus fidei*, they seem implicitly to refer to this gift cluster. A table format allows a clear and compelling presentation of the evidence. See table 1 below.

In the left column, I have placed quotations from Aquinas on faith and the gifts of understanding and knowledge, with one row devoted to theological faith, one to the gift of understanding, and one to the gift of knowledge. In the middle and right columns, I have placed quotations by the Magisterium and other theologians on the *sensus fidei*, respectively, which seem to correspond to how Aquinas characterizes theological faith and the gifts of understanding and knowledge. I have simply placed the quotations by the Magisterium and other theologians in the "gift" row that seems most fitting.

For example, Aquinas says that the gift of understanding "denotes a certain excellence of a knowledge that penetrates into the heart of things" (ST II-II q. 8, a. 1). In the "Magisterium" column of the "gift of understanding" row, I have placed a quote from *Lumen Gentium*, which characterizes the *sensus fidei* as penetration of faith "more deeply with right thinking" (no. 12). Thus, the Magisterium seems to use the term *sensus fidei* implicitly to refer to the gift of understanding as well as to theological faith. Likewise, Aquinas says that the gift of knowledge gives "a sure and right judgment on [things proposed to be believed], so as to discern what is to be believed, from what is not to be believed" (ST II-II q. 9, a. 1). In the "Magisterium" column of the "gift of knowledge" row, I have placed a quote by Pope Benedict XVI, which characterizes the *sensus fidei* as enabling discernment of "whether or not a truth belongs to the living deposit of the Apostolic Tradition."[69] In the "Other Theologians" column of the same row, I have placed a quote by the ITC, which characterizes the *sensus fidei* as "a sort of spiritual instinct that enables the believer to judge spontaneously whether a particular teaching or practice is or is not in conformity with the Gospel and with apostolic faith."[70] Thus, the Magisterium and theologians seem to use the term *sensus fidei* implicitly to refer to the gift of knowledge as well as to theological faith.

---

[68] Möhler, *Symbolism*, 122.
[69] Benedict XVI, "Address to the International Theological Commission."
[70] International Theological Commission, Sensus Fidei *in the Life of the Church*, no. 49.

In addition to such implicit reference to these specific gifts of the Holy Spirit in their characterization of the *sensus fidei*, a few authors, including the ITC,[71] speak explicitly of a relationship between the *sensus fidei* and other gifts of the Holy Spirit.[72] Such explicit discussion of a relationship between the *sensus fidei* and specific gifts of the Holy Spirit seems further to support my proposal, perhaps to the point of proving it unoriginal! However, these authors do not articulate the precise way that they think the *sensus fidei* is related to the other gifts. David A. Tamisiea, for instance, specifically considers the gifts of understanding and knowledge as related to the *sensus fidei*, but it is unclear whether he thinks that the gifts of understanding and knowledge are constitutive of the *sensus fidei*, or whether they are distinct but help to ensure the *sensus fidei*. With respect to the latter, Tamisiea might think that the gifts of understanding and knowledge help perfect the *sensus fidei*, insofar as they help perfect theological faith. While I am open to this understanding of the relationship between the *sensus fidei* and the gifts of understanding and knowledge, I appeal to the Magisterium's and other theologians' implicit characterization of the *sensus fidei* as including the gifts of understanding and knowledge to defend my proposal that the *sensus fidei* is best understood as referring to the gift cluster. At minimum, I hope to have shown that the *sensus fidei cluster* is a plausible development of consensus point 2 (the *sensus fidei* pertains to faith and is a gift of the Holy Spirit).

The clear metaphysical referent of the *sensus fidei cluster* also has more to recommend it with respect to the theological consensus and dissensus points listed above. I will now outline some ways in which the *sensus fidei cluster* benefits theological discussion of the *sensus fidei*. The first point is specific to the inclusion of the gifts of understanding and knowledge in the referent; the second and third points pertain even if *sensus fidei* refers only to the connatural aspect of theological faith.

First, understanding the *sensus fidei* as the *sensus fidei cluster* strengthens the conception of the *sensus fidei* as indicating a "realm of knowledge, but where knowledge is understood to be a form other than discursive reasoning"[73] (consensus point 3). Speaking of the gift of

---

[71] International Theological Commission, Sensus Fidei *in the Life of the Church*, no. 58.
[72] See Sara Butler, "The Instinct That Guides Christians," *L'Osservatore Romano* (2014): 14; Tamisiea, "Vatican II, St. Thomas Aquinas, and the *Sensus Fidelium*," 103–104.
[73] Burkhard, "*Sensus Fidei*: Recent Theological Reflection since Vatican II: II. 1985–1989," 133.

wisdom,[74] Aquinas says that it is right judgment based on "sympathy or connaturality for Divine things," rather than "right judgment about Divine things after reason has made its inquiry" (ST II-II q. 45, a. 2). In this, Aquinas distinguishes two modes of knowing: knowing on the basis of a graced connaturality for Divine things, and knowing on the basis of discursive human reasoning. For Aquinas, all infused virtues and gifts of the Holy Spirit seem to have this intuitive or connatural quality, due to the indwelling Holy Spirit.[75] In this vein, the ITC document states, "The *sensus fidei* is the form that the instinct which accompanies every virtue takes in the case of the virtue of faith."[76] However, recall that the infused virtues perfect human reason, albeit supernaturally, while the gifts of the Holy Spirit perfect the individual's response to the promptings of the Holy Spirit (ST I-II q. 68, a. 2). Thus, though Aquinas does not say so explicitly, plausibly he thinks that the gifts of the Holy Spirit have an even stronger connatural quality than the infused virtues. Indeed, Aquinas does not speak explicitly of the connatural aspect of faith, but, as I have indicated, Aquinas says that the gift of knowledge involves "a sure judgment of truth, without any discursive process, *by simple intuition*" (ST II-II q. 9, a. 1). Thus, the inclusion of the gifts of understanding and knowledge in the *sensus fidei cluster* strengthens the basis on which the *sensus fidei* can be said to indicate an intuitive or connatural "realm of knowledge" (consensus point 3).

Second, understanding the *sensus fidei* as the *sensus fidei cluster* validates the *sensus fidei* as an active quality (consensus point 4) of the whole people of God (consensus point 1). Moreover, the *sensus fidei cluster* enables the import of a wealth of theological reflection on guaranteed and possible avenues of God's grace, benefiting discussions of "who are the whole people of God" (dissensus point 1) and the role of public opinion (dissensus point 3). Through Christian baptism, persons receive, inter alia, the infused virtues (including the theological virtues), along with the gifts of the Holy Spirit, each to a degree sufficient for salvation.[77] Thus, on the Thomistic understanding I have proposed, it is certain that all baptized Christians in a state of grace, laity and bishops alike, have theological faith and the gifts of understanding and knowledge; that is, it is certain that all baptized Christians in a state of grace, laity and bishops alike, are part

---

[74] Wisdom is the gift that perfects the virtue of charity, and, as previously explained, charity enlivens the virtue of faith (ST II-II q. 45, a. 2).
[75] See ST II-II q. 45, a. 2; II-II q. 5, a. 2; Eleonore Stump, "The Non-Aristotelian Character of Aquinas's Ethics: Aquinas on the Passions," *Faith and Philosophy* 28, no. 1 (2011): 37–39.
[76] International Theological Commission, Sensus Fidei *in the Life of the Church*, no. 53.
[77] See *Catechism*, no. 1266.

of the whole "people of God" and share in the *sensus fidei*. Furthermore, understanding the *sensus fidei* as including the gifts of understanding and knowledge, and in particular the gift of knowledge which grants "sure judgment," (ST II-II q. 9, a. 1), secures the active character of the *sensus fidei* for both laity and bishops alike. Note that God may also give prevenient graces akin to theological faith and the gifts of understanding and knowledge to the baptized who are not in a state of grace and to the unbaptized.[78] Therefore, expressions of the *sensus fidei* may not be limited to baptized Christians in a state of grace, and public opinion may have value.

Third, by the same token, the *sensus fidei cluster* is still compatible with consensus point 4, the "limitations, dangers, and temptations"[79] related to the *sensus fidei*, which also has implications for the role of public opinion (dissensus point 3). While it is certain that all baptized Christians in a state of grace share in the *sensus fidei*, those who seem to others to be in a state of grace may not be. In addition, those in a state of grace have theological faith plus the gifts of understanding and knowledge sufficient for salvation, but still imperfectly (ST I-II q. 68, a. 6), which may also account for some imperfection of the *sensus fidei* even among those in a state of grace. For instance, those in a state of grace may yet have false faith-related beliefs. As *Donum Veritatis* notes, "Although theological faith as such then cannot err, the believer can still have erroneous opinions since all his thoughts do not spring from faith" (no. 35). Aquinas clarifies that while neither living nor lifeless faith is compatible with "obstinate disbelief" in "one article of faith" (ST II-II q. 5, a. 3), "simple people" may be misled by others in matters of faith through no fault of their own (ST II-II q. 2, a. 6). Thus, those who have false faith-related beliefs yet are "free from obstinacy in their heterodox sentiments" (ST II-II q. 2, a. 6), Aquinas implies, may still have living faith. Additionally, Aquinas observes that faith is compatible with believing things "more or less explicitly" and with differing degrees of "certitude and firmness" on the part of the intellect, and differing degrees of "promptitude, devotion, or confidence" on the part of the will (ST II-II q. 5, a. 4).[80] Likewise,

---

[78] See *Catechism*, no. 1257.

[79] Burkhard, "*Sensus Fidei*: Recent Theological Reflection since Vatican II: II. 1985–1989," 133.

[80] Thus the possibility of the *sensus fidei*'s growth in the individual: "Since it is a property of the theological virtue of faith, the *sensus fidei fidelis* develops in proportion to the development of the virtue of faith. The more the virtue of faith takes root in the heart and spirit of believers and informs their daily life, the more the *sensus fidei fidelis* develops and strengthens in them" (International Theological Commission, Sensus Fidei *in the Life of the Church*, no. 57). As I noted above, Pope Benedict also suggests that the *sensus fidei* can "be authentically developed" in individuals (Benedict XVI, "Address to the International Theological Commission").

Burkhard has noted the "pilgrim character of all saving knowledge, both for the individual believer and for the whole community of believers."[81] And so it is true that apparent manifestations of the *sensus fidei*, whether in small, orthodox communities or in majority opinion, may not be "authentic manifestations";[82] rather, authentic manifestations must be discerned.

MÖHLER'S CONTRIBUTIONS TO THE *SENSUS FIDEI*

Having established the plausibility, concordance with the literature, and other merits of the *sensus fidei cluster*, I will now at last retrieve Möhler's relevant insights based on where Möhler seems to speak of theological faith and the gifts of understanding and knowledge.[83] I will present four ways in which Möhler can help to illuminate points of consensus and offer balanced responses to points of dissensus, and thus contribute to contemporary discussion on the *sensus fidei*.

First, in response to dissensus point 2 regarding the relationship of the Magisterium to the *sensus fidei*, Möhler's insistence that "God can be known by the individual only in the whole"[84] supports a via media between individualistic and authoritarian understandings of the *sensus fidei*. Möhler contends that "God can be known by the individual only in the whole. As only the All of his revelation reveals him completely, one can truly know him only in the All, living in him, embracing the All with a full heart. This is the mystery of our knowledge of God: only in the whole can he who created the whole be known because he reveals himself completely only in the whole."[85] Möhler explains that individuals are part of a whole both horizontally (united to other

---

[81] Burkhard, "*Sensus Fidei*: Recent Theological Reflection (1990–2001). Part II," 52.
[82] Francis, "Address to Members."
[83] Some (see, for instance: International Theological Commission, Sensus Fidei *in the Life of the Church*, no. 35) see Möhler's "ecclesiastical consciousness" in the following passage as a reference to the *sensus fidei*: "The Church is the body of the Lord: it is, in its universality, his visible form—his permanent, ever-renovated, humanity—his eternal revelation. He dwells in the community—all his promises, all his gifts are bequeathed to the community—but to no individual, as such, since the time of the apostles. This general sense, this ecclesiastical consciousness is tradition, is the subjective sense of the word. What then is tradition? The peculiar Christian sense existing in the Church, and transmitted by ecclesiastical education; yet this sense is not to be conceived as detached from its subject matter—nay, it is formed in, and by this matter, so it may be called a full sense. Tradition is the living word, perpetuated in the hearts of believers" (Möhler, *Symbolism*, 278). However, the understanding of the *sensus fidei* that I have proposed enables deeper probing of Möhler's relevant insights. I believe that the relation of what Möhler says to theological faith and gifts of understanding and knowledge will be apparent, so for the sake of space, I will not argue for the relation each time I present a quote from Möhler.
[84] Möhler, *Unity in the Church*, 153.
[85] Möhler, *Unity in the Church*, 153.

believers through the Church[86]) and vertically (united to God). Both horizontal and vertical elements are necessary for individuals to know God. Individuals cannot know God apart from unity to other believers in the Church. It is a falsity, Möhler argues, to think that we can "lift ourselves"[87] to God apart from other believers in the Church; apart from the horizontal whole, individuals can only ever know God partially.

In this, Möhler indicates one "limitation"[88] of the *sensus fidei* (consensus point 5): the partial knowledge of the individual. Möhler's insight regarding the partial knowledge of individuals helps to explain the importance of "the context of the community of all believers"[89] for the *sensus fidei* (consensus point 1). Moreover, if the *sensus fidei* can be shared "by the individual only in the whole,"[90] then what follows from this is that the *sensus fidei* cannot be invoked in an individualistic or an authoritarian sense. In the language of consensus point 5, individualistic and authoritarian understandings of the *sensus fidei* are both "temptations."[91]

Möhler stresses: "To no individual, considered as such, doth infallibility belong; for the Catholic, as is clear from the preceding observations, regards the individual only as a member of the whole; as living and breathing in the Church. When his feelings, thoughts, and will are conformable to her spirit, then only can the individual attain to inerrability."[92] The *sensus fidei* cannot reliably be said to be operating when individuals have cut themselves off from the Church, and so the *sensus fidei* cannot be understood in an individualistic sense. Rather, individuals participate in the *sensus fidei* insofar as they are united to other believers through the Church. In this, Möhler

---

[86] Möhler does not speak directly about the Church in this section of *Unity in the Church*, however he does make clear in other writings that "the essential form" of this unity of believers is the Church (Möhler, *Symbolism*, 288). Consider, for instance: "for the Catholic, as is clear from the preceding observations, regards the individual only as a member of the whole; as living and breathing in the Church" (Möhler, *Symbolism*, 261). Earlier in *Unity in the Church*, Möhler favorably quotes Irenaeus: "Therefore, none can have a part in the Spirit who have not been nourished to life at the breasts of the mother and who have not received the pure source streaming from the body of Christ (the Church)" (*Against Heresies*, 3.24.1, trans. Möhler, *Unity in the Church*, 84).
[87] Möhler, *Unity in the Church*, 153.
[88] Burkhard, "*Sensus Fidei*: Recent Theological Reflection since Vatican II: II. 1985–1989," 133.
[89] Burkhard, "*Sensus Fidei*: Recent Theological Reflection since Vatican II: II. 1985–1989," 133.
[90] Möhler, *Unity in the Church*, 153.
[91] Burkhard, "*Sensus Fidei*: Recent Theological Reflection since Vatican II: II. 1985–1989," 133.
[92] Möhler, *Symbolism*, 261.

anticipates Pope Benedict XVI's affirmation quoted above: "The *sensus fidei* cannot be authentically developed in believers, except to the extent in which they fully participate in the life of the Church."[93]

That the *sensus fidei* cannot be understood in an "individualistic" sense does not preclude it from having an "individual" sense. Indeed, Möhler's notion of individuals having only partial knowledge of God suggests that the lived reality of the *sensus fidei* will differ in individuals, though the same theological virtue and gifts of the Holy Spirit are operating. Along these lines, a Thomistic framework adds that God grants some individuals gratuitous graces (graces in excess of what is necessary for one's own salvation) of faith and knowledge (ST I-II q. 111, a. 1 and 4). The *sensus fidei* may be possessed and expressed differently, or more completely, by some individuals due to such gratuitous graces.

Just as individuals must not individualistically cut themselves off from the horizontal whole, claiming the *sensus fidei* apart from the Church, so the Magisterium must not cut itself off from the horizontal whole in an authoritarian manner, claiming the *sensus fidei* apart from other believers.[94] This is not to say that the Magisterium cannot teach authoritatively. Möhler upholds "the necessity of a living, visible authority which in every dispute can, with certainty, discern the truth, and separate it from error."[95] Nor is it to say that believers will never feel that Magisterial teaching is an imposition. Indeed, Möhler observes the reality that doctrine "born out of the inspired spiritual fullness of heart and the depth of the first beautiful Christian times now had to be accepted as an austere and rigid law imposed from outside."[96] Rather, Möhler cautions that Magisterial teaching is not true *because* it is taught by authority, but it is true because it teaches what the Holy Spirit teaches to all believers: *"The Catholic's faith was not faith in authority ... but the Catholic had all authority for himself or herself.... All the faithful have one consciousness, one faith, because one divine power forms them."*[97] Here, Möhler opens the door

---

[93] Benedict XVI, "Address to the International Theological Commission."
[94] For discussion of the dangers of an authoritarian Church, see Valadier, "Has the Concept of *Sensus Fidelium* Fallen into Desuetude?"
[95] Johann Adam Möhler, *The Spirit of Celibacy*, trans. Cyprian Blamires, ed. Rev. Emery de Gaál (Chicago: Hillenbrand, 2007), 201.
[96] Möhler, *The Spirit of Celibacy*, 54.
[97] Möhler, *Unity in the Church*, 110. In this, Möhler undermines the division in eighteenth century theology between the *Ecclesia docens* ("teaching Church") and the *Ecclesia discens* ("learning Church"), which grants only a passive role to the laity (contrary to contemporary consensus point 4). John Henry Newman invokes the *sensus fidei* to issue a more stringent warning against an authoritarian Church (John Henry Newman, "On Consulting the Faithful in Matters of Doctrine," in *The Rambler*, New Series [London: Burns and Lambert, 1859]). Newman points to the Arian controversy of the fourth century in which most bishops were Arians, while the laity,

for Pope Francis' instruction referenced above: "For its part, the Magisterium has the duty to be attentive to what the Spirit says to the Churches through the authentic manifestations of the *sensus fidelium*."[98]

Second, Möhler's attention to living faith's preceding and exceeding doctrinal formulations helps to flesh out the *sensus fidei*'s role in the development of doctrine (consensus point 6). For Möhler, that faith is "living" means that development of doctrine is possible, as growth and development are properties of living things: "Since Christianity is seen as a new divine life given to people, not as a dead concept, it is capable of development and cultivation."[99] Furthermore, Möhler sees that the faith living in believers underlies such development of doctrine: before the Church ever puts doctrine into words, the doctrine is already living among the faithful, and living faith always goes beyond what could be put into words. For example, "The doctrine of justifying faith experienced the same fate as all the other fundamental doctrines of Christianity. For fifteen hundred years, Christians had lived in and by that faith, had formed many intellectual conceptions upon it, and had laid down the same in numerous writings, but had withal felt much deeper things than could be comprehended in notions or defined by words."[100] To put this point more in the

---

led by the *sensus fidei*, held fast to the Nicene formula. Newman argued that the Arian controversy should serve as a reminder for the "teaching Church" to listen to the *sensus fidei* expressed by the laity.

[98] Francis, "Address to Members." See also International Theological Commission, Sensus Fidei *in the Life of the Church*, no. 74: "In matters of faith the baptised cannot be passive. They have received the Spirit and are endowed as members of the body of the Lord with gifts and charisms 'for the renewal and building up of the Church', so the magisterium has to be attentive to the *sensus fidelium*, the living voice of the people of God. Not only do they have the right to be heard, but their reaction to what is proposed as belonging to the faith of the Apostles must be taken very seriously, because it is by the Church as a whole that the apostolic faith is borne in the power of the Spirit. The magisterium does not have sole responsibility for it. The magisterium should therefore refer to the sense of faith of the Church as a whole. The *sensus fidelium* can be an important factor in the development of doctrine, and it follows that the magisterium needs means by which to consult the faithful."

[98] Francis, "Address to Members."

[99] Möhler, *Unity in the Church*, 111.

[100] Möhler, *Symbolism*, 118. Likewise, for Möhler, living faith preceded scripture: "The living gospel always preceded the written gospel and went along with it" (Möhler, *Unity in the Church*, 113). The idea that the *sensus fidei*'s preceding and exceeding doctrinal formulations in part underlies the development of doctrine is echoed in the ITC document: "The *sensus fidei fidelis* thus acquires a prospective dimension to the extent that, on the basis of the faith already lived, it enables the believer to anticipate a development or an explanation of Christian practice. Because of the reciprocal link between the practice of the faith and the understanding of its content, the *sensus fidei fidelis* contributes in this way to the emergence and illumination of aspects of the Catholic faith that were previously implicit"

language of Aquinas and contemporary theology: what makes living faith "living" is God Himself, and God, Who always precedes and exceeds human cognition and language, guides the Church's ever deepening understanding of His Revelation through the development of doctrine.[101]

Third, in response to dissensus point 3 regarding the role of public opinion, Möhler's positive appraisal of the role of heresy in the clarification and purification of doctrine helps to underscore the benefit of public opinion, even while the *sensus fidei* is not the same as public opinion. For Möhler, living faith, as I have explained, implies the possibility of growth and development of doctrine; but, for Möhler, the "living" metaphor does not mean that such growth and development of doctrine occur simply in an organic fashion.[102] Rather, Möhler argues that, for example, human freedom operating through heresy stimulates the development of doctrine: "If Church doctrine were established only for itself and not surrounded by the assertions of heretics, our faith could not appear so bright, so proven.... Catholic doctrine is besieged by its contradiction so that our faith might not grow stiff in peace but, moved by practice, become more pure.... She [the Church] is not to be sorrowful that new error always arises so as to elevate her truth."[103] Insofar as it allows faith to appear brighter and purer, Möhler views heresy positively.

For Möhler, heresy allows faith to appear brighter and purer partially because heresy always contains some partial truth. Separated from the fullness of truth (Möhler's first contribution above), heresy cannot be a full, authentic expression of the *sensus fidei*. As I documented earlier, Pope John Paul II, the CDF, Pope Benedict XVI, and Pope Francis have all warned against equating public opinion with the *sensus fidei*, and rightly so, it would seem, in Möhler's view.[104] However, Möhler helps to underscore that public opinion will likely contain what one may call a partial expression of the *sensus fidei*: "The whole heathen world was shot through with fragments of truth and

---

(International Theological Commission, Sensus Fidei *in the Life of the Church*, no. 65).

[101] See ST II-II q. 1, a. 7.

[102] Grant Kaplan and Holly Taylor Coolman, "Development of Doctrine," in *Oxford Handbook of Catholic Theology*, ed. Lewis Ayers and Medi-Ann Volpe (Oxford: Oxford University Press, 2019), 618.

[103] Möhler, *Unity in the Church*, 158–160. See also Möhler, *Unity in the Church*, 243: "A great new danger threatened to tear church apart, yet because of it she drew more firmly together, developed her basic principles more clearly than earlier."

[104] "I am far from being ignorant of the power of the spirit of the age. But I believe we can stand above it, assess it truthfully, and accept only what there is of good in it as not absolutely bad: the rest however we must oppose. What a vast amount would have to be thrown away as outdated if we simply bowed to prevailing opinion!" (Möhler, *The Spirit of Celibacy*, 82).

traces of the divine. In it we encounter deep intimations, dimmer or clearer ideas of a higher world order, a feeling, indeed a desire (however weak) for something better, a widespread yearning for union with the divine. Everything that was believed in its fullness and divinely in Christianity we find foreshadowed in heathendom."[105] Note that the likelihood that public opinion will contain what one may call a partial expression of the *sensus fidei* accords with the understanding of the *sensus fidei* as the theological virtue of faith plus the gifts of understanding and knowledge, given the possibility of prevenient grace, as discussed earlier.[106] Möhler also alludes to the role of such prevenient graces on a few occasions.[107]

Thus, Möhler's positive appraisal of the role of heresy in the clarification and purification of doctrine grounds a posture of being mindful of the "danger"[108] of equating public opinion with the *sensus fidei* (a specification of consensus point 5), while nonetheless taking seriously public opinion, to discern the truth in it (a response to dissensus point 3). The subjects of the *sensus fidei* are not always apparent, and even partial expressions of the *sensus fidei* with an admixture of error can play a positive role in the development of doctrine (a specification of consensus point 6). It is important for theologians and the Magisterium to pay attention to public opinion because public opinion may contain within it, even if distortedly, important truths that will contribute to the development of doctrine.[109]

Fourth, in response to dissensus point 4, Möhler's distinction between antithesis and contradiction can serve as a principle of discerning the *sensus fidei*. Consider Möhler's distinction between true antithesis, which "can be found in unity,"[110] and contradiction,

---

[105] Möhler, *The Spirit of Celibacy*, 31. See also Möhler, *The Spirit of Celibacy*, 43: "For the truth is that under every great error of the human race is a great truth, a deep need of the human heart, a dark mysterious longing and intuition" and Möhler, *Symbolism*, 66: "Even in the breast of the heathens such a divine spark beyond a doubt still glowed."

[106] As also referenced above, Aquinas avers that "a heretic who obstinately disbelieves one article of faith" can have neither living nor lifeless faith (ST II-II q. 5, q. 3). However, Aquinas allows that "if he is not obstinate, he is no longer in heresy but only in error" (ST II-II q. 5, q. 3), leaving the door open for faith.

[107] For example: "The Catholics were wont at times to refer to men, like Camillus, and from their lives demonstrate the moral freedom enjoyed even by the heathens, and the remnants of the good to be found in them. They defended, moreover, the proposition, that God's special grace, communicated for the sake of Christ's merits, working retrospectively, and confirming the better surviving sentiments in the human breast, is undeniably to be traced in many phenomena" (Möhler, *Symbolism*, 67).

[108] Burkhard, "*Sensus Fidei*: Recent Theological Reflection since Vatican II: II. 1985–1989," 133.

[109] For example, public opinion may aid the articulation of truth that has not yet been articulated, the clearer articulation of a truth, etc.

[110] Möhler, *Unity in the Church*, 195.

which is "in opposition" and threatens "danger and destruction."[111] For Möhler, contradiction cannot exist in unity, but antithesis can, and in fact must.[112] Accordingly, among the faith-related propositions that must or may be believed,[113] Möhler thinks there are antitheses, but there cannot be contradictions. Likewise, among authentic manifestations of the *sensus fidei*, there may be antitheses, but there cannot be contradictions. Discernment of whether a particular manifestation of the *sensus fidei* is authentic thus can be aided by consideration of whether the manifestation is an antithesis or contradiction of the deposit of faith. Moreover, Möhler has confidence that such discernment is possible: "For with belief in Christ, as a true envoy of the Father of light, it is by no means consistent, that those who have been taught by him, should be unable to define in what his revelations on divine things consist, and what, on the other hand, is in contradiction to his word and ordinances."[114]

CONCLUSION

In this paper I have proposed the *sensus fidei* is best understood as referring to the gift cluster of the connatural aspect of theological faith as well as the gifts of understanding and knowledge. I have shown the plausibility of this understanding within a Thomistic framework, provided evidence that the Magisterium and theologians already implicitly assume this understanding, and indicated how I believe this understanding benefits theological discussion. With this understanding of the *sensus fidei* in mind, I have retrieved four ways in which Johann Adam Möhler can help illuminate points of consensus and offer balanced responses to points of dissensus.

---

[111] Möhler, *Symbolism*, 7.
[112] Religion can make itself known completely only in an infinity of such variations" (Möhler, *Unity in the Church*, 196); "Unity in its essence is not identity" (Möhler, *Symbolism*, 7).
[113] "True progress would be hindered if the style of presentation for a particular period, the manner of conceiving a doctrine according to a particular age according to that age's explanation and foundations, would be viewed as one as the same thing as the doctrine itself" (Möhler, *Symbolism*, 354).
[114] Möhler, *Symbolism*, xxvii.

Table 1: Comparison of Faith, Understanding, and Knowledge to Descriptions of the *Sensus Fideli*

Gift (Aquinas)	Magisterium on SF	Other Theologians on SF
Theological Virtue of Faith		
• "the substance of things to be hoped for, the evidence of things that appear not" (Hebrews 11:1; ST II-II q. 4, a. 1) • "two things are required that this act may be perfect: one of which is that the intellect should infallibly tend to its object, which is the true" (ST II-II q. 4, a. 5) • "by the habit of faith, the human mind is directed to assent to such things as are becoming to a right faith, and not to assent to others" (ST II-II q. 1, a. 5)	• infallibility in belief; unwavering adherence to "the faith given once and for all to the saints" (*Lumen Gentium*, no. 12) • personal, infallible adherence to the truth (*Donum Veritatis*, no. 35)	• "act of faith"[115] • "act of belief itself"[116] • "the experience of the faith in the Spirit and the faith conviction of the whole community of the faithful";[117] "an interior predisposition for and an internal adhering to the whole revelation"[118] • "the form that the instinct which accompanies every virtue takes in the case of the virtue of faith";[119] "comparable to a vital instinct or a

---

[115] Burkhard, "*Sensus Fidei*: Recent Theological Reflection since Vatican II: I. 1965–1984," 43, citing Magnus Löhrer, *Mysterium Salutis: Grundriss Heilsgeschichtlicher Dogmatik*, ed. J. Feiner and M. Löhrer (Einsiedeln: Benziger, 1965).

[116] Burkhard, "*Sensus Fidei*: Recent Theological Reflection since Vatican II: I. 1965–1984," 54, citing Harald Wagner, "Glaubenssinn, Glaubenszustimmung und Glaubenskonsens," *Theologie und Glaube* 69 (1979): 263–271.

[117] Michael Seybold, "Kirchliches Lehramt und Allgemeiner Glaubenssinn. Ein Reformatorisches Anliegen aus der Sicht des I. und II. Vatikanischen Konzils," *Theologie und Glaube* 65 (1975): 267. Translated by Burkhard, "*Sensus Fidei*: Recent Theological Reflection (1990–2001). Part I," 451–452.

[118] Seybold, "Kirchliches Lehramt und Allgemeiner Glaubenssinn. Ein Reformatorisches Anliegen aus der Sicht des I. und II. Vatikanischen Konzils," 274. Translated by Burkhard, "*Sensus Fidei*: Recent Theological Reflection (1990–2001). Part I," 451–452.

[119] International Theological Commission, Sensus Fidei *in the Life of the Church*, nos. 49, 53.

		sort of 'flair' by which the believer clings spontaneously to what conforms to the truth of faith and shuns what is contrary to it … infallible in itself with regard to its object: the true faith."[120]
Gift of Understanding		
• "denotes a certain excellence of a knowledge that penetrates into the heart of things" (ST II-II q. 8, a. 1)	• penetration of faith "more deeply with right thinking" (*Lumen Gentium*, no. 12) • "a more profound understanding and activation of the word of God" (*Familiaris Consortio*, no. 5)	
Gift of Knowledge		
• "the knowledge of human affairs" (ST II-II q. 9, a. 2) • gives "a sure and right judgment on [things proposed to be believed], so as to discern what is to be believed, from what	• "supernatural discernment" (*Lumen Gentium*, no. 12) • discernment of "whether or not a truth belongs to the living deposit of the Apostolic Tradition"[121]	• "a kind of 'connaturality' or spontaneous knowledge"[123] • "permits each believer to 'seize on what is in harmony with the authentic meaning of the Word of God or

---

[120] International Theological Commission, Sensus Fidei *in the Life of the Church*, nos. 54–55.
[121] Benedict XVI, "Address to the International Theological Commission."
[123] William M. Thompson, "*Sensus Fidelium* and Infallibility," *The American Ecclesiastical Review* 167 (1973): 480. Thompson draws this idea of the *sensus fidei* as "a kind of 'connaturality'" from Aquinas's discussion of the gift of wisdom in ST II-II q. 45, a. 2.

is not to be believed" (ST II-II, q. 9, a. 1) • "to know what one ought to believe, belongs to the gift of knowledge" (ST II-II q. 9, a. 2)	• discernment of "what is truly of God" (*Evangelii Gaudium*, no. 119) • deciphering the signs of the times [122]	what follows from it'" [124] • "capacity to recognize the intimate experience of adherence to Christ and to judge everything on the basis of this knowledge" [125] • "an active capacity for spiritual discernment" [126] • "a sort of spiritual instinct that enables the believer to judge spontaneously whether a particular teaching or practice is or is not in conformity with the Gospel and with apostolic faith" [127]
• primarily and principally indeed, regards speculation, in so far as man knows what he ought to hold by faith; yet, secondarily, it	• a shining forth in the laity of "the power of the Gospel ... in their daily social and family life"	• "enlightens and guides the way in which the believer puts his or her faith into practice" [128]

---

[122] Paul VI, "General Audience: Signs of the Times."
[124] Jean-Marie Roger Tillard, "Autorité et mémoire dans l'église," *Irénikon* 61 (1988): 340. Translated by Burkhard, "*Sensus Fidei*: Recent Theological Reflection (1990–2001). Part I," 454.
[125] Zoltán Alszeghy, "The *Sensus Fidei* and the Development of Dogma," in *Vatican II: Assessment and Perspectives Twenty-Five Years After (1962–1987)*, ed. René Latourelle (New York: Paulist, 1988), 147.
[126] Anglican-Roman Catholic Dialogue (ARCIC-II), "The Gift of Authority," 24.
[127] International Theological Commission, Sensus Fidei *in the Life of the Church*, no. 49.
[128] International Theological Commission, Sensus Fidei *in the Life of the Church*, no. 59.

extends to works, since we are directed in our actions by the knowledge of matters of faith, and of conclusions drawn therefrom" (ST II-II q. 9, a. 3)	(*Familiaris Consortio*, no. 5) • the application of this faith "more fully in ... life" (*Lumen Gentium*, no. 12)	

Gina Maria Noia is Assistant Professor of Theology and Resident Bioethicist at Belmont Abbey College. She received her PhD in Theology and Health Care Ethics from Saint Louis University. She is published in *Christian Bioethics* and the *Journal of Moral Theology*.

Virtue as Birth Control: An Examination of the Account of Rational Participation as a Component of Natural Law in *Humanae Vitae* and the Documents of the Papal Commission

Arielle Harms

WHILE POPE PAUL VI'S 1968 encyclical *Humanae Vitae*'s confirmation of the Church's perennial teaching on birth control was and is still extremely controversial, its influence in the realm of moral theology extends beyond the teaching on contraception.[1] *Humanae Vitae* also served as a major influence on moral theology in general, questioning not just the application of principles, but the principles themselves.[2] Addressing a need for clarification of the Church's teaching in the debate concerning contraception,[3] particular emphasis was given to the perception and status of natural law and its role in the articulation of moral theology and ethics.[4] As Russell Hittinger asserts, *Humanae Vitae* was a catalyst in the post-conciliar renewal of Catholic moral theology in general and natural law in particular. The controversy surrounding the document and the use of natural law arguments by those for and against the document's conclusions revealed a fault line in moral theology.[5] Part of *Humanae Vitae*'s effect on natural law

---

[1] F. Russell Hittinger, "Natural Law and Public Discourse: The Legacies of Joseph Ratzinger," *Loyola Law Review* 60 (2014): 255–257.
[2] See Janet Smith, Humanae Vitae*: A Generation Later* (Washington, DC: Catholic University of America Press, 1991), 9–10. Smith cites Edward MacKinnon, SJ, "*Humanae Vitae* and Doctrinal Development," *Continuum* 6 (1968) 269–75. Disagreement over principles is not categorical. For a thoughtful example of disagreement on the application, see Charles DeKoninck and Maurice Dionne, "The Question of Infertility," Memorandum, January 25, 1965.
[3] Smith, Humanae Vitae*: A Generation Later*, 9.
[4] See J. Bryan Hehir, "Bioethics and Natural Law: The Relationship in Catholic Teaching," *Kennedy Institute of Ethics Journal* 6, no. 4 (1996): 334–335, and Smith, Humanae Vitae*: A Generation Later*, 1.
[5] Hittinger, "Natural Law and Public Discourse," 255. Hittinger argues that both the future Popes John Paul II and Benedict XVI saw this weakness and the end result was *Veritatis Splendor*. Hittinger traces the outlines of this in the referenced paper. The

teaching came from the papal commission that preceded its issuance, formally the Papal Commission for the Study of Problems of the Family, Population, and Birth Rate.[6] The commission issued a report which proposed, on the foundation of natural law, the licitness of contraception as a reasonable method of responsible parenthood and, with it as appendices, a minority opinion that rejects this innovation in morality and a majority response, both making use of natural law. While not following the recommendation of the majority, Paul VI's argument from natural law did not follow the contours of the argument of the minority opinion either. In fact, all three documents display different versions of natural law.

The conflict over the meaning of natural law is not new; natural law has never been a univocal term with one common understanding. Though it has broadly included any system that holds objective moral norms, the structure and foundation has varied greatly among natural law proponents.[7] In fact, in the debate about contraception, Janet Smith identifies at least six different versions of natural law arguments, three of which she finds in *Humanae Vitae* itself.[8] What is peculiar about this particular debate is that, even though the documents differ in conclusions, many of the undergirding elements of natural law appear to be in agreement, dependent as they are on a traditional understanding of the nature of sexuality, marriage, and the authentic good of human persons. The crucial differences lie not in the definition of the goods involved, but in the more fundamental point of the definition of natural law itself. This foundational disagreement exposes the real weakness in Catholic natural law theory.

Thomas Aquinas, referenced in the majority paper of the papal commission and in *Humanae Vitae*, defines natural law as a person's rational participation in eternal law (ST I-II, q. 91, a. 2).[9] As rational participation in the eternal law, natural law includes both a reference to the teleology inherent in created natures by which, through their natural acts, they reach their natural ends, and a reference to human beings' own ordering of their personal acts in a manner that is consistent with and ultimately facilitates the realization of their own

---

argument here is focused on the state of natural law in the discussion at that time, not the answer to the question of birth control, or the broader problems in moral theology.
[6] Smith, Humanae Vitae: *A Generation Later*, 11.
[7] Ernest Fortin, *Classical Christianity and the Political Order*, ed. J. Brian Benestad, (Lanham, MD: Rowman and Littlefield, 1996), 200; see Smith, Humanae Vitae: *A Generation Later*, 98–128.
[8] Smith, Humanae Vitae: *A Generation Later*, 98–99. I am not completely convinced of this. Though many have found their own particular version of natural law, it is not clear that Paul VI is so inconsistent in his own view of natural law.
[9] See Robert G. Hoyt, ed., "The Question Is Not Closed," in *The Birth Control Debate* (Kansas City: National Catholic Reporter, 1968), 70, 72 and *Humanae Vitae*, no. 10.

end. Because the documents in question seem to agree on both the rational nature of human beings and the nature and purpose of human sexuality and marriage, it is the account of rational participation in eternal law that is the central locus of divergence between the commission documents and the encyclical itself. The answer to the question concerning what it means for human beings to rationally participate in the eternal law is different in each of the documents. The minority's most prominent natural law position gives a somewhat passive role to reason and its involvement in morality, while the majority response permits reason a very active role, allowing persons to redirect the natural order.[10] While *Humanae Vitae* does not provide a sustained account of natural law, what can be gleaned from the document's presentation suggests a balanced approach to rational participation, neither giving reason a passive role in natural law nor assigning it directing powers when it comes to the natural order. In this moderate approach, *Humanae Vitae* adequately supports the document's conclusion.

NATURAL LAW IN THE MINORITY OPINION

Despite the agreement with the consistent teaching of the Church, the minority position is unable to provide a substantive argument for continuing to support the traditional prohibition of the use of contraceptives. Three main arguments are used in the statement, two natural law arguments and an argument from Divine Law. Though the document asserts the domain of natural law in its consideration,[11] the stronger defense of the Church's traditional teaching seems to be the unanimity of the tradition itself and the immutable law of God. In fact, the minority opinion provides only the barest account of natural law, with a wavering assertion of how reason fits into the picture, leaving the account open to criticism from the majority position.[12]

The minority paper of the commission presents natural law most frequently as simply the order of creation established by God which human beings discern so that they can act in accord with it. In this account, the Church's magisterium and teaching are of assistance to human beings in their rational participation in eternal law, helping them discern the contents of the law. In the minority paper's affirmation of the constant teaching of the Church, it is not evident that the moral order discerned differs from the physical order and the

---

[10] See Smith, Humanae Vitae: *A Generation Later*, 9. The main report from the commission will not be examined here, as its arguments are not as in depth as those in the major and minor report.

[11] Robert G. Hoyt, ed., "The State of the Question: A Conservative View," in *The Birth Control Debate*, 25–26.

[12] See Smith, Humanae Vitae: *A Generation Later*, 20.

laws the physical order follows. Further, the role of reason is simply discerning this order. The paper explains: "Theologians and the church have considered contraception as a violation not of an affirmative precept, but of a negative precept which obliges always and everywhere: 'Let no one impede human life in its proximate causes,' or 'let no one violate the ordination of this act and processes toward the good of the species.'"[13] The minority opinion thus concludes: "One may not deprive the conjugal act of its natural power for the procreation of new life."[14] Each of these statements is concerned with what is ultimately a physical ordering regarding the nature of acts and causes of generation.

Critiquing the majority's acceptance of artificial contraceptives, the paper affirms a deductive use of reason in natural law: "This view does not do justice to or protect either the competence which the Church has so many times vindicated for herself for the interpretation of the natural law, nor the Church's effective capacity of discerning the moral order established by God, which is so often obscure to fallen man."[15] In promoting this relatively passive view of rational participation, the paper criticizes those who say that rational participation in the eternal law might be understood in a more active manner, whereby the givens of the natural world can be used by human beings to assist them in their own development and the humanizing of culture.[16] The minority document adds to the earlier criticism of the majority conclusion: "Man's own psycho-physical parts are conceived of as having been entrusted to the embodied spirit which is man, so that he may humanize them through his culture in a given set of physical possibilities. Therefore he can frustrate his own biological, sexual function, even when voluntarily aroused, because it is subject to reason for the bettering of the human condition."[17] From the insistence that a person not manipulate the biological processes of his generative organs, the primary argument thus appears to be that contraception is a violation of the ordering of the laws of nature, which human beings are to discern and obey.

In asserting this, the minority document shows a deracinated view of nature, inherited from Francis Bacon.[18] Rather than accepting the

---

[13] Hoyt, "The State of the Question: A Conservative View," 31.
[14] Hoyt, "The State of the Question: A Conservative View," 32.
[15] Hoyt, "The State of the Question: A Conservative View," 50.
[16] This is one of the arguments given in the majority response. See Hoyt, "The Question Is Not Closed," 68.
[17] Hoyt, "The State of the Question: A Conservative View," 51.
[18] Francis Bacon, *Novum Organum*, ed. Joseph Devey (New York: P. F. Collier & Son, 1902), 119–120. Bacon separated knowledge into physics, which includes efficient causality, and metaphysics, which is almost everything else. Metaphysics, which included teleology, he called magic.

four causes of things—material, formal, efficient, and final—important for Aquinas' account of natural law, the document, focusing on functionality, reduces causality to efficient causality, effectively excluding teleology from the conversation. Despite this line of argument, the document insists that it does not want to present a physicalist view of natural law.[19] Perhaps recognizing the inadequacy of the approach, it guardedly explains: "In no way does [the teaching of the church] derive from any philosophy of nature (of the scholastics, stoics, or others) in which the natural physical order is the *general criterion* of the morality of man."[20] This caution leads the drafters of the document to initiate a new line of reasoning, bifurcating the argument. It is not simply the naturalness of the ordering which demands respect: "It does attribute a special inviolability to this act and to the generative process precisely because they are generative of new *human life*, and life is not under man's dominion. It is not because of some philosophy which would make the physical order of nature as such the criterion of the morality of human acts."[21] Human life in its generation is introduced as a value above the created order. While this approach correctly recognizes that the good of the physical order of creation is not reducible to functionality,[22] this is another self-inflicted vulnerability. By presenting generation as an inviolable good, natural law itself is deracinated, by moving a good of the created natural order outside the realm of nature and limiting the scope of natural law to the human good, outside the context of the whole. Once such a view of nature limiting causality to functionality is adopted, appeals to natural law that wish to avoid being an appeal to mere functionality must bypass the ordering of nature and introduce further categories and terms. Language of this kind, protecting some particular and limited good, is a precursor of and shaped by the conversations that would lead to the full exposition of new natural law theories.[23]

In striving to displace the physicalist error of using physical processes (efficient causality) as normative for morality, the new natural law theorists usually conceive of morality as abstracted from things, and instead dependent on what the agent intends. The language that affirms this thinking is present in the document, for example,

---

[19] The Church has been accused of adopting this position. See Smith, Humanae Vitae: *A Generation Later,* 88, and Charles Curran, *Transition and Tradition in Moral Theology* (Notre Dame, IN: Notre Dame Press, 1979), 31.
[20] Hoyt, "The State of the Question: A Conservative View," 34, emphasis in original.
[21] Hoyt, "The State of the Question: A Conservative View," 34.
[22] See Smith, Humanae Vitae: *A Generation Later,* 74–75.
[23] See John Finnis, *Natural Law and Natural Rights* (Oxford: Oxford University Press, 2011), especially chapters 3 and 4. The proponents of New Natural Law were highly involved in the discussion leading up to and following *Humanae Vitae*, so it is no surprise that New Natural Law concepts made it into the reports.

where it asserts that "to have an intention, directly and actively contrary to a fundamental human good is something intrinsically evil."[24] The new natural law tendency to focus on the intention as being intrinsically evil, rather than on the action that deviates from or distorts the normative moral order, is evident in this particular formulation, though it does not appear in the rest of the document.

Finally, in addition to the intentionalism present, in declaring the inviolability of the origin of human life, the minority effectively moves the consideration outside the framework of natural law. Instead these issues become directly dependent on the will of God and are not to be interfered with by human beings. Reference to Divine Law appears later in the document as well, attributing the real failure of accounts that would allow for the utilitarian manipulation of nature to an "insufficient place in human life for the action of the Holy Spirit and his mission of healing sin."[25] While the subsequent reference to virtue leads back to nature and natural law, the condemnation of the technological manipulation of human generation in the context of virtue ethics is only secondary and inconclusive: "Neither is it evident what are the great demands on virtue which are often affirmed in this new tendency."[26] Articulating the argument in such a way that virtue is secondary does not strengthen the natural law argument, but instead introduces a new argument dependent on grace and Divine Law.

The minority report indicates a weak conception of natural law and an insufficient understanding of its foundations. Because of this, the document equivocates on the locus of the malice in the natural law argument against contraception. While initially following a common conception of natural law which states that evil is found in disrespect for the biological laws of generation, the minority paper also places malice in the intention of the agent. By elaborating on the manner in which the created order is not normative and focusing attention on the inviolability of human life (either as a natural good or a separate Divinely-granted gift, subject to Divine Providence), the report calls into question the credibility of a natural law argument supporting Church teaching. As the document moves the evil in the act from the violation of a normative created order to the realm of intention against a human or divine good, the argument's universality is weakened. While an intrinsically evil action is always wrong and can be judged according to a normative moral order, intention is not able to be judged in the same way. Intentions for employing contraceptive methods are not identical, and surely there are many times contraception is

---

[24] Hoyt, "The State of the Question: A Conservative View," 36.
[25] Hoyt, "The State of the Question: A Conservative View," 51.
[26] Hoyt, "The State of the Question: A Conservative View," 51. Precisely how this statement relates to nature will become clear in the section on *Humanae Vitae* below.

employed without an intentional malice toward the good of human life.

The other weakness of the minority paper's natural law argument is the assertion that in matters of human life, the action of the Holy Spirit needs to be respected. While this is true, it is not a natural law argument, and placing it in such a context might lead readers to believe that there is no natural law argument properly speaking, thus leading to the conclusion that the teaching of the Church is a law only for her members, not to be universally applied. Both of these challenges leave room for the critique that the teaching of the Church is not based on a natural law argument at all, a critique that the majority (on the papal commission) makes. Despite its rejected conclusion, the majority correctly recognizes the profound connection between natural law and providence, and the necessity of the complementarity and compatibility of the realms of grace and nature.

THE REPORT OF THE MAJORITY AND NATURAL LAW

While the minority paper hinted at intentionalism, the majority's response hinges on an intentionalist view. In their paper, "The Question Is Not Closed," the larger consensus of the papal commission argued that the use of contraception within marriage is licit according to natural law. In its search to provide a natural law foundation for the proposed change to Church teaching on matters of contraception, the majority coalition in the birth control commission had two tasks. The first would be to show that accepting contraception did not represent a problematic change to Church teaching and natural law, and the second would be to give a different or corrected account of natural law that does not find the use of contraceptives intrinsically evil.[27]

Despite the insistence of the minority that theirs was not a physicalist understanding of natural law, the unfounded sacralizing of the natural order, especially the claim of the "inviolability of the sources of human life,"[28] draws the most criticism, since it does not suggest a place for the use of human reason or satisfactorily consider the person's task before God to be a responsible and prudent steward of creation.[29] The majority explains: "An unconditional respect for nature in itself (as if nature in its physical existence were the expression of the will of God) pertains to a vision of man which sees something mysterious and sacred in nature and because of this fears that any human intervention tends to destroy rather than perfect this

---

[27] Smith, Humanae Vitae: *A Generation Later*, 15.
[28] Hoyt, "The Question Is Not Closed," 68; see 64–65.
[29] Hoyt, "The Question Is Not Closed," 64.

very nature."[30] Accepting the purely functional view of nature put forward by the minority, the majority rejects the conclusion that this version of nature and the concomitant physicalist account of natural law can give any normative guidance.

Against this physicalist consideration of natural law, the majority proposes a version of natural law that gives human beings a more active participation. "The very dignity of man created to the image of God consists in this: that God wished man to share in his dominion. God has left man in the hands of his own counsel."[31] A person is not merely consigned in his moral life to respect nature because it is under Divine providence, but is asked to act according to the dictates of his own reason. He is responsible for discerning the good and acting appropriately. The document explains: "In the course of his life, man must attain his perfection in difficult and adverse conditions, he must accept the consequences of his responsibility, etc. Therefore, the dominion of God is exercised through man, who can use nature for his own perfection according to the dictates of right reason."[32] Nature and its physical laws become a tool of human perfection rather than the source of moral norms.

From a person's rational use of nature for personal perfection, the majority opinion takes a further step: "[Man] feels that he is more conformed to his rational nature, created by God with liberty and responsibility, when he uses his skill to intervene in the biological processes of nature so that he can achieve the ends of the institutions of matrimony in the conditions of actual life than if he would abandon himself to chance."[33] Instead of the inviolability of the created order proposed by the minority, the majority opinion proposes that the created order stands in need of perfection through the application of human reason.[34] It becomes clear that in the majority paper the formal content of natural law, the intelligibility of it, is from human reason, not from the order of biological processes.[35] The paper asserts: "Finalization toward fecundity can formally come only from man though this finality is found materially in the organs. Fecundation must be a personal human act. With the progress of knowledge, man can exercise this dominion and ought to exercise it responsibly."[36] Human reasoning becomes the measure and guide for how to direct

---

[30] Hoyt, "The Question Is Not Closed," 68.
[31] Hoyt, "The Question Is Not Closed," 69.
[32] Hoyt, "The Question Is Not Closed," 69.
[33] Hoyt, "The Question Is Not Closed," 69.
[34] Hoyt, "The Question Is Not Closed," 68.
[35] See Smith, Humanae Vitae: A Generation Later, 24.
[36] "The Question is Not Closed," 71.

things to a particular end.[37]

Despite the need to clarify the assertion that intention constitutes a truly human act, the document does not completely disregard the natural ordering of acts and organs related to this debate. This can be seen in the document's acknowledgement of the material ordering of sexual intercourse: "Intercourse materially considered carries with it some orientation toward fecundation, but this finality must be rationally directed by man according to the means and conditions of human love, size of family, educational needs, etc."[38] Here human beings, through the use of reason, determine whether or not the *natural material* ordering of the particular act should be permitted to reach finality or not, and thus participate in ordering things to their end by choosing to allow something to reach its end. Human reason, not nature, contains and gives final causality. Thus, in the case of the formal account of a particular act of sexual intercourse, a naturally fertile act must be a rational one: a person should intend fecundity. It is into this structure that the permission for contraception is said to fit. People are permitted to use contraceptive means to rationally control fecundity.

Even while asserting the priority of intention in a person's rational participation in the moral order, the majority opinion does not wish to be without some objective standards.[39] In the case of the licit use of contraception, the meaning of sexuality within marriage must be respected. Even in permitting contraception, marriage is always to be ordered to procreation, though there is also the good of mutual self-gift involved.[40] Using the moral teaching of St. Thomas Aquinas, the statement explains regarding love in the context of marriage that "this human act which has one moral specification can be composed of several particular acts if these partial acts do not have some object in itself already specified. And this is the case for matrimonial acts which are composed of several fertile and infertile acts; they constitute one totality because they refer to one deliberate choice."[41] The document ties all these aspects together—the intention of the end, the formal and material ordering of the act—through the person and nature, to address specifically the case of a particular contraceptive act:

> When man intervenes in the procreative process, he does this with the intention of regulating and not excluding fertility. Then he unites the

---

[37] See Hoyt, "The Question Is Not Closed," 71 and the discussion of this in Smith, Humanae Vitae: *A Generation Later*, 26.
[38] Hoyt, "The Question Is Not Closed," 71.
[39] Hoyt, "The Question Is Not Closed," 73.
[40] Hoyt, "The Question Is Not Closed," 74.
[41] Hoyt, "The Question Is Not Closed," 72.

material finality toward fecundity which exists in intercourse with the formal finality of the person and renders the entire process "human." Conjugal acts which by intention are infertile are ordered to the expression of the union of love; that love, however, reaches its culmination in fertility responsibly accepted.[42]

Thus, the majority argues, because of its ordering to union, which itself is ordered to fecundity, a particular contraceptive act can be licit within the whole of a marriage open to life. The two standards for judging liceity are marriage and openness to life that is not completely excluded.

With its attention to finality and the ordering of a marriage as a whole, the majority opinion sees itself as having sufficient regard for the order of nature, which can rightly be used for the good of human beings. The argument is that conjugal acts rendered sterile through contraceptive means can still be ordered to the good of the unity of the couple, which is itself ordered to the good of procreation, even when a particular conjugal act is not.[43] The act in question does not then seem to violate the good of human life, as the specific intention against life through human generation is not present, but rather the act is ordered by a person's intention to its remote finality to the good of conjugal procreation.

This argument, however, fails to take into consideration the importance of the natural species of the act which, while not identical with the moral species, is still included in determining the moral species. For the moral species cannot contradict or ignore the object of the act's natural and *per se* components, it must instead include them to be judged properly by right reason. When determining the moral species of an act, the act itself—that is, what is actually happening—must be considered, along with the natural teleological ordering of the act. The intention of the agent cannot override natural ordering to change the natural or the moral species of an action. In this case, intentionally rendered infertility cannot be actually ordered to a remote procreative end. Intentional and deliberate infertility cannot, by the intention of the agent, be considered one and the same moral act as the sexual acts that are intentionally procreative, or at the very

---

[42] Hoyt, "The Question Is Not Closed," 72.
[43] See Hoyt, "The Question Is Not Closed," 72. While this is an intentionalist argument, Germain Grisez himself, in *Contraception and the Natural Law* (Milwaukee, WI: Bruce, 1964) excludes the reasoning found in the majority report by explaining that "man and wife cannot express love in any genuine sense if they know they are cooperating in an evil act. Hence such cooperation renders the sexual act for those who practice contraception while knowing it to be evil an offense against marital love as well as an offense against procreation" (95).

least do not hinder procreation.[44] It is the type of action that is naturally incapable of this ordering, and thus to do so by intention would be to act against reason. To intentionally order a contraceptive act to the end of procreation is fundamentally irrational. To take a simpler example, it would be irrational to claim that taking poison could be, when considered in the context of a life spent eating real food, ordered overall to the good of nutrition. The type of act that taking poison is is intrinsically opposed to nutrition, even though the same organs are used. In the same way that the good of nutrition cannot be reached through taking poison, the good of procreation cannot be reached through contraceptive acts, no matter the context. They are inherently opposed.

HUMANAE VITAE'S ACCOUNT OF NATURAL LAW

In its own argument, *Humanae Vitae*'s point of departure indicates that the very articulation of the natural law given by the majority response will be subject to close critique:

> Could it not be admitted that the intention of a less abundant but more rationalized fecundity might transform a materializing intervention into a licit and wise control of birth? Could it not be admitted, that is, that the finality of procreation pertains to the ensemble of conjugal life, rather than to its single acts? It is also asked whether, in view of the increased sense of responsibility of modern man, the moment has not come for him to entrust his reason and his will, rather than to the biological rhythms of his organism, the task of regulating birth. (*Humanae Vitae*, no. 3)

---

[44] While this paper is about natural law and not primarily about birth control and the morality of various means of birth control, it seems appropriate to make a comment here about the contraceptive act mentioned in the above discussion and natural family planning's method of using the infertile times of a woman's cycle in such a way as to regulate births. First, it must be said that not having sex is not a sin, so avoiding intercourse during presumed fertility is not in itself sinful. Intercourse outside of the times thought to be fertile remains open to life as long as there are no obstacles placed in the way. These can be either physical obstacles in the case of various means of artificial contraceptives, or intentional obstacles, as in the case of those who would try to use a natural family planning method with a "contraceptive mentality." Both actual contraceptives and intentional contraceptives are morally wrong here, but in different ways. The unobstructed act is not deprived of its natural end. If fertility is miscalculated, conception is not prevented, the act can reach its end under the appropriate conditions. Having a "contraceptive mentality" would make this act that is not wrong in itself wrong though the intention. While the discussion of contraception and natural family planning is a sensitive issue, it is outside the scope of this paper to discuss its uses and abuses, or the situations that make natural family planning difficult. Moral reasoning cannot start with the difficult cases.

In framing the question this way, the specific arguments of the commission are taken into consideration: the need for humanizing the biological processes through a person's use of reason and will, the finality of the act through the overall intention, and the need to take responsibility for personal actions. Paul VI indicates that the answer to the moral question here is in principle founded on natural law and more fully explained in revelation: "Such questions required from the teaching authority of the Church a new and deeper reflection upon the principles of the moral teaching on marriage: a teaching founded on the natural law, illuminated and enriched by divine revelation" (*Humanae Vitae*, no. 4). With these words, he reaffirms the basis of the teaching of the Church in natural law even as he seeks to take on the task of explaining it more clearly.[45]

Humanae Vitae begins its treatment with the question of the end, a decidedly Thomistic starting point, though Aquinas is only cited once. The encyclical states: "The problem of birth, like every other question regarding human life, is to be considered beyond partial perspectives—whether of the biological or psychological, demographic, or sociological orders—in the light of an integral vision of man and of his vocation, not only his natural and earthly, but also his supernatural and eternal vocation" (no. 7). In light of his nature and supernatural vocation the meaning of marriage becomes clear. Paul VI reiterates the ends of marriage which the other two documents had already affirmed and supported: procreation and conjugal love (no. 7). These two ends are inherent in marriage by nature and given supernatural significance in the elevation of the natural institution to a sacrament (no. 8). From these ends of marriage, the pope shows the character of marriage: fully human, total, faithful, exclusive, and fecund (no. 9). Because it is human, marriage demands free acts of the will, consciously chosen, fully-intended acts not based in "instinct and sentimentality." When acting in a properly human manner, human beings act with intention and goals in mind. Actions within a marriage require the full use of human reason, governing choices and intending ends. While passion plays a part, the conscious choice of the means and intention of the end humanize marital love, making it an occasion for virtue. *Humanae Vitae* points out that it is through their shared life that married couples "attain their human perfection" (no. 9).

With the characteristics and ends articulated, the pope shows the aspects of responsible parenthood. He begins: "In relation to the biological processes, responsible parenthood means the knowledge and respect of their functions; the human intellect discovers in the power of giving life biological laws which are part of the human

---

[45] See Smith, Humanae Vitae: *A Generation Later*, 73.

person" (no. 10). Pope Paul VI does not have a physicalist view of natural law in mind here, as the minority opinion tended to, but still holds the same teleological view. For Paul VI, the purpose of human sexuality is of primary importance and biological laws support this. Along with marriage, sexual acts and organs have a purpose, not just a function, and reason takes both of these into account. By paying attention to what is actually happening in fertility cycles, people are able to leave fewer procreative actions to chance, instead using reason to discover the order and finality of human reproduction. Given this knowledge, the person can then choose actions based on his or her goals. According to the document, then, appropriate, fully-human action would require abstinence during fertile times.

Reason is used in two ways here.[46] First in a scientific way, man discerns the order of creation, and second in the judgment of what should be done in the present moment, based on the desired outcome. The first sense is of science or knowledge, knowing the order of things. The second applies this to human action so that the judgment of reason guides instinct and passion. This second use of reason is moral reasoning, the reasoning of natural law. As Martin Rhonheimer explains the encyclical, human beings participate in the "Creator's providence by his own acts of intelligent understanding. This *active, intelligent* participation in divine providence is what properly is called natural law. Man has to judge what is right or what is convenient to do. By simply following his instincts, he could not fulfill the will of his Creator."[47] Active participation requires prudential judgment. Paul VI emphasizes this, asserting: "In relation to the tendencies of instinct or passion, responsible parenthood means that necessary dominion which reason and will must exercise over them" (no. 10). Instinct or passion cannot be allowed to undermine the course of action dictated by right reason. To allow reason to be subverted by instinct or desire for pleasure would be a transgression of the moral order.

The document next specifies what the considerations of reason might be in this regard: "In relations to physical, economic, psychological, and social conditions, responsible parenthood is exercised, either by the deliberate and generous decision to raise a numerous family, or by the decision, made for grave motives and with due respect for the moral law, to avoid for the time being or even an indeterminate period, a new birth" (no. 10). Thus reason must guide and control instinct and passion when it has been decided that now is an inopportune time to bring a child into the world. While the document has not yet excluded technical means of regulating birth, the

---

[46] Smith, Humanae Vitae: *A Generation Later*, 74–75.
[47] Martin Rhonheimer, "Contraception, Sexual Behavior, and Natural Law," *Linacre Quarterly* 56, no. 2 (1989): 38.

force of the argument up to this point seems to indicate an emphasis on virtue—that is, the reasoned governance of the passions—as the proper form of birth control. If it is not reasonable to have a child at this time, the reasonable course of action would be to refrain from activity ordered to producing a child.[48]

The document continues its consideration of responsible parenthood: "Responsible parenthood also and above all implies a more profound relationship to the objective moral order established by God, of which a right conscience is a faithful interpreter. The responsible exercise of parenthood implies, therefore, that the husband and wife recognize fully their own duties towards God, towards themselves, towards the family and towards society, in a correct hierarchy of values" (no. 10). Taken together, these points show the positive injunctions of natural law in the area of marriage. Human beings are to use reason to discover the moral ordering inherent in sexual intercourse and marriage, which bestows on a person a hierarchy of responsibilities. With a well-formed conscience, persons must prudently determine the moral course of action in light of marriage and other concrete circumstances. This discernment should never contradict the requirements of virtue, by which human beings order their passions according to reason, always keeping in mind the natural ordering of sexual acts and the generative organs.

In giving reason the role of governing action, Paul VI introduces a view of natural law that is neither physicalism nor intentionalism but is instead related to virtue. In his treatment of the topic, Rhonheimer explains, the encyclical's "description of what responsible parenthood is, also provides a very precise characterization of the virtue of chastity. Chastity does not simply mean continence, but mastery of one's own sexual drives so as to integrate them into the order of personal love."[49] The sexual appetite requires the governance of prudence, through the virtue of chastity to live out the responsible parenthood envisioned in the encyclical.[50]

The particular uses of reason proposed in the encyclical are different from what the documents of the commission had proposed as the place of reason in natural law. Taking into consideration the distinction between physical and moral ordering insisted on by both documents of the commission, *Humanae Vitae* emphasizes that human

---

[48] While it is not the main point of this paper, it does seem important to note that *Humanae Vitae* and the magisterium of the Church do not completely rule out sexual intercourse in these instances. Using virtue and science, couples avoiding conception refrain from intercourse during the fertile part of the woman's cycle. Couples can track this using various methods; however, the virtue of self-control is still required.
[49] Rhonheimer, "Contraception, Sexual Behavior, and Natural Law," 39.
[50] See Rhonheimer, "Contraception, Sexual Behavior, and Natural Law," 40, and Thomas Aquinas, *Summa Theologiae* I-II, q. 65, a. 1.

beings are not simply reading an order from the laws of nature. The binding content of the order of creation is not limited to recognizing and respecting functionality, but rather recognizing and respecting natural teleology.[51] Functionality would simply view the biological processes and avoid interfering. However, natural teleology has a broader scope, keeping in mind the whole person and the goal of human life. The functionality of the reproductive system is included but it cannot be separated from the bigger picture. The appropriate use of this functionality also helps the human person reach the goal of human life. On this view, however, functionality is a means to the goal, not the end. With natural teleology, then, something different than non-interference is required.[52] Ultimately, human beings must order their actions to conform to their ends in particular circumstances and with specifying requirements, ruling passions through the use of reason in virtue. This includes sexual intercourse in marriage, so that the biological ordering of the reproductive system is seen in the context of human love, marriage, and ultimately the goal of human life. Reason is to guide the use of passion in ordering actions. But the work of reason does not override the ordering of nature or the functionality of nature as the majority of the commission would have it, either. The moral order established by God is still appealed to by the encyclical, and with this come particular ordinances to which human beings must conform. Rationality does not permit them to be their own standard or to bend or change teleology. The encyclical makes this clear:

> In the task of transmitting life, therefore, they are not free to proceed completely at will, as if they could determine in a wholly autonomous way, the honest path to follow; but they must conform their activity to the creative intention of God, expressed in the very nature of marriage and of its acts, and manifested by the constant teaching of the Church. (no. 10)

Nature is still to be respected as reflecting the ordering of God, in

---

[51] Smith, *Humanae Vitae: A Generation Later*, 74–75.

[52] In fact, interference can be permitted. To discuss all the ways this might be the case and addressing biological abnormalities is outside the scope of this paper (the latter also is beyond the author's competence). However, as an example, hormone therapies that are effective contraceptives can licitly be used to treat disease, regulate cycles, and for other health reasons (see HV, no. 13). In this situation, infertility resulting from the hormonal therapies is neither willed nor intended, it is neither a means nor an end, and thus a valid use of the principle of double effect. The particular medical act does not aim at infertility, and it is not the infertility itself which is the means to healing. Infertility is instead a kind of side effect of the hormonal therapy used to treat disease.

marriage and in the acts that properly belong to marriage.

The two ends of marriage and of the conjugal act are written not only into the nature of marriage and human rationality, but into the biological functions of man and woman as well, and should not be separated on either of these levels (*Humanae Vitae*, no. 12). The document explains: "By safeguarding both these essential aspects, the unitive and the procreative, the conjugal act preserves in its fullness the sense of true mutual love and its ordination towards man's most high calling to parenthood" (no. 12).

Biologically, there are natural periods of infertility, and the encyclical explains that performing the conjugal act during these periods is not a separation of the two ends:

> These acts ... do not cease to be lawful if, for causes independent of the will of the husband and wife they are foreseen to be infecund, since they always remain ordained towards expressing and consolidating their union. In fact, as experience bears witness, not every conjugal act is followed by new life. God has wisely disposed natural laws and rhythms of fecundity which, of themselves, cause a separation in the succession of births. Nonetheless, the Church, calling men back to the observance of the norms of the natural law, as interpreted by its constant doctrine, teaches that each and every marriage act must remain open to the transmission of life. (no. 11)

The use of periods of infertility is what the document considers "respecting the laws of the generative process" and thereby acknowledging "oneself not to be the arbiter of the sources of human life, but rather the minister of the design established by the creator" (no. 13).[53] These conjugal acts which happen to be naturally infertile—whether this is known and intended or not—are not immoral or against reason because they have not been deliberately ordered by spouses in such a way as to prevent fecundity. They have not been intentionally and mechanically deprived of their natural end. Spouses are still acting in harmony with their biological and spiritual nature, and the order inherent to it. They are "ministers of the design," rather than dominating it. Thus Paul VI concludes the document's natural law reflection: "In fact, just as man does not have unlimited dominion

---

[53] While the use of periods of infertility for intercourse can still be used with a contraceptive mentality, it is important to note that the Church does not see the act of intentionally using this part of the cycle for intercourse as intrinsically evil. Abstaining from intercourse during periods of fertility still requires self-control and reason to control passions. If the intention to prevent contraception was illicit in a particular case, the evil in these cases would be in the intention, not in the act itself, as in the case of a contraceptive act.

over his body in general, so also, with particular reason, he has no such dominion over his generative faculties as such, because of their intrinsic ordination towards raising up life of which God is the principle" (no. 13).

The argument of the document is not fundamentally against artificiality or interference, and instead points to true humanization and excellence in action, which is not through technical means but through virtue. The licit method of regulating birth when this is acknowledged to be necessary involves abstaining from the procreative act entirely during periods of fertility, a course of action that the document acknowledges will "appear to many to be difficult or even impossible of actuation." This is because "like all great beneficent realities, it demands serious engagement and much effort, individual, family, and social effort. More than that, it would not be practicable without the help of God, who upholds and strengthens the good will of men. Yet to anyone who reflects well, it cannot but be clear that such efforts ennoble man and are beneficial to the human community" (*Humanae Vitae*, no. 20). This statement again calls to mind St. Thomas' teaching on virtue, which demands individual development of habits, cultivated not only through individual acts but also through law (ST I-II, q. 92, a. 1). Virtue "ennobles man" and brings him to his true human perfection, but not without benefit to the human community.[54]

The moral method of regulation of birth thus comes to light as simply the practice of virtue. Virtue, which is the perfection of human beings in appetite and emotion as these are moved in accord with reason, requires that the person take stock of the situation and act reasonably and responsibly in light of the moral demands made on him. It is not acting in ignorance or despite what seems to be responsible but, rather, conforming one's actions and passions to the situation. Contraceptive methods conquer the effects of passions by technology rather than through right reason.

While it is not usually recognized as such, Pope Paul VI offers a clearly Thomistic account of natural law and a reaffirmation of Church teaching against the positions offered in the papers that came out of the papal birth control commission. In his emphasis on virtue and natural teleology over functionality, he adeptly avoids physicalism and a more passive view of reason. Paul VI also escapes the account of human beings' rational participation in eternal law in the majority report, whereby a person uses technology to control nature. Instead,

---

[54] See Aquinas, *Summa Theologiae*, I-II, q. 90, a. 2; q. 92, a. 1. In the first, Thomas explains that law is directed to the common good, in the second that law's end is inculcating virtue. Thus virtue and the common good of the community are very closely connected.

he points to the traditional understanding of the necessity of virtue, the perfecter of human nature, while pointing out the problems, societal and moral, associated with mechanical methods of birth control.

Though he does not offer an expansive explanation of natural law, Pope Paul VI is able to situate married love in the realm of St. Thomas's entire teaching on virtue. The demand for the primacy of reason indicates that reason is to order and direct the lower appetites and emotions through virtue (ST I-II, q. 50 and 56). By drawing attention to the end of married life as the end of the person in human perfection, the document shows that the virtues necessary for human perfection are further specified in married life.[55] Virtue's all-encompassing role in human life, then, must not be excluded in the other characteristics and demands of marriage.

CONCLUSION

The picture of natural law formed through the reading of *Humanae Vitae* is clearly not equal to those given by the papers coming out of the papal commission that preceded its issuance. While all the documents upheld the goods of marriage, the conjugal act, and the generative organs and acknowledged these as having particular ends and purposes naturally and supernaturally, they were not in agreement on how these goods, especially the purpose of procreation, were normative. Though these purposes were seen to be of assistance in forming a natural law teaching concerning the licitness of contraceptive practices within marriage, the other facet of traditional natural law teaching—a person's rational participation—was not a matter of agreement between the documents, and instead led to differences in conclusion.

The minority paper was shown to suffer from bifocalism, at one and the same time wanting human beings to deduce natural law simply from the ordering of nature but also not wanting to equate natural law with mere physical laws of the universe and thus opening the way to intentionalism. The majority paper offered a more active view of human beings' rational participation in natural law, arguing that they should be able to use technology to participate responsibly in the moral order, and at times even reorder the natural order. In the end, *Humanae Vitae* rejected both of these accounts, steering a clear course between a moral law that is no more than physicalism and the position that the physical laws of the universe are to be dominated for a person's intended ends.

Instead, Pope Paul VI offers a remarkably traditional account of natural law, drawing on the thought of St. Thomas Aquinas. In doing

---

[55] See Aquinas, *Summa Theologiae*, I-II, q. 55, a. 1.

this, he refers to the moral ordering of the created universe, which is in some ways inseparable from its natural ordering. Natural law comes to sight as a person's rational participation in this order by the virtuous ordering of personal action to the end or perfection of the human person. Marriage, the acts that belong to marriage, and the generative organs used in those acts all have their own teleological purposes which in the case of sex and the procreative organs are not able to be separated from their biological ends without violating the moral ordering as well. Reason instead responds to these natural ends, by accepting them as integral to the acts performed. By rationally acknowledging the ends given by nature, a person shows understanding of the act being performed. The natural end of the action can licitly be ordered to further ends, provided the integral nature and effects are not ignored or discarded. Thus human beings are best able to order their actions virtuously only when they know the natural ordering of the particular acts and keep these in mind, ordering them intentionally. From this consideration, a person's participation in eternal law, is to use reason to discern the proper modes of acting, and that means acting in virtue. Through virtue, human beings order themselves to the end, and control their lower faculties, allowing them to be ordered by right reason for the good of themselves and their community.

While *Humanae Vitae* and the debates surrounding birth control in regard to the encyclical revealed a weakness in moral theology concerning natural law, *Humane Vitae*'s treatment of natural law sets a tone for future magisterial documents in the area of morality. While *Humanae Vitae*'s treatment of natural law, in which a balanced use of reason is presented where human reason is neither simply a passive reader of the order of nature nor the standard of the moral law is not commonly recognized, this formulation is found and clarified in later magisterial documents. *Veritatis Splendor* elucidates further the teleological character of the moral life,[56] and later magisterial pronouncements in many areas of moral reflection, including ecology, economy, and society demonstrate a similar outlook.[57] This view of natural law encourages persons to see all actions in the context of a life ordered to the true human good and judge whether or not individual actions can legitimately be ordered to this goal. While more work needs to be done with regard to natural law in Catholic moral theology, the magisterial documents seem to be in agreement on what

---

[56] See especially no. 73, on the teleological character of the moral life.
[57] Pope Francis's *Laudato Si'* condemns those who see human reason as the only standard or limit for the encounter with nature. The social encyclicals caution against economies and social ordering that does not strike this balance between passivity and domination.

version of natural law to use.

Arielle Harms is Director of Graduate Theology Programs and Assistant Professor of Theology at Pontifex University. She holds a PhD in theology with a concentration in moral theology from Ave Maria University. Dr. Harms's academic interests include natural law, virtue, nature and grace, Catholic social teaching, sacramental theology, liturgy, and the theology of Thomas Aquinas. Her published work has appeared in peer-reviewed journals and trade publications for catechesis and religious education.

Catholic Social Teaching, Liberalism, and Economic Justice[1]

Jason A. Heron and Bharat Ranganathan

> There is a growing awareness of the exalted dignity proper to the human person, since he stands above all things, and his rights and duties are universal and inviolable. Therefore, there must be made available to all men everything necessary for leading a life truly human, such as food, clothing, and shelter; the right to choose a state of life freely and to found a family, the right to education, to employment, to a good reputation, to respect, to appropriate information, to activity in accord with the upright norm of one's own conscience, to protection of privacy and rightful freedom even in matters religious. (*Gaudium et Spes*, no. 26)

In *After Virtue*, Alasdair MacIntyre decries liberalism. Given that they lack a shared framework in which to deliberate about the good, liberals are at best consumerists or voluntarists. For example, commenting on conflicting views about war, bodily integrity, and the demands of justice, MacIntyre writes: "It is precisely because there is in our society no established way of deciding between these claims that moral argument appears to be necessarily interminable. From our rival conclusions we can argue back to our rival premises ... and the invocation of one premise against another becomes a matter of pure assertion and counter-assertion."[2] Such charges against liberalism make it seem that Catholicism and liberalism have little to learn from one another. Given the pluralism that characterizes our world and (especially) liberal democracies, does such mistrust best serve our common life?

In this article, we argue that Catholic social teaching about

---

[1] All citations of magisterial teaching are taken from the Vatican website (www.vatican.va/content/vatican/en.html) and indicated by paragraph number. References to John Rawls's work use standard abbreviations: *A Theory of Justice*, rev. ed. (Cambridge: Harvard University Press, 1999) = TJ; *Political Liberalism*, exp. ed. (New York: Columbia University Press, 1996) = PL; *The Law of Peoples* (Cambridge: Harvard University Press, 1999) = LP; and *Justice as Fairness: A Restatement*, ed. Erin Kelly (Cambridge: Harvard University Press, 2001) = JF.

[2] Alasdair MacIntyre, *After Virtue: A Study in Moral Theory*, 2nd ed. (Notre Dame: University of Notre Dame Press, 1983), 8.

subsidiarity in a global society characterized by economic inequalities could benefit from conversation with John Rawls's liberal political philosophy. First, we introduce the principle of subsidiarity, commonly understood to be one of the four basic principles in Catholic social teaching, and its utility in the magisterium's engagement with nation states and, to a limited extent, the global economy. Second, we identify how this magisterial engagement has yet to address subsidiary structures between interdependent but radically unequal societies in the era of globalization. Third, we speculate how the Catholic understanding of subsidiarity may benefit from Rawlsian explication of the *basic structure*, especially if the Church is to speak precisely and normatively about global economic inequality. Fourth and fifth, we introduce Rawls's characterization of the basic structure and how it may help us think about global interdependence, especially in the context of radical economic inequality. Sixth and finally, we gesture toward further challenges for both Catholic social teaching and Rawlsian liberalism.[3]

In undertaking this exercise, we write as two scholars with differing confessional, moral, and political commitments nonetheless committed to friendship and solidarity.[4] From this foundation, we disagree and debate about ethics and politics. To our minds, this admission is important because one of us has been trained to think that such a friendship is either unlikely, inherently unstable, or ultimately illusory.[5] Given our friendship, we challenge one another to think more carefully about how we approach the topic under consideration, especially the ways in which we draw upon and converse with Rawls.

In Christian ethics particularly and religious ethics generally, Rawls is approached (if he is approached at all) with either derision or suspicion. Many characterizations of Rawls in the context of Christian and religious ethics, however, depend on problematic readings of his thought. For example, some ethicists (i) *inherit views about* Rawls rather than carefully reading his work themselves; others (ii) *read into* Rawls certain crass characterizations according to which liberalism and libertarianism are synonymous; and others still (iii) *operate by a hermeneutics of fear* according to which views that do not originate in

---

[3] It is beyond our scope in this paper to detail the history of how the tradition of Catholic social teaching has *already* been impacted by its dialogue with traditions of liberalism and to offer normative analysis of this impact. Our focus here is limited to the way dialogue with a certain tradition of liberalism may enrich Catholic social teaching's participation in addressing a discrete contemporary issue.
[4] On intellectual solidarity, see David Hollenbach, *The Common Good and Christian Ethics* (Cambridge: Cambridge University Press, 2002), chap. 6.
[5] See Alasdair MacIntyre, "Is Friendship Possible?" Presented at the de Nicola Center for Ethics and Culture, University of Notre Dame, Notre Dame, IN, November 8, 2019.

scripture and/or magisterial teaching are somehow morally, politically, and theologically compromised.

Our hope is not only to think about the ways the institutions in which we participate contribute to economic equality and inequality but also to encourage practical reflection on the sources upon which ethicists draw and how these sources might help or hinder reflection about our common life.[6]

CATHOLIC SOCIAL TEACHING: SOCIETY AND SUBSIDIARITY

Catholic social teaching summarizes and prescribes the scriptural and magisterial teachings on matters of justice in social life. Catholic social teaching develops over time and offers an ideal-normative vision of a just society. This vision is grounded in both scripture and the collected experience of the Christian community as it responded to economic, political, and social issues. Historically, Catholic social teaching has addressed—among other things—poverty and inequality, the right to and dignity of work, the relationship between the church and state, the nature and function of the family, and environmental degradation and stewardship. As Catholic social teaching has developed, four principles have been identified.[7] Among these principles, *subsidiarity* refers to the ordering of institutions within the social whole.

Within Catholic social teaching, subsidiarity is commonly used to judge the proper cooperation and jurisdiction of the various social institutions. Since social life is in many ways complex and disproportionate, no single authority governs or orders our common life. Instead, we live within a variety of jurisdictions. Given that economic justice is not solely a matter of individual morality and economic interactions are not the sole social interactions among human persons and communities, speaking accurately about economic justice requires a precise understanding of institutions and their relationships to each other.[8] Thus, clarity regarding economic justice

---

[6] We will neither engage nor address the work of contemporary moral theologians on issues related to Catholic social teaching; rather, we will focus narrowly on the authoritative sources with which those theologians must contend, namely the encyclical tradition. Likewise, in the latter half of the essay, we will focus primarily on Rawls and Rawlsians as influential sources in contemporary political philosophy, not on the extensive secondary literature.

[7] They are: (i) the dignity of the human person, (ii) the priority of the common good, (iii) solidarity as a principle and as a virtue, and (iv) subsidiarity as a sign of the healthy functioning of any social whole.

[8] For more on situating economic interactions within a broader social context, see Andrew Beauchamp and Jason A. Heron, "Solidarity in a Technocratic Age: Commercialization, Catholic Social Teaching, and Moral Formation," *Journal of Religious Ethics* 47, no. 2 (2019): 356–76.

requires clarity on subsidiarity.

In the history of Catholic reflection on subsidiary relations, the most often quoted teaching is Pius XI's social encyclical, *Quadragesimo Anno* (1931). Pius writes:

> The supreme authority of the State ought, therefore, to let subordinate groups handle matters and concerns of lesser importance, which would otherwise dissipate its efforts greatly. Thereby the State will more freely, powerfully, and effectively do all those things that belong to it alone because it alone can do them.... Therefore, those in power should be sure that the more perfectly a graduated order is kept among the various associations, in observance of the principle of "subsidiary function," the stronger social authority and effectiveness will be [and] the happier and more prosperous the condition of the State. (no. 80)

To understand his caution against overbearing state authority, it is essential to consider the socio-political circumstances of the nineteenth century informing Pius's teaching. Put succinctly, the Catholic Church since at least 1789 had been contending with a developing nation-state that had designs on much of the social activity of the Church. From 1789 to 1945, the Church's social magisterium was developed in dynamic tension with the nation-state. The latter was often perceived by the magisterium as attempting to wrest authority from the Church and the family, ostensibly in order to centralize and streamline social services like education and healthcare. Because of this prolonged and complex relationship, we observe throughout modern Catholic social teaching uncertainty about the modern iteration of the political body.[9]

Thus, some contemporary interpreters understandably read subsidiarity in late capitalist societies as a bulwark against inefficient government intervention at the lower levels of society. Contemporary

---

[9] Offering a Christian reflection about the political body (Romans 13), Paul is clear that the state has a divinely authorized vocation. So, the tension between Church and state in the modern period should not be interpreted as agnosticism about the natural good that is the state. In fact, it is the Church's vision of the state's vocation that funds its energy in dialoguing with the modern nation-state regarding jurisdiction, competence, and usurpation. See Leo XIII, *Rerum Novarum*, no. 37: "Rights must be religiously respected wherever they exist, and it is the duty of the public authority to prevent and to punish injury, and to protect every one in the possession of his own. Still, when there is question of defending the rights of individuals, the poor and badly off have a claim to especial consideration. The richer class have many ways of shielding themselves, and stand less in need of help from the State; whereas the mass of the poor have no resources of their own to fall back upon, and must chiefly depend upon the assistance of the State. And it is for this reason that wage-earners, since they mostly belong in the mass of the needy, should be specially cared for and protected by the government."

reflection on the principle of subsidiarity is often focused on the "local" and the "lower" in an almost libertarian preference for state minimalism. This characterization of subsidiarity deprives the principle of its true range of meaning. A fuller characterization does not prioritize localism over other tiers of governance.[10] Rather, subsidiarity properly characterized exhorts every sphere—no matter its location in the gradual array of institutions—to assess its duty to the common good.

In *Quadragesimo Anno*, Pius's criticism of the state is not designed to minimize state authority. Rather, Pius situates state authority in its proper context within a social array. The bodies in this array extend from the individual human person to the universal Body of Christ, and each possesses duties to the common good. The priority of the common good requires that each institution in the array be free and efficient in the exercise of its power. In other words, subsidiarity exhorts every institution to understand its proper role. So understood, institutions—including the state—play a critical role in making possible a real and necessary measure of order and peace. The state's role is all the more critical in terms of defending the basic rights of those most vulnerable to the coercions of severe poverty.

That the state has a duty to care for the most vulnerable signals subsidiarity's anthropological foundation. One can justifiably call subsidiarity a sign of a *healthy* social whole inasmuch as subsidiary structuring is a sign that every sphere of a social whole is contributing freely and efficiently, according to its unique competency and duties, to the flourishing of the persons comprising the whole. So, the principle of the Church's commitment to subsidiarity reflects a concern that human persons be regarded according to their irrevocable dignity. Who or what may so regard human persons? The individuals, institutions, and polities of which they are a part.[11] In short, individual

---

[10] See Russell Hittinger, "Social Roles and Ruling Virtues in Catholic Social Doctrine," *Annales Theologici* 16, no. 2 (2002): 295–318; "The Coherence of the Four Basic Principles of Catholic Social Doctrine: An Interpretation," *Nova et Vetera* 7, no. 4 (2009): 791–838.

[11] This characterization mirrors developments since the late 1980s in Anglophone human rights theory. In such human rights theory, the obligations that correspond to someone's human rights claims may be understood "institutionally" or "interpersonally." Many Rawlsians (e.g., Thomas Pogge, *World Poverty and Human Rights*, 2nd ed. [Cambridge: Polity, 2008]) conceive human rights as institutional: the primary obligation to fulfill the substance of another's human rights falls on economic and political institutions. For interpersonalists (e.g., Peter Singer, "Famine, Affluence, and Morality," *Philosophy and Public Affairs* 1, no. 3 [1972]: 229–243), individuals hold human rights claims universally, that is, in relation to each and every other individual. Some thinkers (e.g., Simon Caney, "Global Poverty and Human Rights: The Case for Positive Duties," in *Freedom from Poverty as a Human Right: Who Owes What to the Very Poor?*, ed. Thomas Pogge [New York: Oxford University

people require subsidiarity if the societies of which they are members are not to become either neglectful or overbearing.

This historical development of the Catholic magisterium's exhortation to the modern state to conduct itself according to the principle of subsidiarity is instructive for understanding the more contemporary question of the global economy's social jurisdiction. The history of the magisterium's engagement with the modern state has shaped, but not fully prepared, the magisterium's ability to speak to economic matters on a global scale. If we look back at the period from 1789 to 1945 as the historical arena in which the magisterium engaged the modern nation-state, then from 1945 forward to our own time, the magisterium has had to increase its engagement with a global capitalist economy. Three magisterial interventions stand out in this engagement, each representing a different moment in a rapidly changing global-economic context.

First, in 1991 Pope John Paul II issued *Centesimus Annus*. In light of the symbolic fall of the Berlin Wall, *Centesimus Annus* is an optimistic exhortation of liberal democracy and capitalism to humanize the world left behind by communism's demise.[12] Second, in 2009 Pope Benedict XVI issued *Caritas in Veritate*. In light of the global financial crisis of 2008, *Caritas in Veritate* is less optimistic. Instead, as we will see below, it can be read as an acknowledgement that if the global economy is to be humanized, it will become so because we have begun to govern it according to the principle of subsidiarity. Despite this acknowledgement, however, Benedict does not work out in any detail what such governance should look like.[13] Finally, in 2015 Pope Francis issued *Laudato Si'*, which treats environmental degradation and global poverty as intertwined phenomena. The optimism of *Centesimus Annus* is absent. Benedict's cautious confidence that there is some way to humanize a global economy is muted, if not absent. What remains in Francis's letter is a hope that micro-solutions will somehow help some of us resist the darker consequences of global capital.[14]

NEED FOR PRECISION

Since it is ideal-normative, Catholic social teaching does not pronounce with significant detail on how the ideal should be realized in historical praxis. Granted, the tradition of Catholic social teaching features magisterial interventions in social issues that always have

---

Press, 2007], 275–302) argue that institutional and interpersonal accounts need to be articulated together in hybrid fashion.
[12] See John Paul II, *Centesimus Annus*, nos. 22–29.
[13] See Benedict XVI, *Caritas in Veritate*, nos. 21–26, 41–42, 60, and 67.
[14] See Francis, *Laudato Si'*, nos. 105, 202–227.

historical shape and content. Magisterial interventions in social life provide principles, guidelines, exhortations, cautions, and the like, as they should. Popes and bishops who teach do so as experts in humanity, not as experts in economics, environmental conservation, or warfare.

Even within the ideal-normative register, however, greater precision is possible and necessary. This precision is lacking when it comes to articulating the actual subsidiary structures of the global society in which we now live. Specifically, within the relationships that obtain among different subsidiary arrays, we are interested in developing a clearer way of speaking about disparity, inequality, and injustice not only "up and down" within a single array, but also "across" the relationships between arrays. To clarify, consider the following way of understanding our current context.

Imagine a society (i.e., the nation-state) as a cone. On standard treatments within Catholic social teaching, subsidiarity most often refers to the relationships between "higher" and "lower" levels within a single cone. Sometimes, these levels within a single cone are treated as "remote from" and "proximate to" specific issues within that society. For example, the federal government is remote from certain issues to which a local school district is more proximate. Sometimes, these levels within a single cone are treated as more or less authoritative with regard to those same issues. Thus, on conventional portraits of subsidiarity, the question of the proper ordering of the institutions within society is a question of hierarchical ordering indexed to social issues that must be addressed according to the competence most suited to them.

In our contemporary globalized and interconnected world, however, questions regarding institutional ordering require rethinking and further precision because of the ways in which we implicate both those inside and outside the nation-state. In other words, how do we (re)conceive the meaning and relevance of subsidiary relations for our understanding of order *between* cones? Given facts about national and international interdependence, can subsidiarity assist us in normatively evaluating injustice and inequality not only *within* but also *across* such a vast society? It seems natural enough that Catholic social teaching's principles of human dignity, solidarity, and the common good could function as guides for just this sort of normative evaluation. Moreover, given that the four principles function as a synthetic whole, it would make sense for the precision we seek to come from within the tradition of Catholic social teaching itself. How?

According to the social magisterium, the dignity of the human person demands that we address injustice and inequality wherever it diminishes the flourishing of our fellow humans. The moral demand voiced by each person's inherent dignity is only reinforced by the reality of solidarity among persons and groups. We are not only individual moral agents. We are also biologically, socially, politically, economically, and historically bound to each other in webs of interdependence. Moreover, in Catholic social teaching, we speak of our interdependence as the reality of solidarity. It is a human fact, and also a moral possibility. Solidarity is at once an actual state-of-affairs and a potential field of human action. Put most succinctly, we can get better at living solidarity.[15]

It would seem then that we have the resources within Catholic social teaching to speak normatively about the demands of justice and equality both "up and down" the subsidiary array of a single cone and "across" or "between" the cones of a global society. What good would subsidiarity do in the global context? The word "subsidiarity" carries within it a signal that there is more to this principle than institutional ordering up and down a single hierarchy. The root of the word is the Latin *subsidium*, which refers to help given and even to a cohort of soldiers sent to aid. If we attend to the word itself, we find more than a way of speaking about who does what in a hierarchy of powers. We find a way of speaking about the help, assistance, or aid institutions within a society give to the parts and the whole. Without leaving the question of hierarchical ordering behind, we are faced with the question of the free and efficient exercise of each society's power *to help*. Subsidiarity has built within it a vocational element, exhorting not only the members, but the institutions of society to help each other toward flourishing.

In the nineteenth century social magisterium, this vocational element was clearly articulated by Pope Leo XIII in his opposition to socialism and exhortation to rich people. Consider Leo's teaching in *Quod Apostolici Muneris* (1878), specifically his concern with the relationship between government and the distribution of goods. His chief concern in addressing this relationship is the proper and effective care of those who were unlucky enough to be born poor by those who were lucky enough to be born rich. After noting the ongoing role of the Church in administering charity for those in need, he reminds rich people that they have a vocation to "give what remains to the poor." Leo does not use the language of solidarity or subsidiarity at all here.

---

[15] See John Paul II, *Sollicitudo Rei Socialis* (1987), nos. 26, 38–40; *Centesimus Annus* (1991), nos. 41, 49, and 51. Over and against "procedural justice," some of Rawls's critics have argued that justice is not only a set of principles but also an ethos. See, e.g., G. A. Cohen, "Incentives, Inequality, and Community," in *The Tanner Lectures on Human Values*, vol. 13, ed. Grethe Peterson (Salt Lake City: University of Utah Press, 1992), 261–329; and "Where the Action Is: On the Site of Distributive Justice," *Philosophy and Public Affairs* 26, no. 1 (1997): 3–30.

But the question of how to best deploy help to those in need within a hierarchical array is precisely the point. So, within the single cone of nineteenth century Italy, France, or Germany, the obligation to help in response to economic inequality is a "grave precept" that must be kept if society is to flourish. Throughout the rest of his social magisterium, Leo's perspective does not change about this vocation of rich people to send help to poor people.

In the 1960s, we find Pope Paul VI translating for a new, more global context Leo's exhortation to rich people. In *Populorum Progressio* (1967), Paul writes of "mutual solidarity—the aid that the richer nations must give to developing nations" (no. 44). This encyclical stands as the first significant magisterial effort to attend to a globalizing world. In *Sollicitudo Rei Socialis* (1987) and *Centesimus Annus* (1991), John Paul II further develops magisterial teaching about solidarity. The entirety of Pope Francis's encyclical *Laudato Si'* (2015) can be read as a culmination of the effort to speak of Leonine charity in terms of something *mutual*: something respecting the real but mutable bonds of solidarity. Within the magisterial teaching on global relations in the contemporary context, Pope Benedict XVI's encyclical *Caritas in Veritate* (2009) stands out as a signal that there is more work to be done on the place of subsidiarity in a global web of interdependence.

Benedict's teaching in nos. 53–67 on "the cooperation of the human family" is relevant, with nos. 57 and 59 being especially notable. Exhorting global society to a "deeper critical evaluation of the category of relation" (no. 53), Benedict explores the role of subsidiarity in a world where the obligation to care for the poor continues to involve international development aid. In no. 57, Benedict rehearses the traditional teaching about subsidiarity. The Pope states that subsidiarity is "the most effective antidote against any form of all-encompassing welfare state." And so, in our current context, "subsidiarity is particularly well-suited to managing globalization and directing it towards authentic human development." Indeed, if we are to avoid a "dangerous universal power of a tyrannical nature," subsidiarity is essential.[16] Granted, Benedict writes, the

---

[16] See Immanuel Kant, "Perpetual Peace: A Philosophical Sketch" in *Kant's Political Writings*, ed. Hans Reiss, trans. H. B. Nisbet (Cambridge: Cambridge University Press, 1970), 93–130. In his *The Law of Peoples*, Rawls draws from Kant's views to argue against cosmopolitan liberalism and for the limitations of global governance. For Rawls, a global government "would either be a global despotism or else would rule over a fragile empire torn by frequent strife as various regions and peoples tried to gain their political freedom and autonomy," LP, 36. While many Rawlsians reject Rawls's view in *The Law of Peoples*, the limited view of liberalism he expresses has found support among Catholic thinkers. See, e.g., Russell Hittinger, "John Rawls: The Basis of Social Justice and Intercultural Dialogue in a Globalized World," in *Doctor

process of globalization "certainly requires authority, insofar as it poses the problem of a global common good that needs to be pursued. This authority, however, must be organized in a subsidiary and stratified way, if it is not to infringe upon freedom and if it is to yield effective results in practice" (no. 57).

Given the context of globalization and the implications of the global financial crisis, Benedict's reflection on subsidiarity, global authority, and human development turns to economic matters. In no. 59, he reminds us that development is not *only* economic. Instead, economic development ought to take place within the broader context of concrete cultures, each of which has the capacity to contribute to a human dialogue about the global common good. He writes:

> Technologically advanced societies must not confuse their own technological development with a presumed cultural superiority, but must rather rediscover within themselves the oft-forgotten virtues which made it possible for them to flourish throughout their history. Evolving societies must remain faithful to all that is truly human in their traditions, avoiding the temptation to overlay them automatically with the mechanisms of a globalized technological civilization.

It is an understatement to say that the ongoing dialogue regarding charity, paternalism, distribution, and justice, both within the single cones of society and between the many cones of global society, is fraught with difficulties. In the increasingly interdependent global society of which John Paul II, Benedict, and Francis write, "mutuality" remains an unrealized goal difficult to imagine. The word *mutuality* connotes reciprocity, equal agency, and even, in its Latin roots, the act of borrowing. But consider the interdependence between the Global North and the Global South. How can we conceive of mutuality between such parties? How would we work for it and why? What are the conditions necessary for its achievement?

So far, magisterial teaching has not provided us with significant guidance regarding mutual global social relations. Benedict's intervention is not even really a development. It is simply an acknowledgment that subsidiarity must somehow guide globalization.[17] If Catholic social teaching is to move past general

---

communis fasc. 1–2—*Persona, legge naturale, diritti umani in una società complessa e globale* (Città Del Vaticano: Pontificia Academia Sancti Thomae Aquinatis, 2007), 142–164.

[17] Pope Francis's encyclical *Laudato Si'* and his apostolic exhortation *Evangelii Gaudium* could be read as developments of Benedict's call to let the principle of subsidiarity guide the interdependent dynamics of globalization. For example, in no. 54 of *Evangelii Gaudium*, Francis cautions against naive faith in trickle-down theories of global economic development. Francis's caution could be read as an implicit call

exhortations to solidarity and mutuality and toward a "deeper critical evaluation of the category of relation" in a global context, then perhaps Rawls's basic structure argument will prove an essential asset. As we will suggest, the Rawlsian idea of the basic structure provides an avenue through which the ideal-normative vision of Catholic social teaching may be fruitfully developed. More specifically, the Rawlsian idea of the basic structure can provide Catholic social teaching with something it does not currently have: a way to speak precisely and practically about the principle of subsidiarity in a context of radical inequality between societies. Rawls's emphasis on the basic structure challenges and refines Catholic social teaching's ability to judge the hierarchical relations that obtain between rich and poor people in our actual context. This challenge is essential in a world where both liberalism and Catholic social teaching are vocationally bound to address the inequality between rich and poor people.[18]

BASIC STRUCTURE AS THE SUBJECT OF JUSTICE

To put Rawls in conversation with Catholic social teaching, we identify in this section, first, what Rawls means by the *basic structure* and, second, why Rawls privileges the basic structure as the *site* of justice. In comparison to other ideas in his theory of justice, Rawls's development of the basic structure is relatively brief and "whether Rawls himself was ultimately committed to the basic structure argument," Arash Abizadeh notes, "is a matter of some interpretive ambiguity."[19] Moreover, Rawls's theory of justice is long and complicated, so we will not offer here a full exegesis or reconstruction of the various interlocking parts of his theory. Rather, we will focus

---

for subsidiary relations where all members of a hierarchical global society take responsibility for offering their help (*subsidium*) to those in need. Furthermore, throughout both documents, Francis's sensitivity to the negative consequences of social exclusion can also be read as a call for subsidiary relations, where all participants in global society are given the opportunity to participate in the pursuit of their flourishing and to foster bonds of mutual solidarity (see *Evangelii Gaudium*, no. 59; *Laudato Si'*, nos. 48–52). Finally, in *Evangelii Gaudium* nos. 234–237, Francis addresses the fundamental issue underlying subsidiarity: the relation of the part to the whole. His idea of society as a *polyhedron* rather than a *sphere* could be read as a gesture toward the need for a more precise, systematic, and practical way of speaking about the inequitable relations between parts of a global whole. Nevertheless, each of these examples is a possible interpretation and not a deliberate effort to bring the principle of subsidiarity into the normative assessment of global inequalities.

[18] On the one hand, perhaps the imprecision of the term *mutuality* explains why it is found nowhere in *Caritas in Veritate*. On the other hand, Benedict does use the words *reciprocal* and *reciprocity*. In no. 57, he uses the word *reciprocity* once, emphasizing its role in subsidiary relations. In no. 59, his preferred word is *cooperation*.

[19] Arash Abizadeh, "Cooperation, Pervasive Impact, and Coercion: On the Scope (not Site) of Distributive Justice," *Philosophy and Public Affairs* 34, no. 4 (2007): 319, n. 3.

on Rawls's arguments for the basic structure and its importance for thinking about economic inequality.[20]

In his *A Theory of Justice*, Rawls claims that "justice is the first virtue of social institutions," adding that "laws and institutions no matter how efficient and well-arranged must be reformed or abolished if they are unjust" (TJ, 3). Rawls groups a society's major economic, legal, political, and social institutions under the heading of the "basic structure," which is the "primary subject of justice." "Taken together as one scheme," he writes, "the major institutions define men's rights and duties and influence their life prospects, what they can expect to be and how well they can hope to do" (TJ, 6–7). The effects the basic structure has on people's lives are "profound and present from the start" (TJ, 7). Given that we cannot control the contingencies from which we start life, for example, the native talents we are gifted or the socioeconomic class or circumstances into which we are born,[21] the justness of the basic structure is necessary to ensure that we are able to be equal participating members of our society's political community.

Moreover, a society needs to ensure that all people have the all-purpose means necessary to pursue their lives as members of the moral and political communities—that is, to pursue their own respective vision of the good and cooperate with one another such that others are able to do so as well. A just society, then, cannot countenance deep inequalities among its members, whether economic, political, or social, for such inequalities will pervasively affect who we are and might become (JF, 10). Regardless of our vision of the good, there are certain material, political, and social goods—for example, "rights, liberties, and opportunities, and income and wealth" (TJ, 79)—whose presence or absence will play a central role in who we are and might become. Rawls calls these material, political, and social goods "primary social goods." They are *primary* insofar as they are "things which it is supposed that a rational man wants whatever else he wants." They are *social* insofar as they are connected to the basic structure: "Liberties and opportunities are defined by the rules of the major institutions and the distribution of income and wealth is regulated by them" (TJ, 79).

Given that the basic structure is responsible for distributing primary social goods, Rawls devises a thought-experiment according to which citizens deliberate about how such goods should be justly distributed, aiming to mitigate the effects of the natural and social

---

[20] Several arguments and interpretations in this section draw from Bharat Ranganathan, "On Helping One's Neighbor: Religious Ethics, Obligations to Others, and Severe Poverty" (ms.).
[21] Rawls calls these contingencies the "natural and social lotteries." See TJ, 65.

lotteries. According to Rawls, we should articulate the terms according to which our lives will be organized (i.e., "the principles of justice"[22]) starting from what he calls *the original position*. In order to ensure that no one is unjustly advantaged or disadvantaged, in the original position we should imagine ourselves behind what he calls the *veil of ignorance*. "Among the essential features of this situation," he writes, "is that no one knows his place in society, his class position or social status, nor does any one know his fortune in the distribution of natural assets and abilities, his intelligence, strength, and the like" (TJ, 11). On Rawls's view, the original position provides a position of equality from which we can propose principles to justly govern our cooperative lives together.

Underwriting Rawls's theory are three values privileged in liberal moral and political theory: autonomy, equality, and reciprocity.[23] By *autonomy*, we mean that each individual person has their own distinct vision of the good they wish to pursue. For liberals, we have freedom *to* pursue this vision and freedom *from* others when we pursue it. On our view, autonomy should not be understood as an end state, where one is permitted to pursue whatever good simply because one chooses it, but rather as a side constraint, which makes demands on both self and other.[24] By *equality*, we mean that every person is an equal member of the moral and political communities, that is, every person counts as much as the next simply by virtue of being human. Relatedly, equality demands that every person requires (and may hold a justified claim to) the all-purpose means in order to pursue their distinct vision of the good. By *reciprocity*, we mean that every person recognizes others as cooperating members of society, however widely or narrowly conceived, with whom we need to deliberate and justify ourselves. Because we recognize one another as such members, we not only provide reasons to one another when we deliberate about policy but also provide the means by which we are all to pursue our own good. Whether these values are reflected in the principles of

---

[22] The two principles of justice are: "First, each person is to have an equal right to the most extensive scheme of equal basic liberties compatible with a similar scheme of liberties for others. Second, social and economic inequalities are to be arranged so that they are both (a) reasonably expected to be to everyone's advantage, and (b) attached to positions and offices open to all" (TJ, 53).

[23] To say that these three values are privileged by liberals does not entail concomitantly suggesting that all liberals agree on the content of these values nor how they are to be balanced with one another.

[24] "In contrast to incorporating rights into the end state to be achieved," Robert Nozick writes, "one might place them as side constraints upon the actions to be done: don't violate constraints C. The rights of others determine the constraints upon your actions ... The side-constraint view forbids you to violate these moral constraints in the pursuit of your goals," *Anarchy, State, & Utopia* (Oxford: Blackwell, 1974), 29. For Rawls (PL, 365–366), arrangements that violate basic liberties are void *ab initio*.

justice will in turn affect how they are upheld by the basic structure.

Furthermore, in theorizing about justice, it is important to distinguish between the *site* and *scope* of justice. For Rawls, the basic structure is the *site* of justice. For something to be the site of justice means that it is governed by the principles of justice.[25] On this characterization, an evaluation of the justness or unjustness of a society does not need to consider what each and every person in that society is doing; rather, an evaluation of the site of justice informs us about the terms according to which members of that society interact with and implicate one another through shared institutions and whether the distribution of primary goods is justifiable to those it governs. If the distribution of primary goods sustains deep inequalities among people, the principles that govern the basic structure would not be just nor would the principles be justifiable to those governed by them.

While Rawls limited his concerns about justice to the domestic basic structure, in our globalized and interconnected world it is important to ask about the *scope* of justice. Consonant with Catholic social teaching's emphasis on the common good, the scope of justice refers to the range of people "who have claims upon and responsibilities to each other arising from considerations of justice."[26] To be sure, because we interact with and implicate members of our own country and local communities through domestic public policy, we all fall within this limited scope of justice. While we do not set policy in other countries through the voting booth, we interact more and more with those who live beyond our borders through, for example, the goods we consume, the economic sanctions we impose, and the immigration policies we enact. Given that we now live in *one world*,[27] do considerations of justice include everyone and not just our compatriots? If so, on what terms? These questions, to which we will return below, present new opportunities for both Catholic social

---

[25] The regulative principle for a thing, Rawls holds, depends on the nature of the thing (TJ, 47). The distinction between principles for institutions and principles for individuals is important because Rawls articulates his deontological account of justice during a period when utilitarianism was the regnant normative theory. Utilitarianism uses the same evaluative standard (i.e., the maximization of utility) for both institutions and individuals. Moreover, while noting that his theory of justice is not disconnected from moral considerations, Rawls claims that his theory is not a complete moral theory accounting for a full but rather only a limited range of considerations, that is, whether the institutions that make up the basic structure uphold the principles of justice. This limited range of considerations is captured by Rawls's motto that justice as fairness is "political not metaphysical." See TJ, 15, and PL, Lecture I.

[26] Abizadeh, "Cooperation, Pervasive Impact, and Coercion," 323.

[27] On this phrasing and conception, see Peter Singer, *One World: The Ethics of Globalization* (New Haven: Yale University Press, 2002).

teaching and liberal theories of justice to think about the site and scope of justice.

In sum, Rawls holds that theorizing about justice focuses on society's major economic, legal, political, and social institutions, that is, what he calls the basic structure of society. Because we both govern and are governed by the basic structure, we interact with and implicate people who we will never know and with whom we will never come into direct contact. For the institutions that make up the basic structure to be just, they must deliver on the substance of the principles of justice, promoting and protecting autonomy, equality, and reciprocity. By doing so, we work toward making the basic structure just; in turn, we ensure that we mitigate the potentially deleterious effects of the natural and social lotteries on people's lives, confronting the deep inequalities that permeate our social lives and providing the goods necessary for us to pursue our ends.

THE BASIC STRUCTURE AND GLOBAL JUSTICE

Like Catholic social teaching, it is important to note that Rawls's theory of justice is also ideal-normative,[28] with Rawls emphasizing—for the greater part of his career and in his philosophical corpus—justice *within* the nation-state. We do not have to think hard to identify deep inequalities in the interactions between the Global North and the Global South. These inequalities are especially salient because of the increasing economic, political, and social interdependence between the two. How might we draw from and extend the moral and philosophical insights of the Rawlsian basic structure argument to think about economic inequalities between states? Rawls himself repeatedly prioritized and emphasized justice within domestic basic structure (JF, 11), giving rise to the view that he was himself an anti-cosmopolitan.[29] Drawing inspiration from some Rawlsian thinkers, however, we will briefly sketch how we might confront the deep inequalities that exist between states.

In the non-ideal real world, Thomas Pogge notes, affluent people,

> consciously or unconsciously, try to get around [moral] norms by arranging their social world so as to minimize their burdens of

---

[28] Commenting on his aim in his *Theory of Justice*, Rawls writes: "What I have attempted to do is to generalize and carry out to a higher order of abstraction the traditional theory of social contact as represented by Locke, Rousseau, and Kant," TJ, xviii.

[29] Rawls's anti-cosmopolitanism is on display in his *The Law of Peoples*. On Rawls's anti-cosmopolitanism, see also Philip Pettit, "Rawls's Peoples," in *Rawls's* Law of Peoples: *A Realistic Utopia?*, ed. Rex Martin and David A. Reidy (Malden, MA: Wiley-Blackwell, 2006), 38–55.

compliance. Insofar as agents succeed in such norm avoidance, they can comply and still enjoy the advantages of their dominance. Such success, however, generally reduces not merely the costs and opportunity costs of moral norms for the strong, but also the protections these norms afford the weak.[30]

Because of their disadvantaged position—consequences of the natural and social lotteries and unjust economic, political, and social institutions—people who live under conditions of inequality are unable to defend themselves against those whose affluence enables them to uphold an unjust state-of-affairs. Thus, severe inequalities persist because they are self-reinforcing, with severely poor people living subject to a vicious cycle.

In contrast to those unjust and vicious people who actively try to benefit from a radically unequal state-of-affairs, morally conscientious and virtuous people seek to act justly, recognizing and acting in accord with what autonomy, equality, and reciprocity demand. Without the institutional oversight provided by the basic structure, major risks to the justness of society, whether domestic or global arise. While we may start from fair conditions, Rawls argues (PL, 266), over time the aggregation of our separate interactions, along with the effects of the natural and social lotteries, will make free and fair interactions within such a system impossible. Thus, as the site of justice, the basic structure's role is to secure the conditions against which our individual actions take place. Only through such regulation, Rawls holds, will fair and just conditions continue to obtain.

But in a society united together through civic friendship rather than bound together via justice,[31] would not the basic structure be unnecessary? "The fact that everyone with reason believes that they are acting fairly and scrupulously honoring the norms governing agreement," Rawls responds, "is not sufficient to preserve background justice" (PL, 267). On background justice, Rawls writes: "Individuals and associations cannot comprehend the ramifications of their particular actions viewed collectively, nor can they be expected to foresee future circumstances that shape and transform present tendencies" (PL, 268). Despite our best intentions, Rawls believes, our epistemic foresight is limited and our moral inclinations flawed. Thus, the basic structure is necessary, on his account, to secure the very conditions against which justice may be realized.

How might these insights be extended to the global arena? To be sure, there is no neat overlap between justice within a state and justice

---

[30] Pogge, *World Poverty and Human Rights*, 5.
[31] See, e.g., Aristotle, *Nicomachean Ethics*, trans. Terence Irwin (Indianapolis: Hackett, 1999), 1155a24.

between states. We nonetheless believe that Rawls's basic structure argument can be constructively developed to think about global justice. Instead of arguing for a basic structure similar to that found within the state, we will focus on what may be called an *institutional scheme*. Such a scheme includes the institutions that facilitate our interactions with and interdependence on one another across state borders, whether economically, politically, or socially.[32] Through these shared institutional interactions, we structure together, to varying degrees of extensity and intensity, our disparate lives. We can belong to an institutional scheme so long as we interact with others via shared institutions, which provide benefits for some and burdens for others.[33] In a globalized world, these interactions are usually mediated by supra- and trans-national institutions including, for example, multinational corporations.[34]

Important to note, on this Rawlsian view, is the fact that the demands for justice within an institutional scheme are not triggered merely by an awareness of another's existence; rather, they are triggered by participation in that scheme. Thus, an institutional account of justice does not stem from pre-institutional concerns about benevolence or fairness or (more problematically) sentimentality.[35] Instead, the fact that we interact with and are interdependent on one another requires that the terms of interaction be justifiable to the relevant parties; and for these terms to be justifiable requires that they honor autonomy, equality, and reciprocity. Moreover, focusing on an institutional scheme does not mean we rectify institutions for the sake of rectifying institutions; rather, we identify and improve on the just-making features of such institutions to ensure that the people who are

---

[32] See Thomas Pogge, *Realizing Rawls* (Ithaca: Cornell University Press, 1989), 8.

[33] Even those who attempt to extricate themselves from such institutional interactions, A. J. Julius notes, "help to enforce its policies, for example by paying taxes" ("Nagel's Atlas," *Philosophy and Public Affairs* 34, no. 2 [2006]: 185).

[34] For further discussion of supra- and trans-national institutions that mediate people's interactions see, e.g., Pogge, *World Poverty and Human Rights*, chaps. 8–9; Pogge, *Politics as Usual: What Lies Behind the Pro-Poor Rhetoric* (Cambridge: Polity, 2010), chaps. 3–5.

[35] On standard philosophical views, justice is an enforceable duty we have to others; for Rawlsians in particular, justice becomes an enforceable duty by virtue of the fact that we participate in and implicate one another via the basic structure. In contrast, simply appealing to something being the good or right thing to do, for example, does not tell us why that thing is good or right, who is responsible, and on what terms, especially with regard to economic, political, and social institutions. In other words, such appeals may become sentimental rather than enforceable, leaving them open to criticism from skeptics who do not believe we have widespread and enforceable duties of justice. On such skepticism, see Jan Narveson, "We Don't Owe Them a Thing!: A Tough-Minded but Soft-Hearted View of Aid to the Faraway Needy," *The Monist* 86, no. 3 (2003): 419–433.

part of such institutional schemes are recognized and respected as equal members of the moral and political communities.

Understanding justice in our globalized world holds that duties of justice obtain wherever people are participating members of an institutional scheme not delimited by national boundaries. For example, multinational corporations and regional trading blocs are institutions in which we participate that are not limited to one state. Duties of justice require us to deliberate and justify ourselves to one another when we are trying to formulate the principles that will govern our interactions, however narrowly or expansively, together. The justness and justifiability of these principles is especially important when the outcomes of the interactions they govern pervasively impact other people's material prospects, with "interdependence produc[ing] benefits and burdens." "The role of a principle of distributive justice," Charles Beitz thus observes, "would be to specify what a fair distribution of those benefits and burdens would be like."[36] Our interactions with one another are no longer limited to our local communities or nation-state; rather, through shared institutions, they extend to and throughout the global arena. For the Rawlsian, such interactions demand that we uphold autonomy, equality, and reciprocity.

CONCLUSION: THINKING TOGETHER CATHOLIC SOCIAL TEACHING AND RAWLS'S BASIC STRUCTURE

We have discussed subsidiarity and Rawls's basic structure, especially how institutions that make up either a subsidiary array or the basic structure address economic inequality. To our minds, there is significant overlap between Catholic social teaching and Rawlsian liberalism. Both begin from the inviolable dignity of the human person. Both regard institutions as critical for realizing justice in society. So, according to both, a given society's economic arrangements must be normatively assessed with regard to human dignity and the demands of justice. In light of this important consonance, in this concluding section, we will explore how Catholic social teaching might incorporate insights from Rawls's argument in a practical and synergistic way.

Popes from Paul VI to Francis have highlighted both the importance of global relations and the moral gravity of inequality; moreover, in *Caritas in Veritate*, Benedict XVI indicates that there is a need for a "deeper critical evaluation of the category of relation" in the global context. In these exhortations, subsidiarity is a critical component. Despite these developments, as noted above, the Catholic

---

[36] Charles Beitz, *Political Theory and International Relations*, rev. ed. (Princeton: Princeton University Press, 1999), 152.

Church's social magisterium has thus far not provided significant guidance about institutional and individual morality in light of global interdependence. If Catholic social teaching is to move beyond general exhortations to normatively efficacious accounts of solidarity and mutuality, then Catholic social teaching about subsidiarity would benefit from dialogue with Rawlsian basic structural thinking in the following ways.

First, the basic structure argument would fortify Catholic social teaching against the charge of sentimentalism in exhorting affluent people to send *subsidium* to severely poor people. Because participation in the basic structure implicates the affluent and the poor, the near and the far, the terms according to which participants interact must be justifiable to all the relevant parties. For example, on what terms may rich people be taxed (i.e., provide the all-purpose means for the flourishing of all)? To what extent are they entitled to provide for their own material well-being (i.e., pursue their own vision of the good)? By the same token, the dignity of those being helped requires that they interact on terms that recognize them as free and equal. That is to say, if people do not work to counteract rejected inequalities, then they are not acting on terms that are interpersonally justifiable.[37] Thus, the provision of material aid must accompany a willingness to acknowledge that it is a means to flourishing and not flourishing in and of itself. Though magisterial teaching refrains from prescribing detailed action, exhortations to all persons of good will to fulfill their duties to poor people will always stand in need of justification. Rawls's argument for the basic structure in a society provides a justification that is un-sentimental. It is also consonant with the foundations of Catholic social teaching: scripture and natural law. Though the natural law tradition will raise questions about what a Rawlsian means by the "autonomy," "equality," and "reciprocity" protected by a society's basic structure, we view this dialogue about key terms as essential to the task of performing Benedict's evaluation of relations in our globally interdependent society.

Second, this dialogue between Rawlsian basic structure thinking and Catholic social teaching would provide both Catholic social teaching and liberal theorists with nuance regarding the role of institutions in forging together disparate people and nations into a global society. While it is an open question whether we truly live in Singer's one world,[38] we are now more than ever globally interdependent. Despite this interdependence, the inequality between the Global North and South is now the greatest observed in post-

---

[37] See A. J. Julius, "Basic Structure and the Value of Equality," *Philosophy and Public Affairs* 31, no. 4 (2003): 322.
[38] See Singer, *One World*.

colonial times. If we do in fact live in one world, it is a single world suffering from a lack of authentic mutuality, where we are not neighbors to one another, but strangers. What is the role of institutions, then, in remedying such a situation? While there are increasing exhortations about global relations, papal recommendations currently suffer from a lack of content. But this is not an issue for Catholic social teaching alone. Thomas Nagel, for example, believes that while questions concerning domestic politics are well understood, those concerning international politics are not.[39] Given that the role of the nation-state continues to evolve in an unfamiliar context, the present dialogue provides us with ways to assess why a global authority remains difficult to conceive and what that difficulty means for more localized work toward achieving justice and equality.

Third, basic structural thinking can be extended to give an account of why and how it matters that we participate in globally interconnected institutional schemes. In other words, Catholic social teaching need not wait to work out what a global authority might look like. Catholic social teaching can and must speak normatively about what just participation in global institutional schemes really looks like.[40] This is an ideal complement to the magisterial teaching on subsidiarity. Though the principle of subsidiarity was refined in a more national context, the social, political, and economic issues prompting magisterial intervention were issues of participation, authority, and competence. In short, they were issues of coercion and how to justify it.[41] Rawlsian arguments about the basic structure, participation, and justification can help Catholic social teaching articulate a defense of the human person in a context where billions of people are coerced unjustifiably.[42]

Neither Catholic social teaching nor Rawlsian liberalism is immune from the contemporary challenge of thinking carefully about the evolving structures and implications of globalization. The ongoing

---

[39] See Thomas Nagel, "The Problem of Global Justice," *Philosophy and Public Affairs* 33, no. 2 (2005): 113–147.

[40] One might interpret the difference between Benedict XVI and Francis's social magisteria in this way. In *Caritas in Veritate*, Benedict speculates about global institutional authority. In *Laudato Si'*, Francis speculates about participation in unjust schemes.

[41] In Leo XIII's social magisterium alone, the issues of matrimony and education are two examples. On matrimony, see *Arcanum* (1880); on education, see *Spectata Fides* (1885).

[42] *Coercion* is commonly understood as getting someone to do something against their own will, for example, threatening someone's life unless they hand over their wallet. On this understanding, coercion is unjust: we do not have a legitimate claim upon someone to do something or refrain from doing something else. Coercion can be just and therefore legitimate, for example, in democratic societies where the state imposes and upholds laws that regulate our individual and communal behavior.

impasse between cosmopolitanism, on the one side, and nationalism and localism, on the other, is sufficient evidence that the task of understanding human community, duty, and obligation is in no way complete. Both Catholic social teaching and Rawlsian liberalism provide resources for thinking of community, duty, and obligation in a global context. These resources must continue to be honed against the reality of our current context. In the spirit of friendship and solidarity, we have endeavored here to start a conversation toward this end.[43]

Jason A. Heron is S. Wilma Lyle Assistant Professor of Theology at Mount Marty University. His research interests include Catholic social teaching, modern economic thought, social theory, and virtue ethics. His articles have appeared in the *Journal of Moral Theology*, the *Journal of Religious Ethics*, *New Blackfriars*, and *Nova et Vetera*.

Bharat Ranganathan is Brooks Professor of Social Justice and Religion at the University of Nebraska at Omaha and Clinical Ethics Fellow at the MacLean Center for Clinical Medical Ethics at the University of Chicago. His research and teaching interests include religious ethics, philosophy of religion, and theology.

---

[43] We presented an earlier version of this essay at New Wine, New Wineskins (2018). Thanks to our colleagues for their comments on that occasion. Further thanks to Dallas Gingles, Jamie Pitts, Alessandro Rovati, Gordon Warren, Matthew Whelan, and two anonymous reviewers for their helpful criticisms.

A Good Moral Teacher Must Be a Good Pre-Moral Teacher: On the Pedagogical Limits of US Constitutional Law

Justin Menno

IN HER 2012 BOOK *LAW'S VIRTUES*, Cathleen Kaveny outlines a new framework for wise lawmaking on contentious "life issues" through her model of "law as moral teacher." Kaveny proposes this framework in order to overcome the limits of two dominant and opposing models of law in the US. The first model, the "firewall model," attempts to settle fraught "life issues" like abortion and euthanasia through imposing a morally neutral permissiveness toward each in law.[1] The second, the "enforcement model," attempts to do the same, but through imposing a morally absolute prohibition of each in law. Kaveny criticizes the first for giving "too little weight to the socially important message of law."[2] She faults the second for viewing "the moral message as the only relevant factor."[3] In contrast, Kaveny promotes her "third way" as neither indifferent to nor idealistic about the moral message of law. In fact, she argues that her "law as moral teacher" model is "at once optimistic about the effectiveness of moral pedagogy without being utopian, and realistic about moral disagreement without being relativistic."[4]

In support of her argument, Kaveny claims that her model is able to harmonize better what she calls the dual "legal virtues" of autonomy and solidarity in pluralistic liberal democracies like the US. These two virtues are not simply two among many. In fact, Kaveny asserts that they are the "overarching" virtues of law and social life in the US.[5] Given the pluralistic character of US moral traditions, she states that the virtues of autonomy and solidarity stand out not only for their

---

[1] Cathleen Kaveny, *Law's Virtues: Fostering Autonomy and Solidarity in American Society* (Washington, DC: Georgetown University Press, 2012), 1. The phrase "life issues" is Kaveny's. This phrase, in principle, is expansive. For the purposes of her book, Kaveny uses it primarily in reference to euthanasia and most especially to abortion. In what follows, I use the phrase "life issues" in much the same way.
[2] Kaveny, *Law's Virtues*, 1.
[3] Kaveny, *Law's Virtues*, 1.
[4] Kaveny, *Law's Virtues*, 2.
[5] Kaveny, *Law's Virtues*, 7.

broad-based appeal, but also their apparent ability to promote individual and communal flourishing. To justify the selection of each virtue, Kaveny appeals to two primary sources. The first is Aquinas's treatment of general justice, the second is Alasdair MacIntyre's application of practical reason to political communities.[6] Going further still, Kaveny then roots the content of each legal virtue in the work of two other sources. Specifically, she conceives autonomy as a "configuration" of the virtue of prudence according to the work of legal philosopher Joseph Raz,[7] and formulates solidarity as an extension of the virtue of justice according to the work of John Paul II.

With these important preliminaries in place, Kaveny then applies her model to various forms of American law. Importantly, in the context of US constitutional law, she evaluates two sets of constitutional cases on distinct "life issues" to see whether each adequately teaches the virtue of solidarity. In the first set of abortion-related cases, Kaveny argues that *Roe* (1973) and *Casey* (1989) each pay insufficient attention to the dependency and vulnerability of all human beings.[8] They largely underemphasize, if not outright ignore, the virtue of solidarity.[9] However, in the second set of euthanasia-related cases, Kaveny argues that *Glucksberg* (1997) and *Quill* (1997) better balance the legal virtues of autonomy and solidarity.[10] In contrast to the former cases, she claims that these latter ones better emphasize the protection of the vulnerable, the constitutional value of federalism, and judicial deference to legislators in hard cases.[11]

Like Kaveny, I agree that the Supreme Court's reasoning in *Glucksberg* and *Quill* is more adequate morally and jurisprudentially than in *Roe* and *Casey*. I also agree that Kaveny's "law as moral teacher" framework is more adequate morally and jurisprudentially than the "firewall" or "enforcement" models. Nonetheless, I do not think that the solidarity prong of Kaveny's framework can be adequately applied to US constitutional law for historical, internal, and

---

[6] See Kaveny, *Law's Virtues*, 28–33, 50–52. Kaveny principally draws on Aquinas' "Treatise on Law" in *Summa Theologiae* (ST) I-II qq. 90–108, and MacIntyre's discussion of practical reason in *Whose Justice? Which Rationality?* (Notre Dame, IN: University of Notre Dame Press, 1988).
[7] Kaveny summarizes Raz's conception of autonomy as "the capacity to be the 'part-author' of one's own life by making a successive series of choices that forge a more or less coherent narrative" (*Law's Virtues*, 53).
[8] *Roe v. Wade*, 410 US 113 (1973), *Planned Parenthood v. Casey*, 505 US 833, 846 (1989).
[9] Kaveny, *Law's Virtues*, 75–76.
[10] *Washington v. Glucksberg*, 521 US 702 (1997), *Vacco v. Quill* 521 US 793 (1997).
[11] Kaveny, *Law's Virtues*, 163–164.

formal reasons.[12] To be clear, I do not take issue with the application of this prong to US federal law,[13] nor do I take issue with its application to state law, tort law, family law, or any other type of law.

To understand why, it is important to turn to some of the formal presuppositions of the virtue of solidarity, especially as these relate to the union and distinction of interpersonal encounters. In John Paul II's thought, the virtue of solidarity unites symmetrical *and* asymmetrical interpersonal encounters. That is, it preserves the distinct notions of encounter between equal agents *and* unequal agents. In contrast, US constitutional law has not exhibited the same capacity to unite these two types of encounters. In fact, given its contractarian anthropological presuppositions, US constitutional law has tended to interpret all interpersonal encounters through the controlling ideal of symmetrical or equally agential encounters.[14] Consequently, it has tended to subsume asymmetrical or unequally agential encounters under this ideal. In light of this tendency, I argue that US constitutional law cannot adequately internalize or inculcate the virtue of solidarity. Building on this argument, I further claim that, given its apparent presuppositions, US constitutional law cannot competently address the asymmetrical encounters specific to contentious "life issues" like abortion.

Before going any further, I want to clarify my use of the term

---

[12] Formally, US constitutional law is concerned with the right ordering and relation of the three co-equal branches of the US government: executive, judicial, and legislative. This is what makes US constitutional law the type of law that it is. Inasmuch as the structure of the US Constitution applies to all articles and amendments, I suggest that there is a distinct tendency in US constitutional law to see legal encounters among persons or branches of government as symmetrical encounters of equals. In what follows, I will say more about how this tendency has played out in the historical and formal presuppositions of US constitutional law.

[13] Materially, US federal law primarily concerns Acts of Congress. But it likewise includes Senate treaties, regulations issued from the executive branch, and case law from the federal judiciary. Nonetheless, unlike US constitutional law, it is not formally structured according to the right ordering and relation of the three co-equal branches of the US government. In principle, it is open to legal encounters between equal and unequal agents.

[14] This statement certainly does not settle the issue of the anthropological presuppositions of US constitutional law. I think there are *at least* four positions one can take on the issue: 1) US constitutional law has an empty anthropology, such that there is no original or internal priority for symmetrical encounters; 2) it has a malleable anthropology, such that even if it had an original priority for symmetrical encounters, subsequent judicial decisions or amendments can revise it at will; 3) it has an original, but not controlling contractarian anthropology, such that it remains congenial to the inclusion of asymmetrical encounters in its formality; 4) it has an original and controlling contractarian anthropology, such that it remains relatively uncongenial to the inclusion of asymmetrical encounters in its formality. I subscribe to the final position, and I explain why in the first two sections of this article.

competency in the context of law. In her 2018 book *Ethics at the Edges of Law*, Kaveny addresses the issue of competency in making judgments, especially in law. Drawing on the work of Jeffrey Stout, Kaveny characterizes competent judges as those who "are able to appreciate excellent instantiations of the goods internal to their respective practices."[15] She further elaborates that one "becomes a competent judge by demonstrating one's ability to make assessments in cases that are increasingly difficult, but that have a clear resolution according to the standards of the practice."[16] I think Kaveny's description provides a succinct practical understanding of the issue of competency in making judgments, especially in law. In examining this same issue, I draw primarily on Aquinas' treatment of the subject. For Aquinas, competency in making legal judgments principally refers to 1) formal notions 2) inherent to specific forms of human law, 3) whose basis rests properly "in" the minds of the law's authors.[17] In contrast to Kaveny then, in assessing the issue of competency in making legal judgments, I focus more on the *formal presuppositions* of competency in law rather than its *functional effects*. In Thomistic terms, I focus more on the measuring-measure (*mensura-mensurans*) of law itself rather than the measured-measure (*mensura-mensurata*) of the human mind making judgments about it.[18] In this regard, I emphasize that US constitutional law can only competently give or teach to what is outside itself notions internal to itself.

In what follows, I plan to unfold my argument in five parts in critical and constructive engagement with Kaveny's work. First, I will survey the historical and internal presence of contractarian anthropological presuppositions in US constitutional law. Second, using James Mumford's work, I will examine how these presuppositions limit the recognition of asymmetrical interpersonal encounters, especially in cases of contentious "life issues." Third, I will summarize the union of symmetrical and asymmetrical interpersonal encounters in John Paul II's thought on the virtue of solidarity. Fourth, I will trace the major lines of Aquinas' thought on competency in making legal judgments. Finally, in sketching two approaches to address better legal protections for the most vulnerable, I will outline how the principle of subsidiarity can not only supplement but strengthen Kaveny's framework for wise lawmaking.

---

[15] Cathleen Kaveny, *Ethics at the Edges of Law: Christian Moralists and American Legal Thought* (New York: Oxford University Press, 2018), 76.
[16] Kaveny, *Ethics at the Edges of Law*, 76.
[17] See especially ST II-II q. 60.
[18] For more on this distinction, see ST I-II q. 93, a. 1, ad. 3, and I-II q. 93, a. 4.

THE EMERGENT IDEAL OF SYMMETRICAL ENCOUNTERS IN US CONSTITUTIONAL LAW

Historians have long recognized the presence of social contractarian presuppositions in the US Constitution and constitutional law.[19] In *The Social Contract in America*, Mark Hulliung documents how seventeenth century political philosopher John Locke's social contract theory played a decisive role in shaping the US Constitution.[20] Hulliung details how Locke's theory, laid out in his *Second Treatise on Government*, influenced notable framers like Alexander Hamilton, Thomas Jefferson, and James Madison. Additionally, he makes clear that Locke's theory did not just influence the early American elite. In fact, he notes that, in the immediate pre-Revolutionary period, Locke's theory was so revered that "Loyalists sometimes plotted to steal the *Second Treatise* from the rebels."[21] Turning to other social contract theories debated in pre-Revolutionary America, Hulliung highlights the distinctive content of Locke's theory. In so doing, he emphasizes at least three important contrasts between Samuel Pufendorf's and Locke's theory. First, he notes that Locke bases his theory on the "natural asociability" of human beings in the state of nature.[22] Second, in light of this "natural" independence, he writes that Locke maintains that government arises through ongoing acts of consent of, by, and for the people.[23] Finally, in light of the primacy of these acts, and these acts *alone*, he summarizes that Locke presents the social contract as a "revocable trust," and not as an "irreversible contract of submission."[24] For Locke, then, through acts of symmetrical interpersonal consent, the people put the government on a type of "permanent probation."[25]

Legal scholars have similarly recognized the presence of social contractarian presuppositions in US constitutional law.[26] Michael

---

[19] Bernard Bailyn, *The Ideological Origins of the American Revolution*, fiftieth anniversary edition (Cambridge, MA: Belknap, 2017), 58–59; Gordon Wood, *The Creation of the American Republic, 1776–1787* (Chapel Hill, NC: The University of North Carolina Press, 1969), 282–291; Steven Dworetz, *The Unvarnished Doctrine: Locke, Liberalism, and the American Revolution* (Durham, NC: Duke University Press, 1994); Thad W. Tate, "The Social Contract in America, 1774–1787: Revolutionary Theory as a Conservative Instrument," *William and Mary Quarterly* (1965): 375–391.

[20] Mark Hulliung, *The Social Contract in America: From the Revolution to the Present Age* (Lawrence, KS: University of Kansas Press, 2007).

[21] Hulliung, *The Social Contract in America*, 18.

[22] Hulliung, *The Social Contract in America*, 20.

[23] Hulliung, *The Social Contract in America*, 35.

[24] Hulliung, *The Social Contract in America*, 18.

[25] Hulliung, *The Social Contract in America*, 35.

[26] See David A. J. Richards, *Toleration and the Constitution* (New York: Oxford University Press, 1986); Richard B. Stewart, "The Reformation of American

Dorf, for example, affirms that "social contractarian political theory" has "deep roots in American legal thought,"[27] and draws attention to a variety of court decisions in support.[28] Anita Allen likewise argues that "social contractarian thought" has played a significant role in American case law.[29] Going further than Dorf, she cites at least two dozen other court cases throughout the history of US constitutional law to shore up her argument.[30] Additionally, Richard Garnett echoes the respective judgments of Dorf and Allen in his own examination of the influence of social contractarianism in US constitutional law.[31] Unlike Dorf and Allen, he focuses much more on the influence of its anthropological presuppositions. Garnett notes that, in social contractarian thought, the human person is conceived as originally "un-tethered, un-situated, and alone."[32] He finds this vision "flawed" for a number of reasons. Yet despite its flaws, Garnett concedes that US constitutional law historically rests upon this "unsteady foundation."[33]

Finally, in his recent book *What It Means to Be Human*, O. Carter Snead has gone further than any other legal scholar in describing the characteristics and implications of this very foundation. In this work, Snead evaluates the "anthropological frame" underlying much of American law, and US constitutional law in particular, on "vital conflicts" like abortion.[34] He calls this frame "expressive individualism," and then elaborates at length on how it has advanced a significantly attenuated vision of human identity and flourishing. Like the legal scholars above, Snead traces "expressive individualism"

Administrative Law," *Harvard Law Review* 88 (1975): 1667, 1718; Gerald L. Neuman, "Whose Constitution?" *Yale Law Journal* 100 (1991): 909, 923–927.

[27] Michael Dorf, "Integrating Normative and Descriptive Constitutional Theory: The Case of Original Meaning," *Georgetown Law Journal* 85 (1997): 1774.

[28] Dorf, "Integrating Normative and Descriptive Constitutional Theory," 1774, footnote 41. For Dorf, these decisions include, but are not limited to *Chisholm v. Georgia*, 2 US (2 Dall.) 419 (1793); *Calder v. Bull*, 3 US (3 Dall.) 386 (1798); *United States v. Verdugo-Urquidez*, 494 US 259 (1990).

[29] Anita Allen, "Social Contract Theory in American Case Law," *Florida Law Review* 51 (January 1999): 2–40.

[30] Some of the cases she cites deal with sovereignty: *Kawanakoa v. Polybank*, 205 US 349 (1907); Congressional non-delegation: *Bank One Chicago v. Midwest Bank & Trust Co.*, 516 US 264 (1996); Public health: *Jacobson v. Massachusetts*, 197 US 11 (1905); Civil forfeiture: *United States v. 785 St. Nicholas Ave.*, 983 F.2d 396 (2d Cir. 1993). For a more complete list, see Allen, "Social Contract Theory in American Case Law," 6–9, n. 17–40.

[31] Richard Garnett, "Christian Witness, Moral Anthropology, and the Death Penalty," *Notre Dame Journal of Law, Ethics and Public Policy* 541 (2003): 541–558.

[32] Garnett, "Christian Witness," 555.

[33] Garnett, "Christian Witness," 555.

[34] O. Carter Snead, *What It Means to Be Human: The Case for the Body in Public Bioethics* (Cambridge, MA: Harvard University Press, 2020), 5.

to the thought of social contract theorists like Locke.[35] Similarly, he notes that, like social contractarianism, "expressive individualism" characterizes human identity and flourishing as fundamentally transactional. In such a frame, Snead writes that human relationships are reduced to "agreements, promises, and consent for the mutual benefit of the parties involved."[36] Likewise, he asserts that human encounters are reduced to the binary option of "collaborative or contending wills, pursuing their own individual goals."[37] Shriveled as this frame is, Snead nonetheless acknowledges that it underwrites much of American law on "vital conflicts," and most especially in constitutional jurisprudence on abortion law.[38]

In her own work, Kaveny seems to suggest that social contractarian presuppositions inform the origins of US constitutional law. In her 2016 book *Prophecy without Contempt*, Kaveny examines the interchangeable uses of "covenant" and "contract" in early Puritan New England.[39] She charts how the meaning of these two terms developed culturally and legally. In particular, she comments on how the shift from a more theological to a more natural rights-based framework influenced the meaning of these two terms. Quoting seventeenth century preacher George Walker, she notes that a contract was conventionally understood in Puritan New England to involve "a mutual promise, bargain, and obligation between two parties."[40]

In Kaveny's account, the growing legal use of contracts in seventeenth-century Puritan New England can be considered important for at least two reasons. First, it seemed to inform and even re-interpret the theological notion of covenant. Kaveny notes that, through the analogy of the common law of contracts, the notion of

---

[35] Snead, *What It Means to Be Human*, 74–75, 90.
[36] Snead, *What It Means to Be Human*, 6.
[37] Snead, *What It Means to Be Human*, 6.
[38] In his section on the "Anthropology of American Abortion Law," Snead states that this area of law "proceeds from the assumption that the core unit of reality is the atomized and isolated self, lacking any unchosen constitutive attachments, along with the obligations and benefits that might flow from them." Thus, it "reduces the person to a lonely agent of desire, defined by the will and the capacity to make choices, whose highest thriving is self-definition and the pursuit of economic and social aspirations" (*What It Means to Be Human*, 168). Despite this deficient assumption, Snead nonetheless argues that US constitutional law can be reformed through the integration of what he calls a more adequate "anthropology of embodiment." In section five below, I outline my agreement with Snead on the goal of US constitutional law recognizing the greater adequacy of this "anthropology of embodiment." In the same section, I acknowledge my disagreement with Snead on the means to achieve this goal.
[39] Cathleen Kaveny, *Prophecy without Contempt: Religious Discourse in the Public Square* (Cambridge, MA: Harvard University Press, 2016): 135–235.
[40] Kaveny, *Prophecy without Contempt*, 169, quoting George Walker, *The Manifold Wisdom of God* (London: Hodgkinson, 1641), 39.

God's covenant came to be reconceived as God's free entry into agreement with humanity, albeit in such a way as to bind, but not compromise his sovereignty.[41] Second, it seemed to promote a new ideal of interpersonal encounter. Regardless of inequalities in other areas, Kaveny remarks that increasingly "in the realm of bargained-for-exchange" even "the prince and pauper could meet as equals."[42] Thus, through the growing legal use of contracts in Puritan New England, these two developments seemed to advance a symmetrical ideal of interpersonal encounter.

The re-conception of contracts and covenants in terms of this symmetrical ideal was no doubt a significant intellectual and historical development. But in an important caveat, Kaveny acknowledges that, even though this re-conception presented the two parties in a contract as *theoretically symmetrical*, it did not necessarily presume them to be *naturally symmetrical*. In fact, Kaveny notes that, in English common law, the legal notion of a contract or covenant was "unique in its capacity to accommodate a negotiated relationship between vastly unequal parties."[43] Nonetheless, over the course of the eighteenth century, the idea of a natural asymmetry in covenantal or contractual relations seemed to fade in accounts of interpersonal encounter. In Kaveny's account, the waning of this idea seemed to involve three distinct developments. First, in the seventeenth-century, covenantal relations between God and human beings were increasingly characterized in Puritan preaching in "transactional images."[44] Second, throughout the eighteenth century, these relations were increasingly subordinated in Puritan New England to the transactional interests of commerce.[45] Third, by the Revolutionary era these relations were effectively displaced in American political life through "the Lockean framework of natural rights and the social contract made in the state of nature."[46] Kaveny does not explicitly discuss how this final development impacted the drafting of the US Constitution. Given

---

[41] Kaveny elaborates that "God's sovereignty was protected by the federal theologians' claim that He had voluntarily entered into this pact. God's essential unknowability was safeguarded by their insistence that the covenant did not describe God's internal life but only His freely chosen pattern of behavior toward humanity" (*Prophecy without Contempt*, 138–139).

[42] Kaveny, *Prophecy without Contempt*, 137.

[43] Kaveny, *Prophecy without Contempt*, 135.

[44] Kaveny, *Prophecy without Contempt*, 168.

[45] Kaveny, *Prophecy without Contempt*, 179, 202–203. In concert with this growing focus on commerce in the eighteenth century, Perry Miller claims that "covenant theology, having conceived and cradled the principle of voluntary consent, set the New England mind at work destroying that theology" (*The New England Mind: From Colony to Province* [Cambridge, MA: Belknap, 1953]: 267), quoted in Kaveny, *Prophecy without Contempt*, 202.

[46] Kaveny, *Prophecy without Contempt*, 222.

the thrust of her account and the work of the scholars like Hulliung mentioned above, it seems fair to suggest that the emergent ideal of symmetrical interpersonal encounter likely informed it.

THE PRE-MORAL LIMITS OF THE IDEAL OF SYMMETRICAL ENCOUNTER

No one has examined the ethical implications of theories of interpersonal encounter more than James Mumford. In his 2013 book *Ethics at the Beginning of Life*, Mumford evaluates the influence of two major theories of interpersonal encounter in ethics, medicine, and law. In particular, he assesses how each theory has informed these areas, especially in debates about beginning-of-life ethics. Mumford calls the first major theory of authentic interpersonal encounter the "contractarian" model and the second the "empathetic" model. He traces the first to the work of Locke in his seminal *Second Treatise* on government.[47] He attributes the second to the work of twentieth century dialogical philosopher Martin Buber in his influential "I-Thou" and "I-It" schema of interpersonal encounter.[48]

Though different in origin, Mumford claims that both models tend to idealize symmetrical interpersonal encounters in ethical reflection. He notes that the "contractarian" model regards interpersonal encounters as authentic so long as they are mutually arranged and equally willed. He likewise remarks that the "empathetic" model regards the same as authentic so long as they are mutually open, reciprocal, and suffused with rich emotion and inter-subjectivity. Each model then judges interpersonal encounters as authentic *if and only if* they are symmetrical, voluntary, foreseen, and highly agential. Encounters falling short of these characteristics are not only deemed inauthentic, but sub-personal and even sub-human. In Buber's schema, they belong to the I-It polarity. In Mumford's account, the limits of each model of interpersonal encounter are important for at least three reasons.

First, it seems that the two models above have not only proposed symmetrical encounters as ideal, but have become entrenched as a controlling ideal in much of legal and ethical thought, especially on contentious "life issues." In the "contractarian" model, Mumford notes that the prioritizing of symmetrical encounters has made the status of fully-fledged agents normative for all other encounters.[49]

---

[47] James Mumford, *Ethics at the Beginning of Life: A Phenomenological Critique* (Oxford: Oxford University Press, 2013), 82–90.
[48] Mumford, *Ethics at the Beginning of Life*, 31–42.
[49] In his critique of the "anthropological frame" of expressive individualism, Snead seems to find this same norm operative in much of American law. Key to this frame

That is, it has set forth the arranged encounter of two equal agents as the measure for all encounters. In this transactional model, symmetry obtains inasmuch as both agents mirror each other in their distinct capacities of willing, deliberating, and promising. Similarly, in the "empathetic" model, Mumford notes that the equivalent prioritizing of symmetrical encounters has accomplished much the same. He elaborates that it has put forth the inter-subjective encounter of two mutually-awakened agents as the norm for all encounters. In light of these two models and their near-identical measures, it is no surprise that encounters between unequally-capacitated agents have been accorded lower status in much of legal and ethical thought, especially on contentious "life issues."

Kaveny seems to agree with the thrust of Mumford's first point. In her criticism of *Roe*, she asserts that the Court's lack of emphasis on positive obligations toward unequally-capacitated subjects like pre-natal children is no mere "legal anomaly."[50] In fact, she claims that *Roe* is the "logical end" of "those strands of American law that content themselves with negative prohibitions that suffice for those in the full vigor of life."[51] Kaveny makes clear that the lack of positive obligations toward the weak and vulnerable in American law is a serious deficiency. In response, she proposes the inclusion of a compensating "vulnerable person" standard in US law.[52] Kaveny argues that this standard would not only better address current inequities in US law, but would provide a more comprehensive standard for acting. She concludes that the inclusion of a "vulnerable person" standard would pave the way toward evaluating how "solidarity should be legally instantiated" in the US.[53]

I do not dispute that a "vulnerable person" standard can be included in areas of law like US federal and state law. I am skeptical that it can be included in US constitutional law without distortion to the concept of vulnerability and the necessary relations of dependence and non-reciprocal care inherent to it. Inasmuch as constitutional law seems to

---

is an "image of the human person" "fully formed" and "at the height of his cognitive powers" (*What It Means to Be Human*, 90).
[50] Kaveny, *Law's Virtues*, 79.
[51] Kaveny, *Law's Virtues*, 79.
[52] Kaveny, *Law's Virtues*, 80–81. In line with her effort to build bridges between American legal theory and the Catholic moral tradition, Kaveny appeals to the respective work of Alasdair MacIntyre and Martha Albertson Fineman on the status of vulnerable persons. Though each differs substantively on contentious "life issues," they both share a commitment to advancing something like a "vulnerable person" standard in political communities. See MacIntyre, *Dependent Rational Animals* (Chicago: Open Court, 1999): 73–74 and Fineman, "The Vulnerable Subject: Anchoring Equality in the Human Condition," *Yale Journal of Law and Feminism*, no. 1 (2008): 1–23.
[53] Kaveny, *Law's Virtues*, 80.

admit contractarian presuppositions, it seems to suppose a derivative controlling ideal of symmetrical interpersonal encounter between independent, fully-fledged agents. Inasmuch as this is the case, it seems to be internally uncongenial to standards of encounter between those who are unequally-capacitated either temporarily or permanently.[54]

Second, it seems that the controlling ideal of symmetrical encounters has fostered a restricted vision of human encounter in much of ethical and legal thought, especially on contentious "life issues." Mumford argues that this ideal has served to obscure the actual "working of things" in the vast and varied range of human encounters.[55] In other words, he argues that this ideal is not only theoretically insufficient, but descriptively inadequate. The contractarian and empathetic models are each attuned to see human encounters in the full vitality of mature adult life. Like those who are at once far- and near-sighted, they are each limited in seeing less than fully-capacitated agents at the edges of life. Moreover, as these models

---

[54] In her discussion of vulnerability and its application to American law, Kaveny draws on Alasdair MacIntyre's critique in *Dependent Rational Animals* of the normative view of human persons as "autonomous, independent," and "self-contained" (*Law's Virtues*, 79–80). In his own discussion of the same, Snead draws even more so on MacIntyre's critique. Specifically, in his appraisal of the anthropological frame of expressive individualism, Snead indicts it for failing "to respond to the reality of embodied human lives regarding their mutual dependence, integrated constitutive goods and histories, and shared unchosen obligations to one another." In response, Snead seeks to correct this frame through the inclusion of a more thoroughgoing "anthropology of embodiment" in American law. Drawing on MacIntyre, he states that in such an anthropology "the virtues of acknowledged dependence" like generosity, hospitality, and misericordia can be better cultivated and practiced. He concludes that one thereby becomes "capable of the relationships of giving and receiving that characterize human flourishing" (*What It Means to Be Human*, 94, 99). In their own ways, Kaveny and Snead seem to suggest that the implied anthropology of US constitutional law can be enlarged and reformed through greater attention to human vulnerability. Nonetheless, given the apparent formal contractarian lens of US constitutional law, I think it less likely that this implied anthropology is enlarged through such attention, and more likely that the full reality of human vulnerability is once again obscured from view through being re-interpreted along the lines of symmetrical encounter. In section five, using the principle of subsidiarity, I propose that the resolution of contentious "life issues" in American law might be better addressed through delegating such issues to those areas of law more internally congenial to the recognition of symmetrical and asymmetrical encounters like statutory and family law.

[55] Mumford, *Ethics at the Beginning of Life*, 80. Snead seems to endorse this point in his analysis of the Supreme Court's abortion law jurisprudence. There he states that "the anthropological assumptions of the Court obscure from view the networks of relationships in which the parties are embedded—relationships of family (including, but not limited to maternal-fetal biological kinship), community, and polity—that could and should be responsive to the basic needs that arise from unwanted or unplanned pregnancy" (*What It Means to Be Human*, 169).

control the vision of much ethical and legal thought on contentious "life issues," they in turn control its application to considerations of who is and who is not subject to ethical and legal concerns. In sum then, paraphrasing Wittgenstein, Mumford claims that much of ethical and legal thought is held "captive" to a picture that prevents it from seeing what it ought to see.[56]

In *Ethics at the Edges of Law*, Kaveny seems to agree with the thrust of Mumford's second point. In fact, like Mumford, she explicitly endorses Wittgenstein's warning against distorted pictures in the context of legal and ethical thought. Using what she calls "Wittgensteinian therapy," Kaveny cautions against intellectual impediments to seeing the world as it is, especially "in hard cases" in law.[57] Quoting Stout, she affirms that considerations of these cases should "direct our attention away from our subjective states to how things and persons are in the world."[58] They should direct our attention to "how things and persons would be if we revised our norms."[59] I agree that those making judgments in law can and should revise their norms and pictures to better fit the world. I am not convinced that forms of law like US constitutional law can always do the same. Given the apparent contractarian presuppositions of US constitutional law, it seems like this form of law is held relatively captive to a picture of symmetrical interpersonal encounter.

In the ethical and legal realm, nowhere do the limits of this "picture" seem more evident than in its application to human emergence. Mumford asserts that, in the "extraordinary encounter" between a mother and what he calls her "newone," the contractarian and empathetic models of human encounter each cannot see the prenatal child as he or she really is.[60] To justify this point, he notes that the transparency of agents appearing to each other is a key threshold condition of each model. This very condition is lacking in pregnancy, inasmuch as the relative "hiddenness" of the newone is an essential feature.[61] Turning to the work of Luce Irigaray and Iris Marion Young, Mumford notes that in pregnancy "the newone is hidden from the world and from the mother" at the same time.[62] In fact, the newone

---

[56] Mumford, *Ethics at the Beginning of Life*, 79.
[57] Kaveny, *Ethics at the Edges of Law*, 75.
[58] Kaveny, *Ethics at the Edges of Law*, 75, quoting Jeffrey Stout, *Democracy and Tradition* (Princeton, NJ: Princeton University Press, 2004), 276.
[59] Kaveny, *Ethics at the Edges of Law*, 75, quoting Stout, *Democracy and Tradition*, 276.
[60] Mumford, *Ethics at the Beginning of Life*, 69.
[61] Mumford, *Ethics at the Beginning of Life*, 25–26, 72.
[62] Mumford, *Ethics at the Beginning of Life*, 25. In discussing the essential "hiddenness" of the newone from the mother and the world, Mumford draws on Luce Irigaray's book *Sharing the World* (London: Continuum, 2008) and Iris Marion

remains especially hidden to the mother with whom he or she has a "privileged relation."[63] It is only over time that the newone becomes more apparent to his or her mother. Even then the newone does so only in degrees. In the "extraordinary encounter" in pregnancy, transparency is not so much an instantaneous condition from the very start as the relative fruit of an ongoing relationship. Thus, to make the transparency of agents appearing to each other a controlling norm for pregnancy seems like a category mistake.

Nonetheless, it seems that the Supreme Court still relies, more or less, on the threshold conditions of symmetry, transparency, and reciprocity in its approach to abortion-related cases. To cite but one example, in *Box v. Planned Parenthood* (2019), Justice Ginsburg seems to have relied on these very conditions in her recent dissent.[64] For the most part, Ginsburg discusses what legal standard to apply in this case. She argues against the majority's use of the rational basis standard.[65] In turn, she proposes the use of the stricter undue burden standard outlined in *Casey*.[66] What is relevant here is that, in defense of this point, Ginsburg seems to rely on the ideal of symmetrical human encounter in her constitutional evaluation of pregnancy. In support of her argument, she asserts without qualification that "a woman who exercises her constitutionally protected right to terminate a pregnancy is not a 'mother.'"[67]

Unsurprisingly, critics were quick to reject Ginsburg's assertion on logical, biological, and metaphysical grounds.[68] Given Ginsburg's

---

Young's article "Pregnant Embodiment: Subjectivity and Alienation," in *On Female Body Experience: "Throwing like a Girl" and Other Essays* (Oxford: Oxford University Press, 2005), 46–61.
[63] Mumford, *Ethics at the Beginning of Life*, 69.
[64] *Box v. Planned Parenthood* 587 US (2019).
[65] See *Box v. Planned Parenthood*, at 1 (Ginsburg, J., dissenting).
[66] *Box v. Planned Parenthood*, at 2, n. 2.
[67] *Box v. Planned Parenthood*, at 2, n. 2.
[68] See Ed Whelan, "Contra Michael Dorf on Justice Thomas' *Box* Concurrence—Part 2," *National Review*, May 31, 2019, www.nationalreview.com/bench-memos/contra-michael-dorf-on-justice-thomass-box-concurrence-part-2. In his article, Whelan quotes Adam White, who criticizes Ginburg's remarks as an "intellectual gerrymander." He additionally quotes Robert George, who similarly criticizes her remarks as question-begging to say the least. In this vein, George remarks that "if a woman seeking an abortion (and who is therefore by definition pregnant) is not a mother, then a pregnant woman who is happy to be pregnant and is not seeking an abortion is not a mother either. She may think she is, and say she is, but she can't be. Not if Justice Ginsburg is right." Finally, Snead joins the others above in taking exception to Ginsburg's comments. Inasmuch as Ginsburg seems to imply that it is "solely the intention to parent that determines parenthood rather than biological reality," Snead asserts that such a premise rejects the "anthropology of embodiment" he outlines, for in this framework parenthood is not merely some contractual relationship, but "the most fundamental network of uncalculated giving and graceful

apparent controlling ideal of symmetrical human encounter, her assertion is actually not all that surprising. Insofar as such encounters involve the arrangement and reciprocity of presumably autonomous agents, it is not difficult to see how encounters that fall below these threshold conditions are judged inauthentic. Insofar as they are judged inauthentic, they apparently fail to realize the controlling norm and *relation* of symmetry. In the case of pregnancy, then, any encounter that does not meet the threshold conditions above does not just fall into the realm of inauthentic encounter. More importantly, it does not realize *any relation at all*. Thus, in pregnancy, this controlling model of human encounter maintains that there is indeed no mother-prenatal child relation to consider. In other words, a woman does not 'exist' as a mother, and a child does not 'exist' at all, until the norm and relation of symmetry obtains between the two. To maintain this picture of human encounter brings us back again to the question of whether arranged encounters, especially as they are apparently formally embedded in US constitutional law and jurisprudence, are theoretically and descriptively adequate or not.[69]

Finally, it seems that the controlling ideal of symmetrical encounters has served to situate all human encounters in a fundamentally "asocial" context in much of ethical and legal thought, especially on contentious "life issues." The primacy of arranged encounters has fostered a picture of reality wherein agents are conceived as originally isolated. Thus, it is only through equally-capacitated agents forging agreements that social life is brought into being. There is no relation to others prior to the free choice and consent of fundamentally isolated agents. In this sense, social life is not a natural condition for all human encounters, but a posterior artifact of arranged encounters alone. In other words, social life does not take place within a fundamental relation of communion, but through a discrete creation and recreation of arranged relations.

Mumford attributes the controlling paradigm of arranged human encounter in much of ethical and legal thought to Locke's theory of

---

receiving essential to life as humanly lived" (*What It Means to Be Human*, 294–295, endnote 146, 181).

[69] Snead seems to think not, given the anthropology of expressive individualism that these arranged encounters are apparently premised on. He insists that this anthropology "does not supply a justification for the payment of those debts in nonreciprocal and unconditional fashion to others who have nothing to offer by way of recompense." Applying this point to US constitutional law on abortion, he emphasizes that the "primary relationship that is invisible to expressive individualism, and by extension, the Court's abortion jurisprudence, is that of parents and children." Thus, Snead asserts that "the Court's prescriptive framework" is not just "gravely misguided," but "indeed, inhuman" (*What It Means to Be Human*, 94, 172).

the social contract.[70] He notes that Locke grounds society not in terms of an original communion with God and all others, but in terms of trade. In turn, Locke reconceives society in commercial and transactional terms. Mumford claims that Locke's re-conception of society is no mere alternative origin story. In fact, it is nothing less than an inversion of the natural order of human encounters in social life. In particular, Mumford argues that Locke's theory reverses the fundamental status of fortuitous and arranged encounters in the natural order of social life. Given the predominance of Locke's theory in much of modern Western thought, the negative effects are not insignificant.

By raising arranged encounters to normative status, Mumford makes clear that most human encounters are relegated to secondary or inauthentic status. The first encounter to be demoted in this inverted order is our original arrival in the world. Mumford notes that the "extraordinary" encounter between a mother and her newone in pregnancy cannot be characterized as mutually arranged, reciprocal, and transparent. All human beings arrive in the world in a largely fortuitous, radically dependent, and completely hidden way. Thus, in making arranged encounters paradigmatic, the extraordinary encounter between a mother and her newone is not just obscured, it is dismissed as neither normative nor even instructive for any other human encounter.

But this dismissal is far from conclusive. Modernity critics have long contested Locke's "asocial" picture of reality.[71] Mumford enlists a few of these critics in his attempt to argue that in the "real world" fortuitous encounters are "primary" and arranged encounters are "derivative."[72] Using Heidegger, he states that we are "thrown into" encounters long before we ever arrange them. Nowhere is this made clearer than in "the most fundamentally contingent" encounter of them all: the maternal-newone encounter.[73] Citing maternal testimony, Mumford asserts that this originary encounter is not just distinctively

---

[70] See Mumford, *Ethics at the Beginning of Life*, 82–102.
[71] Mumford includes the work of several modernity critics across the philosophical spectrum, including Seyla Benhabib's *Situating the Self: Gender, Community, and Postmodernism in Contemporary Ethics* (Cambridge, MA: Harvard University Press, 1992); Martin Heidegger's *Being and Time* (1927), trans. John Macquarrie and Edward Robinson (Oxford: Blackwell, 1962); Leszek Kolakowski's *Modernity on Endless Trial* (Chicago: University of Chicago Press, 1990); Alasdair MacIntyre's *After Virtue* (Notre Dame, IN: University of Notre Dame Press, 1981); and John Milbank's *Theology and Social Theory: Beyond Secular Reason*, 2nd ed. (Oxford: Blackwell, 2006).
[72] Mumford, *Ethics at the Beginning of Life*, 102.
[73] Mumford, *Ethics at the Beginning of Life*, 107.

fortuitous, even if hoped for,[74] but *"asymmetrical"* throughout.[75] That is, it is characterized by the radical and particular dependency of one party upon another from origin to arrival. In this light, Luce Irigaray claims that it is only by denying "the help that has been given to us in order to enter the word" that the reduction of authentic relationships to "partnerships" can be idealized.[76] Mumford likewise concurs that it is only by forgetting where we came from that "the illusion of the asocial" can be sustained.[77]

Once again, Kaveny seems to agree with the thrust of Mumford's third and final point. In *Ethics at the Edges of Law*, Kaveny states that any "sound institution points toward all forms of excellence as ideals worth striving for."[78] But she insists that it should not "base its operational practices on the illusion that most participants in those practices have already achieved the ideal."[79] Nonetheless, US constitutional law seems to presume that the ideal of symmetrical interpersonal encounter has in fact been achieved. Furthermore, it seems to presume that even in cases where the ideal has not been achieved, it should still normatively measure them. In this regard, US constitutional law seems to base its own operational practices not just on "illusion of the asocial," but on the presumptively achieved ideal of symmetrical interpersonal encounter. Given these apparent presuppositions, whether US constitutional law can adequately inculcate or even recognize an essentially social virtue like solidarity seems questionable.

THE UNION OF SYMMETRICAL AND ASYMMETRICAL ENCOUNTERS IN SOLIDARITY

In *Law's Virtues*, Kaveny roots her discussion of the virtue of solidarity in the thought of John Paul II. In fact, she uses John Paul II's definition of solidarity as "a firm and persevering determination to commit oneself to the common good" as the departure point for her own treatment.[80] Kaveny then applies this definition to American law and political life. In so doing, she affirms that the "call to solidarity

---

[74] In both natural and artificially assisted reproduction, Mumford affirms that there are "enough contingent factors involved in procreation, even in artificial procreation, that to view the phenomenon as an automatic process, a straightforward instance of cause and effect, is to impose a falsifying vision on the phenomenon" (*Ethics at the Beginning of Life*, 106).
[75] Mumford, *Ethics at the Beginning of Life*, 107. Italics in the original.
[76] Irigaray, *Sharing the World*, 117 quoted in Mumford, *Ethics at the Beginning of Life*, 117.
[77] Mumford, *Ethics at the Beginning of Life*, 117.
[78] Kaveny, *Ethics at the Edges of Law*, 134.
[79] Kaveny, *Ethics at the Edges of Law*, 134.
[80] Kaveny, *Law's Virtues*, 54, quoting John Paul II, *Sollicitudo Rei Socialis*, no. 38.

supports justice by pressing lawmakers and citizens to attend to the unseen members of their community whose lives will be affected by their actions."[81] Yet, given the apparent controlling ideal of symmetrical interpersonal encounter in US constitutional law, it is questionable whether this form of law has the adequate internal resources to see these "unseen members" as they are. Furthermore, as just mentioned, given the asocial presuppositions of US constitutional law, it is questionable whether it has the adequate internal resources to inculcate the virtue of solidarity. In order then to further evaluate Kaveny's treatment of the virtue of solidarity and its application to US constitutional law, it is important to turn to John Paul II's thought on the subject of solidarity.

The range of John Paul II's thought on the virtue of solidarity is vast. The range of reflections on his thought is similarly vast. Yet, few have focused on the anthropological presuppositions of John Paul II's thought on the virtue of solidarity.[82] In turning to this subject, I aim to show how, in his commentary on this virtue, John Paul II unites symmetrical and asymmetrical interpersonal encounters without confusion or separation. By contrast, I intend to highlight how US constitutional law tends to collapse asymmetrical encounters into symmetrical ones.

In John Paul II's thought, three documents stand out for their thematic attention to the virtue of solidarity. These include *Sollicitudo Rei Socialis* (1987), *Centesimus Annus* (1991), and the *Compendium of the Social Doctrine of the Church* (2004).[83] For the purposes of my argument, the substantive contours of John Paul II's thought are important for at least three reasons.

First, unlike US constitutional law's vision of interpersonal *origins* as symmetrically constituted, John Paul II affirms just the opposite in

---

[81] Kaveny, *Law's Virtues*, 54.
[82] Notable exceptions include Donal Dorr, "Solidarity and Integral Human Development," in *The Logic of Solidarity: Commentaries on Pope John Paul II's Encyclical on Social Concern*, ed. Gregory Baum and Robert Ellsberg (Maryknoll, NY: Orbis Books, 1989): 149, 153–154; Kevin Doran, *Solidarity: A Synthesis of Personalism and Communalism in the Thought of John Paul II* (New York: Peter Lang, 1996), 40–42. Though generally complimentary, Dorr thinks John Paul II needs to supplement his thought on "interpersonal relationships" with a more "affective dimension" (149, 153). For his part, Doran concentrates on John Paul II's debt to Max Scheler and the latter's thought on "person-community," a type of ideal form of solidarity (40–41).
[83] Though John Paul II did not author the *Compendium*, he not only formally initiated its development, but greatly influenced its content. In his "Letter" introducing the *Compendium*, Cardinal Angelo Sodano states that John Paul II's "three great Encyclicals," *Laborem Exercens*, *Sollicitudo Rei Socialis*, and *Centesimus Annus* "represent fundamental stages in Catholic thought" in the area of "Catholic social doctrine."

his treatment of solidarity. In the created order, John Paul II sets solidarity in the context of a fundamental asymmetrical encounter between God and human beings. John Paul II was indeed unique in conceiving solidarity as a "moral" and "social" virtue.[84] Among modern popes, he was not unique in rooting solidarity in the context of the created order. In fact, every major pope from Pius XII, who first explicitly used the term, to John Paul II situated solidarity broadly in this very context.[85] Even so, John Paul II sets himself apart in his thematic link of solidarity to God's gratuitous action of creation.

In *Sollicitudo Rei Socialis*, John Paul II notes that our "gift" of being created in God's "image and likeness" (Genesis 1:26) is a gift given with the task of remaining dependent on the will of God (no. 29). In this light, we are each in turn called to live out this very asymmetrical relation as a "duty" not only to cultivate creation, but to foster the "full development of all others" (no. 30). Only after the basic context and character of this "duty" has been laid out does John Paul II define solidarity as a "firm and persevering determination to commit oneself to the common good" (no. 38). Delimited within the political and social order, it might seem like solidarity would be characterized in terms of symmetrical relations and reciprocal duties. But John Paul II says otherwise. In fact, he makes clear that solidarity is first and foremost a commitment to "lose oneself" for the sake of another and to "serve" without expectation of return (no. 38).

In *Centesimus Annus*, John Paul II builds on this very point. Given our "essential 'capacity for transcendence,'" he insists that it is only through the "free gift of self" that we "truly" find ourselves (no. 41). To refuse this "capacity" then is not just to fail to live out "the experience of self-giving," regardless of reciprocity (no. 41). It is to deprive ourselves of "entering into that relationship of solidarity and communion with others" for which God has "created" us (no. 41).

In the *Compendium*, the virtue of solidarity is likewise set within the fundamental asymmetrical relations of gift and gratuitousness. In fact, the entirety of the Church's social doctrine is set within the context of these very relations. The *Compendium* opens with an explicit discussion of "God's gratuitous presence" in salvation history and "God's gratuitous action" in creation (nos. 20–27). To call this presence and action of God "gratuitous" is no mere rhetorical flourish. Rather, it is to express the right and proper response of gratitude found

---

[84] For a brief history of the explicit use of the term 'solidarity' in papal documents, see the *Compendium*, no. 194, n. 421.
[85] For representative examples, see Pius XII, *Summi Pontificatus* (1939), nos. 35–36; John XXIII, *Mater et Magistra* (1961), nos. 23, 42, 63; Paul VI, *Populorum Progressio* (1967), nos. 16, 17, 22, 27, 44, 48; John Paul II, *Sollicitudo Rei Socialis* (1987), nos. 9, 29, 30, 38, 39.

in "Israel's profession of faith" (no. 26). In other words, it is to grasp "the original extent" of the Creator's "gratuitous and merciful action" on our behalf *from the very beginning* (no. 26). Furthermore, in the practices of the sabbatical and jubilee years, the *Compendium* notes that God's gratuitous action is not just made manifest, but presented as primary pedagogy for the virtue of solidarity. In this light, it notes that these practices do not just show how solidarity is inspired by God's original gratuitous action. Rather, they indicate how they must become "normative points of reference" for every generation and in every social arena (no. 25). In sum, the fundamental asymmetry of God's gratuitousness sets the intrinsic terms not only of solidarity's horizon, but its pedagogical significance for all social forms.

Once this fundamental asymmetry in the created order is laid out, the *Compendium* discusses how solidarity embraces symmetrical interpersonal encounters. Specifically, it discusses how solidarity embraces these encounters in the contexts of civil society (no. 417), democracy (no. 417), economic activity (no. 351), and international cooperation (no. 448), to name a few. The *Compendium* indicates that solidarity does not collapse the symmetrical interpersonal encounters above into the fundamental asymmetrical encounter between God and human beings. Nor does it separate the two. To cite but one example, the *Compendium* suggests that solidarity unites symmetrical and asymmetrical encounters in the context of political community, an area where persons are "*organically* united among themselves as a people" (no. 385). In elaborating on this area, it first makes clear that insofar as political community originally "comes from God," it remains "an integral part of the order that he created" (no. 383). This is not to say that the content of the political community is subsumed in this transcendent relation. In fact, the *Compendium* notes that, in the created order, solidarity is realized in the political community, insofar as horizontal relations cooperate to promote the common good (nos. 383, 391). Thus, in the outline and detail of magisterial teaching, and especially that of John Paul II, it seems fair to say that the virtue of solidarity unites symmetrical and asymmetrical interpersonal encounters without confusion or separation.

Second, unlike US constitutional law's vision of interpersonal *dynamics* as symmetrically constituted, John Paul describes them otherwise in his treatment of solidarity. In the natural order, John Paul II sets solidarity in the context of a basic asymmetrical encounter. In *Sollicitudo Rei Socialis*, John Paul II gestures toward the application of solidarity to the family, "the basic social community" (no. 33). But in *Centesimus Annus*, he makes this application explicit. In this latter encyclical, John Paul II claims that "*a concrete commitment to solidarity and charity*" must begin "in the family" (no. 49). In this "first and fundamental structure" of society, each of us receives our first formative instruction "in what it means to love and be loved" (no. 39). In other words, we each receive our first formative instruction "in what it actually means to be a person" (no. 39). Inasmuch as this instruction takes place in a setting formally *"founded on marriage,"* it is structured in terms of "the mutual gift of self by husband and wife" (no. 39). Given this formal setting, it is an instruction in life and living always materially initiated in the basic asymmetrical relation between children and parents. John Paul II elaborates that in and through this relation we all "develop" our "potentialities" and "prepare to face" our "unique and individual destiny" (no. 39). Thus, he concludes that it is right and proper to call the family not just a *"sanctuary of life,"* but "a community of work and solidarity" (nos. 39, 49).

Drawing largely upon John Paul II's thought, the *Compendium* grounds solidarity even further in the context of asymmetrical encounters in family life. The *Compendium* affirms that the family is "the principal place of interpersonal relationships" (no. 211), making clear that these relationships are neither constituted nor idealized in terms of mutual dependence, symmetry, and voluntariness. Family life, the "prototype of every social order," is not established upon a controlling model of arranged encounter (no. 211), but in terms of an encounter whose essential terms include "disinterested availability, generous service, and solidarity" (no. 221). In other words, it is established upon a model of gratuitous asymmetrical encounter.

Given this model, it is important to reiterate that the *Compendium* insists that solidarity is no added feature to family life. In fact, it clearly maintains that "solidarity belongs to the family as constitutive and structural element" (no. 246). In this regard, solidarity takes shape first in the interpersonal encounter of self-giving, and *not of mutual arrangement*. In other words, it is "not limited by the terms of a contract" (no. 212), because solidarity derives from the very essence and structure of the family. The *Compendium* notes that this structure arises above all else in the fortuitous relationships "following the generation or adoption of children" (no. 212). Inasmuch as solidarity takes shape in such relationships, it is a virtue rooted in asymmetrical encounter, that is, in openness to less-capacitated agents like the vulnerable and dependent. Thus, in its application to all other social forms, the *Compendium* maintains that the virtue of solidarity is able "to bring every situation of distress to the attention of institutions" (no. 246).

Now, in emphasizing the asymmetrical dimensions of solidarity in family life, magisterial teaching does not neglect the symmetrical dimensions internal to it. John Paul II locates the basic form of symmetrical interpersonal encounter in the mutual self-giving of spouses. In *Familiaris Consortio*, John Paul II notes that this form does not just set an ideal, but actively promotes the "authentic and mature communion between persons within the family" (no. 43). Inasmuch as it promotes this "mature communion" within the family, he affirms that it serves to stimulate "broader community relationships marked by respect, justice, dialogue, and love" (no. 43). For John Paul II, then, just as solidarity unites symmetrical and asymmetrical encounters without confusion or separation in the order of social life, so too does it do the same in the natural order.

Finally, unlike US constitutional law's vision of interpersonal *relations* as contractually constituted, John Paul II denies this very theory in his treatment of solidarity. It is important to note that magisterial teaching firmly opposes all theories proposing to make arranged encounters socially normative, without categorically rejecting the limited use of these theories within law and politics. Nonetheless, it seems clear that it condemns the comprehensive and controlling imposition of such theories to these very areas.

Nowhere does this seem to be clearer than in its pointed criticism of contractarian theories of social order. The *Compendium* affirms that society is rooted in the human person, a being who is essentially relational. In this light, it deems it right and proper for society to be characterized as essentially relational *from the very beginning*. Furthermore, in applying this point, the *Compendium* states that it is "evident that the origin of society is not found in a "contract" or "agreement," but in human nature itself" (no. 149, n. 297). To think otherwise is not just to commit a logical error according to the *Compendium*, it is to sanction the "false anthropology" of the "ideologies of the social contract" (no. 149, n. 297). To be clear, this is no minor fault. In one of the most searing comments in the entire text, the *Compendium* concludes that magisterial teaching has declared such "ideologies" as nothing less than "openly absurd" (no. 149, n. 297).

THE COMPETENCE OF LAW TO JUDGE INTERPERSONAL ENCOUNTERS

To this point, I have elaborated on some of the historical and internal reasons for why US constitutional law is relatively incapable of addressing asymmetrical encounters. By extension, I have indicated why it is relatively incapable of inculcating the virtue of solidarity. Nonetheless, it is possible for US constitutional law to still be *formally* capable of addressing asymmetrical encounters and so, by extension, be capable of inculcating the virtue of solidarity. That is, the influence of the historical and internal factors mentioned above might just be accidental and contingent. In principle, US constitutional law thereby remains capable of recognizing and judging asymmetrical encounters as such. If this is the case, then it is reasonable to think that flaws in judging asymmetrical encounters in US constitutional law are attributable to flaws in judgments of the law, *not the form of law itself.*

In her evaluation of current jurisprudence on abortion law, Kaveny indicates that US constitutional law "plays an important role in inculcating solidarity with the unborn—or in failing to do so."[86] In turn, she emphasizes how "*Roe* and its progeny" have failed in this role due to flaws in judgments of the law, not in the form of law itself.[87] In other words, Kaveny emphasizes how these judicial decisions are failures of competent judgments of US constitutional law, not failures of the competence of US constitutional law itself. In response, I would like to consider whether these failures of judgment are more symptomatic of failures of the law. That is, I would like to consider whether the failures of these decisions are primarily attributable to the limited competence of US constitutional law, not just to the flawed competence of judgments of the law. To do so, I now turn to Kaveny's discussion of competence in law and Aquinas' treatment of the same in the *Summa*.[88]

To reiterate, in *Ethics at the Edges of Law*, Kaveny characterizes competence in law in more functionalist terms. She describes competence as a judge's "ability to make assessments in cases that are increasingly difficult, but that have a clear resolution according to the standards of the practice."[89] In *Law's Virtues*, Kaveny elaborates on

---

[86] Kaveny, *Law's Virtues*, 84.

[87] Kaveny takes special exception to Justice William Brennan's infamous comment in *Beal v. Doe* (1977) that "abortion and childbirth, when stripped of the sensitive moral arguments surrounding the abortion controversy, are simply two alternative medical methods of dealing with pregnancy" (quoted in *Law's Virtues*, 84–85). In response, she insists that "the fundamental task facing the pro-life movement now is to demonstrate how deeply mistaken Justice Brennan's view is" (*Law's Virtues*, 85).

[88] In commenting on Aquinas' treatment on competence in law, I rely on Russell Hittinger's important article "Thomas Aquinas on Natural Law and the Competence to Judge," in *St. Thomas Aquinas and the Natural Law Tradition: Contemporary Perspectives*, ed. John Goyette, Mark S. Latkovic, and Richard S. Myers (Washington, DC: Catholic University of America Press, 2004): 280–283. There are quite a few considerations of Aquinas' treatment of authority in law. Some of the more notable include John Finnis, *Natural Law and Natural Rights* (Oxford: Oxford University Press, 1980); Robert George, *Making Men Moral: Civil Liberties and Public Morality* (Oxford: Oxford University Press, 1995); Mark C. Murphy, *Natural Law in Jurisprudence and Politics* (Cambridge: Cambridge University Press, 2006); Jean Porter, *Ministers of the Law: A Natural Law Theory of Legal Authority* (Grand Rapids, MI: Eerdmans, 2010). In my own research and in conversations with Hittinger, it seems that Hittinger's article is the only thematic consideration of Aquinas' treatment of competence in law, at least in the English language.

[89] Kaveny, *Ethics at the Edges of Law*, 76.

the subject, albeit implicitly, at even greater length.[90] In her discussion, Kaveny first draws attention to Aquinas's appeal to Isidore of Seville's list of characteristics for sound human law. Like Aquinas, Kaveny then comments on several of these characteristics. These include, but are not limited to, Isidore of Seville's insistence that law be "virtuous," "necessary," "useful," "possible to nature," "suitable to time and place," and "according to the custom of the country."[91] Kaveny notes that only after these characteristics have been considered can wise law-making take place. Even then, this consideration remains only a preliminary step.

Kaveny then remarks that a further set of factors concerning a law's prospects for success needs to be considered. These include, but are not limited to, the "power of the lawmaker, the type of law at issue, and the character of the subjects involved."[92] Wise lawmaking must not just involve the inclusion of sound characteristics, but the implementation of proper means. Even then, Kaveny asserts that there is no guarantee that laws having passed through these two steps will achieve their intended ends. There are simply too many contingent factors regularly in play to ensure a law's complete success. Given these factors, Aquinas offers practical counsel about the limitations of law. He devotes an entire question in the *Summa* to this subject.[93]

Kaveny distinguishes Aquinas' counsel about the limitations of law into three general types.[94] The first type is most relevant here, for it pertains to the competence of law. Kaveny locates this type of limitation in Aquinas's discussion of what acts human law is competent to judge.[95] Gesturing toward Aristotle's dictum that "everyone judges well of what he knows,"[96] Aquinas claims that human beings only "can make laws in those matters" they are "competent to judge" (ST I-II, q. 91, a. 4). To bring this issue into focus, Aquinas evaluates whether we are competent to judge interior acts, exterior acts, or both. In regard to exterior acts, he answers in the affirmative, for such acts appear to us. In regard to interior acts, he answers in the negative, for such acts remain hidden from us. Aquinas concludes that human law is not competent to judge interior acts, for human law can neither "sufficiently curb" nor "direct" these acts (ST I-II, q. 91, a. 4).

Kaveny does not discuss the issue of the law's competence any

---

[90] Kaveny, *Law's Virtues*, 30–31.
[91] Kaveny, *Law's Virtues*, 30–31, quoting ST I-II, q. 95, a.3.
[92] Kaveny, *Law's Virtues*, 58.
[93] See ST I-II, q. 96, "On the Power of Law."
[94] Kaveny, *Law's Virtues*, 59–61.
[95] Kaveny, *Law's Virtues*, 59, referencing ST I-II, q. 91, a. 4.
[96] See ST II-II, q. 60, a. 1.

further in the context of the *Summa*. In this regard, she limits Aquinas' treatment of competence in law to *judgments of the law* and *those things measured by the law* like interior or exterior acts. But Aquinas' treatment of this subject goes further. In particular, Aquinas does not just discuss competence in law in regard to those things measured by the law, but even in regard to *the measure of law itself*. In other words, Aquinas does not just discuss competence in law *ad extra*, but *ab intra*. In reference to the latter, he does so in three important ways.

First, in his discussion of whether human law can be divided into different types, Aquinas answers in the affirmative (ST I-II, q. 95, a. 4). As a general principle, he notes that a thing can be properly divided in and of itself according to whether it possesses a certain formal principle. In the case of an animal, it can be properly divided according to whether it possesses rationality or not. Likewise, in the case of human law, Aquinas states it can be properly divided, for it possesses many different formal principles. To illustrate his case, Aquinas points to the formal division between the law of nations and civil law. He notes that each is divided according to whether it possesses the formal principle of securing agreements necessary to common life. Aquinas claims that the law of nations possesses this principle inherently, but civil law does not. In support, he elaborates on how this principle is derived in each as a matter of human law. In the case of the law of nations, he comments that this principle is derived directly and necessarily like a conclusion from premises. In the case of civil law, it is derived indirectly and contingently through a particular and customary determination. This principle belongs to the law of nations essentially, but to civil law only accidentally. Thus, Aquinas indicates that specific types of human law are more competent in certain matters than others, inasmuch as they are able to apply inherent formal principles more adequately and directly.

Second, in his discussion of whether unjust human laws are binding, Aquinas argues against flawed measures in law (ST I-II, q. 96, a. 4). In this effort, Aquinas identifies three ways a human law can be unjust. These include: 1) laws opposed to the common good (*ex fine*), 2) laws enacted through improper authority (*ex auctore*), and 3) laws imposing unequal benefits and burdens (*ex forma*).[97] Aquinas makes clear that, if a human law lapses in any of these three ways, it is not a proper law, but a corruption of law. Thus, he insists that no judgment should be based on an unjust law, for the measure of an unjust law is flawed from the very start. In rendering legal judgments then, Aquinas indicates that competence in applying the measure of a law derives first and foremost from the competence of the measure

---

[97] For a more extended commentary on this subject, see Hittinger, "Thomas Aquinas on Natural Law and the Competence to Judge," 280–283.

itself.

Finally, in his discussion of whether judgment is an act of justice, Aquinas sets forth the necessary conditions for right judgment (ST II-II q. 60, a. 1). In answering this question, he emphasizes that these conditions are especially important in the context of law, for judgment "properly denotes the act of a judge as such" (ST II-II q. 60, a. 1). Aquinas identifies two essential conditions for right judgment. These include 1) "the virtue itself that pronounces judgment" and 2) "the disposition of the one who judges" (ST II-II q. 60, a. 1, ad. 1). In reference to the first condition, Aquinas notes that justice is needed to incline one toward right judgment. In reference to the second, he comments that prudence is needed to render right judgment. In the ordering of right judgment then, the first condition is preeminent. For Aquinas, there can be no right judgment unless the virtue of justice or *a subspecies of justice* is present. Aquinas explicitly applies the two necessary conditions of right judgment to those who properly measure out the law. These two conditions seem to apply principally to the measure of law itself, and only derivatively to those who measure it out. Thus, the competence of right judgment in law seems to be based principally on the inherence of the virtue of justice in law itself.

Together, these three points provide an important framework for evaluating whether US constitutional law is relatively competent to judge asymmetrical encounters and inculcate the virtue of solidarity. First, inasmuch as certain formal notions belong properly to specific forms of law, it is best for these notions to be addressed in the most competent forms. If the formal notion of asymmetrical encounters does not belong properly to US constitutional law, it is best for it to be addressed in another type of American law. Second, if justice in law can only be adequately measured out with the proper form or measure of law, then it is necessary for the just treatment of certain subjects to be addressed by the most competent form. Thus, if justice is to be adequately rendered in cases of asymmetrical encounters, and if US constitutional law cannot properly address them internally, the just treatment of these cases is properly considered elsewhere. Finally, even if right judgments are made about certain issues in law, they are subject to instability if not properly assigned to and judged by a more competent measure. Even if the Supreme Court renders more just judgments in cases of asymmetrical encounters, these decisions would likely not be well-settled, so long as they rely on the contractarian measure of US constitutional law.[98]

---

[98] Though it is certainly true that partial and provisional justice is better than no justice at all, it is nonetheless a primary purpose of law to settle cases and controversies in an enduring and proper way.

TWO WAYS FORWARD FOR JUDGING ASYMMETRICAL ENCOUNTERS IN LAW

Given the preceding reasons for the apparent incapacity of US constitutional law to address asymmetrical encounters and inculcate the virtue of solidarity, I want to turn, in this final section, to two possible remedies. The first approach aims to break open this apparent incapacity by leveraging other areas of American law more congenial to the inclusion of asymmetrical encounters. In contrast, the second approach seeks to corral this incapacity by delegating the evaluation of asymmetrical encounters to more competent areas like family law. Each approach has its merits and offers distinct ways forward in addressing contentious "life issues" in the context of US constitutional law. In different ways, Kaveny and Snead seem to endorse the first approach. In her attempt to find models in American law capable of fostering solidarity with the vulnerable, Kaveny identifies at least three promising examples in US federal law. These include the Americans with Disabilities Act (ADA), the Family and Medical Leave Act (FMLA), and the Patient Protection and Affordable Care Act (ACA).[99] In these three pieces of federal legislation, Kaveny sees not just a series of positive mandates, but an important pedagogy of solidarity at work. She asserts that all three "attempt both to teach and to instantiate the virtues of autonomy and solidarity, with particular attention given to the vulnerabilities that attend to human beings because we are embodied beings."[100]

Kaveny then applies this pedagogy of solidarity to thinking about abortion in the context of American law in general, and constitutional law in particular. As previously mentioned, she emphasizes that the law "plays an important role in inculcating solidarity with the unborn—or in failing to do so."[101] She then proceeds to catalog how US constitutional jurisprudence has largely failed to do so since *Roe*. In response, Kaveny calls for American law to "expand beyond rights talk and move toward the virtue of solidarity—solidarity with the unborn, solidarity with others who are vulnerable, and solidarity with those upon whom these most vulnerable persons depend."[102] She draws attention to some positive, albeit highly limited, movement toward this goal in *Casey*, wherein the Court explicitly acknowledged the state's legitimate interest in unborn life from the very beginning. Outside of this decision and the three pieces of federal legislation mentioned above, she sees challenges ahead. In fact, she asserts that much of "American law is sorely deficient in solidarity in that most

---

[99] Kaveny, *Law's Virtues*, 82–84.
[100] Kaveny, *Law's Virtues*, 84.
[101] Kaveny, *Law's Virtues*, 84.
[102] Kaveny, *Law's Virtues*, 85.

states do not impose even a minimal 'duty to rescue' another person in distress, absent special circumstances."[103] Nonetheless, in highlighting positive examples of solidarity in American law, Kaveny seems to suggest they can be leveraged to promote the virtue of solidarity in US constitutional law on abortion.

Like Kaveny, Snead seeks to enlarge the constrained vision of US constitutional jurisprudence on abortion. But unlike Kaveny, he aims to do so through a more exacting critique of the anthropological premises of this jurisprudence. For Snead, the primary problem with US constitutional jurisprudence on abortion is not its inattention to legal models of solidarity external to it, but an apparent lack of any such model internal to it. As mentioned earlier, Snead indicts US constitutional jurisprudence for its underlying anthropology of "expressive individualism." In such an anthropology, with its reductive emphasis on the will and the capacity to make choices, Snead notes that human embodiment is obscured and even ignored. In light of this, he maintains that US constitutional jurisprudence, especially on abortion, is "blind to the reality of vulnerability, dependence, and natural limits."[104] Blind to this reality, it "fails to consider the networks of uncalculated and graceful receiving that are necessary for the survival of embodied beings, as well as vital to their development."[105]

To remedy this blindness, Snead seeks to re-envision US constitutional jurisprudence on abortion through a more fitting and complete "anthropology of embodiment." Within such an anthropological framework, Snead writes that law would better recognize the whole of human life as relatively dependent and vulnerable, and promote practices like "just generosity, hospitality, and accompaniment of others in suffering (misericordia)."[106] Furthermore, it would "seek to strengthen the familial and social ties that serve these ends," including roles for civil society and

---

[103] Kaveny, *Law's Virtues*, 87. Though it is true that there is no legal obligation to rescue vulnerable others in much of American law, there is a legal duty to care for them in situations where we create the vulnerabilities or dependencies at issue. For example, although there is no legal duty to rescue someone who is drowning, there is a legal duty to care for this person if we have pushed him into the water, and so have created the vulnerability and dependency at issue. Thus, in counterpoint to Kaveny, I think American law might be even more congenial to the virtue of solidarity than she allows, especially in the context of ordinary instances of pregnancy, inasmuch as American law emphasizes positive duties of care for vulnerabilities and dependencies that are caused or created.
[104] Snead, *What It Means to Be Human*, 171.
[105] Snead, *What It Means to Be Human*, 171.
[106] Snead, *What It Means to Be Human*, 177–178.

government.[107] Of all the ties it would seek to fortify, Snead emphasizes that the bond of parenthood would be most central. In the anthropology of embodiment, the law would not just recognize this bond, but affirm it as "the most fundamental network of uncalculated giving and graceful receiving essential to life as humanly lived."[108] Snead makes clear that this "family and community-oriented framework" is no mere check on the anthropology of expressive individualism in American law.[109] Rather, he maintains that it is a more adequate and necessary precondition for addressing the full range of human needs at issue in US constitutional jurisprudence on abortion. There is much to commend in Snead's goal of getting US constitutional law to recognize a more adequate "anthropology of embodiment." But there may be better prudential means to achieve it. The second approach below, with its emphasis on corralling, not converting the current anthropology of US constitutional law, offers another way forward.[110]

In contrast to Kaveny and Snead, Helen Alvaré seems to endorse the second approach,[111] through delegating the evaluation of asymmetrical encounters in US constitutional law to areas of American law more competent to treat them. Like Snead, Alvaré sees

---

[107] Snead, *What It Means to Be Human*, 178. Snead acknowledges the possibility of a "very robust role for government," especially in situations where "people find themselves with the support and security of networks of giving and receiving" (178).

[108] Snead, *What It Means to Be Human*, 181.

[109] Snead, *What It Means to Be Human*, 184.

[110] Like Snead, I agree that an "anthropology of embodiment" better captures the integral reality of human life, and that US constitutional law can and should *recognize* its superior adequacy, especially in its jurisprudence on abortion. I differ with Snead on how US constitutional law can and should be remedied *in light of this recognition*. Again, in response to the deficiencies of the apparent "anthropology of expressive individualism" in US constitutional law, Snead makes the case that US constitutional law "must expand and augment its grounding conception of human identity and flourishing" (*What It Means to Be Human*, 68). In the context of abortion jurisprudence, he argues for a reform of US constitutional law through an *expansion* of its current anthropology. In contrast, in the same context, I argue for a reform of US constitutional law through an *express limitation* of its current anthropology. Inasmuch as US constitutional law can and should recognize the constraints of its apparent contractarian anthropology, it not only can and should limit its evaluation of asymmetrical encounters between mothers and pre-natal children, but can and should delegate this evaluation to areas of law more competent to evaluate them, like family law. In sum, whereas Snead argues for the *scope* of US constitutional law's current anthropology to be more generous and expansive, I argue for the *application* of US constitutional law's current anthropology to be more humble and constrained. I say more about this in my analysis of Helen Alvaré's approach below.

[111] See Helen M. Alvaré, *Putting Children's Interests First in US Family Law and Policy* (New York: Cambridge University Press, 2018) and Helen M. Alvaré, "*Gonzales v. Carhart*: Bringing Abortion Law into the Family Law Fold," *Montana Law Review* 69, no. 2 (Summer 2008): 409–445.

a "flawed "anthropology"' at work in much of US constitutional jurisprudence on abortion.[112] She terms this anthropology "sexual expressionism," and describes it as "valorizing" acts of consent whose content is limited to the immediate desires and interests of the adults involved.[113] Alvaré does not deny that this underlying anthropology affirms "profound and individualized human goods, such as dignity, freedom, equality, and identity."[114] She insists that this "starkly individualistic" framework has obscured family-oriented goods like partner stability, marital status, and relationships of dependence.[115] In sum, Alvaré indicates that the anthropology of "sexual expressionism" has made symmetrical encounters normative in US constitutional jurisprudence on abortion, and asymmetrical encounters incidental at best.

Unlike Snead though, Alvaré seems more circumspect about the possibility of enlarging US constitutional law through a different anthropology. Alvaré sees the anthropology of "sexual expressionism" at work in much of US legislative and executive policy on sex and family life,[116] being most prominent in US constitutional jurisprudence on the same. She asserts that in the area of sex and family life the Court is "the most prolific and emphatic author of sexual expressionism."[117] In support, Alvaré catalogs how the Court has increasingly emphasized the "sexual rights and interests of the *individual*" in several significant cases over the past half century.[118] In turn, she traces how this development in US constitutional jurisprudence can be attributed to at least three factors. First, Alvaré draws attention to historical factors external to US constitutional law like changing cultural values on sex and family life in the second half of the twentieth century. Second, she focuses on historical factors internal to *interpretations of US constitutional law* like more permissive readings of the Fourteenth Amendment's Due Process Clause. Finally, she emphasizes formal factors internal to *US*

---

[112] Alvaré, *Putting Children's Interests First*, 103.
[113] Alvaré, *Putting Children's Interests First*, 2.
[114] Alvaré, *Putting Children's Interests First*, 8.
[115] Alvaré, *Putting Children's Interests First*, 2, 8. Alvaré further notes that this framework has obscured "the reality that children's family structure is regularly determined at their conception" (8).
[116] For various examples, see Alvaré's thematic discussion of "Sexual Expressionism and the Executive and Legislative Branches," in *Putting Children's Interests First*, 30–47.
[117] Alvaré, *Putting Children's Interests First*, 16.
[118] Alvaré, *Putting Children's Interests First*, 26. Alvaré cites several cases, including but not limited to those on contraception like *Eisenstadt v. Baird*, 405 US 436 (1972), on abortion like *Roe v. Wade*, 410 US 113 (1973) and *Planned Parenthood v. Casey*, 505 US 833, 846 (1989), on same-sex relations like *Lawrence v. Texas*, 539 US 558 (2003), and same-sex marriage like *Obergefell v. Hodges*, 135 S. Ct. 2584 (2015).

constitutional law itself like the apparent absence of two key presumptions found in family law.

The apparent absence of these two presumptions plays a significant role in Alvaré's critique of the Court's relative incompetence to judge asymmetrical encounters. She makes the case for why this is especially true in the context of abortion law. Alvaré identifies the two "axiomatic" presumptions in family law at issue as 1) the existence of a "strong natural bond" between parents and children and 2) the "self-evident" vulnerability of children.[119] In reference to the first, she notes that family law has long recognized a *duty to preserve* the parent-child bond in ordinary circumstances. In reference to the second, she notes that it has long recognized a *duty to protect* dependents in the same circumstances. Alvaré posits that the acknowledgment of each presumption is key to larger efforts to balance "individual rights and family solidarity" in American law.[120] Given the sexual expressionist framework of much American law and its "excessive individualism," she maintains that this balance remains a challenge.[121]

For Alvaré, nowhere is this challenge to balance "individual rights and family solidarity" more stark than in US constitutional jurisprudence on abortion. Alvaré claims that since *Roe* the Court no longer presumes a "strong natural bond" between mothers and prenatal children. Rather, it presumes a relation of "confrontation" between the two.[122] Given this re-conception, Alvaré maintains that the Court has transformed a relation involving the duties to dependents into a contest of interests. Whenever the interests of mothers and prenatal children conflict, separation is not just presented as possible, but desirable. Thus, "in the face of claims that a born child burdens a woman's ability to realize her interests," Alvaré emphasizes that the Court has demonstrated "a preference for terminating relationships rather than preserving them."[123]

In saying this, Alvaré does not deny that the Court can, in principle, consider the two key presumptions of family law mentioned above. She notes that the Court has employed these presumptions in several pre-*Roe* cases on family life,[124] and that it has done so in at least one

---

[119] Helen M. Alvaré, "*Gonzales v. Carhart*," 412–413, 419.
[120] Alvaré, *Putting Children's Interests First*, 117.
[121] Alvaré, *Putting Children's Interests First*, 117.
[122] Alvaré, "*Gonzales v. Carhart*," 420.
[123] Alvaré, "*Gonzales v. Carhart*," 420.
[124] These cases include but are not limited to *Meyer v. Nebraska*, 262 US 390, 400 (1923); *Pierce v. Society of Sisters*, 268 US 510, 535 (1925); *Prince v. Massachusetts*, 321 US 158, 166 (1944); and *Lehr v. Robinson*, 463 US 248 (1983).

post-*Roe* case on abortion law.[125] Nor does Alvaré deny that these presumptions can at least be adopted as *extrinsic* principles of evaluation in US constitutional jurisprudence. She even suggests that this jurisprudence remains tentatively open to "an ethic of solidarity, generosity, and even altruism" toward post-natal and even pre-natal children.[126] Nonetheless, Alvaré seems somewhat skeptical that US constitutional jurisprudence can accommodate such an ethic, especially in the context of abortion law. Among the reasons for this apparent incapacity, she cites the implied anthropology of "expressive individualism" in US constitutional jurisprudence, its internal bias toward autonomy, and its volatility of interpretation.[127]

In the end, Alvaré seems to suggest that, in the context of abortion law, the evaluation of asymmetrical encounters is best delegated to family law, inasmuch as it more adequately balances "individual rights and family solidarity." Alvaré does not explicitly invoke the principle of subsidiarity, but it seems to be at work in her suggested approach. To be clear, this principle seems to be at work not in the misunderstood sense of simply providing a smaller scale solution to unique social problems, but in the more proper sense of recognizing the unique competencies of specific social forms to resolve unique social problems. Russell Hittinger emphasizes that the principle of subsidiarity does not delegate judgments to the "lowest possible level," but the "proper level."[128] He clarifies that "proper" denotes what belongs to thing, person, or institutional form. He maintains that, inasmuch as this principle presumes "a normative structure of plural forms," with irreducible functions and competencies specific to each, it recognizes that each form has a "proper" role to play "with regard

---

[125] In light of the *Gonzales* case, Alvaré tentatively states that the Court seems to have brought "abortion jurisprudence into greater conformity with family law's presumptions about parent-child relations" ("*Gonzales v. Carhart*," 426).

[126] Alvaré, *Putting Children's Interests First*, 142.

[127] In her article on *Gonzales* in 2007, Alvaré admits that the Court's opinions on abortion are quite "volatile" and subject to change. Despite this concession, she sees in this opinion tentative clues to the better alignment of US constitutional jurisprudence on abortion with the key presumptions of family law. By the time her book on family law appeared in 2018, Alvaré seems to have grown considerably less sanguine about the possibility. The Court's opinion in *Whole Women's Health v. Hellerstedt* (2016), making pro-life legal challenges apparently more difficult to survive judicial scrutiny, certainly seems to have influenced her thinking, but this does not seem to be the only factor.

[128] Russell Hittinger, "The Coherence of the Four Basic Principles of Catholic Social Doctrine: An Interpretation," in Margaret S. Archer and Pierpaolo Donati, eds., *Pursuing the Common Good* (Vatican City: Pontifical Academy of Social Sciences, 2008), 110.

to the common good."[129]

In the context of law, the principle of subsidiarity can be understood to presume a normative structure of plural legal forms, with irreducible functions and competencies specific to each. Given these competencies, it can be understood to recognize that each form has a role to play in law's contribution to the common good. Applied to Alvaré's analysis, it seems that family law, given its two key presumptions, is more *internally* competent to evaluate asymmetrical encounters. Finally, inasmuch as it is more internally competent to do so, it seems that in the world of American law family law is more *formally* competent to evaluate the encounters at issue in abortion law.

CONCLUSION

In applying Kaveny's dual-virtue framework on wise lawmaking to US constitutional law, I have argued that as currently construed, US constitutional law cannot adequately inculcate the virtue of solidarity. I have based this argument in part on John Paul II's account of the union of symmetrical and asymmetrical encounters in the virtue of solidarity and the apparent lack of this union in US constitutional law. Specifically, I have claimed that so long as its contractarian presuppositions control its vision, US constitutional law cannot adequately recognize asymmetrical encounters. By extension, I have claimed that it cannot competently judge the asymmetrical encounters implicated in abortion law. In support of this latter point, I enlisted Aquinas' account of how specific forms of law are competent to judge, inasmuch as they have notions internal to them adequate to address specific legal questions.

In light of this supposed inadequacy, I outlined two possible ways to remedy the apparent incapacity of US constitutional law to address asymmetrical encounters. I noted that the first approach seeks to leverage other areas of American law more congenial to the inclusion of asymmetrical encounters. I further noted that the second seeks to corral this incapacity by delegating the evaluation of asymmetrical encounters to more competent areas like family law. I suggested that the second approach is more competent to address the interpersonal encounters at stake in abortion law. I based this judgment on the key presumptions and competencies of family law. In the wider context of

---

[129] Russell Hittinger, "The Coherence of the Four Basic Principles of Catholic Social Doctrine," 110. Hittinger notes that in Pius XI's commentary on subsidiarity, the word "functions" translates the Latin term "*munera*," meaning "having roles to play or gifts to give." See Hittinger, "Social Roles and Ruling Virtues in Catholic Social Doctrine," *Annales Theologici* 16 (2002): 391. In his own commentary on the principle of subsidiarity, Johannes Messner translates the Latin word "*munera*" as "competencies." See Johannes Messner, *Social Ethics in the Natural Law Tradition*, trans. J. J. Doherty (St. Louis, MO: Herder, 1965), 210.

American law, I further supported this judgment through the use of the principle of subsidiarity, with its emphasis on resolving issues on the "proper" level of law, not just on the lowest level.

In the end, I think Alvaré is right to conclude that family law best balances "individual rights and family solidarity." In Kaveny's terms, it best balances the legal virtue of autonomy with the legal virtue of solidarity in matters dealing with relationships of dependence and care in family life. I think Alvaré is right to suggest that family law is most competent to address the asymmetrical encounters at stake in abortion law. M

Justin Menno, PhD, is instructor of theology at Catholic Central High School in Grand Rapids, MI. His research and writing focus on issues surrounding the intersection of theology, anthropology, and law, and especially on issues surrounding the burial of the dead.

The Healing Power of the Body of Christ: An Ecclesial and Neurological Argument for Social Connection Despite Social Distancing

Christopher Krall, SJ

THE CORONAVIRUS HAS SICKENED the human population not only through its contagious infections. Social distancing and mandatory quarantines certainly helped flatten the curve of positive cases and slow the spread of the virus. However, the effective tactics used to fight the global pandemic have also accelerated a slowly increasing trend of social disengagement and isolation especially in modern American culture. Distancing, social isolation, and individualistic pursuits, while beneficial for finding prayerful peace,[1] may also have detrimental consequences with severities comparable to viruses. Fracturing in human relationships, families, and communities leaves wounds of isolation that cause a decrease in life expectancies and an increase in existential longings for connection, meaning, and fulfillment.[2] When breakdowns of families and communities occur, feelings of loneliness can permeate into a person's consciousness and way of living.[3] Research shows that the

---

[1] See Matthew 6:6 (NAB): "When you pray, go to your inner room, close the door, and pray to your Father in secret. And your Father who sees in secret will repay you." See also "The Cell," in Mary Margaret Funk, OSB, *Tools Matter for Practicing the Spiritual Life* (New York: Continuum, 2007), 70–77; Chester L. Tolson and Harold G. Koenig, *The Healing Power of Prayer: The Surprising Connection between Prayer and Your Health* (Grand Rapids, MI: Baker, 2003), 111–120; Thomas Merton, *Contemplation in a World of Action* (Garden City, NY: Doubleday, 1971).

[2] See Matthew D. Lieberman and Naomi I. Eisenberger, "A Pain by Any Other Name (Rejection, Exclusion, Ostracism) Still Hurts the Same: The Role of Dorsal Anterior Cingulate Cortex in Social and Physical Pain," in *Social Neuroscience: People Thinking about Thinking People*, ed. John T. Cacioppo, Penny S. Visser, and Cynthia L. Pickett (Cambridge MA: MIT Press, 2006), 167–187; Teresa E. Seeman, Tina M. Lusignolo, Marilyn Albert, and Lisa Berkman, "Social Relationships, Social Support, and Patterns of Cognitive Aging in Healthy, High-Functioning Older Adults: MacArthur Studies of Successful Aging," *Health Psychology* 20, no. 4 (2001): 243–255.

[3] There is a growing field of research delving into the silent epidemic of loneliness. See John T. Cacioppo and William Patrick, *Loneliness: Human Nature and the Need for Social Connection* (New York: W. W. Norton, 2008); Lissa Rankin, *Mind Over Medicine: Scientific Proof You Can Heal Yourself* (Carlsbad, CA: Hay House, 2013),

effects of loneliness have possible links to depression, inactivity, proclivity to smoking and risk-taking behavior, higher rates of coronary heart disease and stroke, low self-esteem, sleep disorders, dysregulated stress response, cognitive decline, and increased chances of developing Alzheimer's disease.[4] While social distancing and quarantined separation certainly prevent the passage of microscopic virus strains from the nasal cavity of one person to that of another, physical and psychological distancing propagate deep-seated loneliness and a cascade of physical, psychological, neurological, and spiritual disorders.

A healing remedy for the disorders of separation is what I will term a *supra-ecclesial community*. When Christians gather in communities of prayer and participate in liturgy, they are inspired to grow in knowledge of and devotion to the Trinitarian God of love as well as to develop a collective consciousness of a unified body rather than holding on to individualistic perspectives.[5] The work of the twentieth-century Dominican theologian Yves Congar develops a vision of the Church portraying human persons flourishing as parts of a diverse yet unified catholic community. He emphasizes the benefits of participating in the one communal body of the Church. When people enact their God-given charisms, they strengthen loving human relationships and conform their lives to the will of God. Congar's vast and influential writings can provide a vision for the healing power of the living and unified Body of Christ.

This article is divided into three sections. The first section describes the detrimental consequences of isolation and the spiritual perils of social distancing and human separation. The second section

---

65–119; Julianne Holt-Lunstad, Timothy B. Smith, and J. Bradley Layton, "Social Relationships and Mortality Risk: A Meta-analytic Review," *PLoS Medicine* 7, no. 7 (2010): 1–20; Susan Pinker, *The Village Effect: How Face-to-Face Contact Can Make Us Healthier, Happier, and Smarter* (New York: Spiegel and Grau, 2014).

[4] See Aparna Shankar, Anne McMunn, James Banks, and Andrew Steptoe, "Loneliness, Social Isolation, and Behavioral and Biological Health Indicators in Older Adults," *Health Psychology* 30, no. 4 (2011): 377–385; Nicole K. Valtorta, Mona Kanaan, Simon Gilbody, Sara Ronzi, and Barbara Hanratty, "Loneliness and Social Isolation as Risk Factors for Coronary Heart Disease and Stroke: Systematic Review and Meta-Analysis of Longitudinal Observational Studies," *Heart* 102, no. 13 (2016): 1009–1016; Andrew Steptoe, Natalie Owen, Sabine R. Kunz-Ebrecht, and Lena Brydon, "Loneliness and Neuroendocrine, Cardiovascular, and Inflammatory Stress Responses in Middle-aged Men and Women," *Psychoneuroendocrinology* 29, no. 5 (2004): 593–611; John T. Cacioppo and L. C. Hawkley, "Perceived Social Isolation and Cognition," *Trends in Cognitive Sciences*, 13, no. 10 (2009): 447–454; L. C. Hawkley and John T. Cacioppo, "Loneliness Matters: A Theoretical and Empirical Review of Consequences and Mechanisms," *Annals of Behavioral Medicine* 40, no. 2 (2010): 218–227.

[5] See Tyler J. VanderWeele, "Religious Communities and Human Flourishing," *Current Directions in Psychological Science* 26, no. 5 (2017): 476–481.

develops Congar's theological insights into how community, especially through the sacramental activity of the Church and the grace of the Holy Spirit, allows for participation in the life of the Trinitarian God. The third section applies Congar's theological principles to practical pastoral healing remedies for the tendencies of division within the present age, especially dealing with the global pandemic. Neuroscientific studies are pointing toward the importance of social connections. Congar's ecclesiological wisdom offers a healing contrast to the isolation and alienation of our time by articulating a vision of the human person as part of the Body of Christ. People who seek prayerful solitude form loving relationships, unite in communal worship of God, and love their neighbors, support and depend upon each other as members of a *supra-ecclesial* community that can exist here on earth as in heaven.

THE SOCIAL FRAGMENTATION OF HUMANITY

The flourishing of human life requires loving relationships and strong communities while social isolation and divided societies are lethal. Money, fame, and honors are often identified as the marks of a successful life in society. However, many psychological, sociological, and neurological studies reveal that social connection is far more important than material wealth.[6] The obsession for wealth and honor can drive people to despair or fuel desperate measures. Aaron Kheriaty's research on suicide found that "rising rates of suicide, drug abuse, and depression can all be traced to increased social fragmentation. Since the 1980s, reported loneliness among adults in the US increased from 20% to 40%."[7] Supporting the sad reality of Kheriaty's insight about social fragmentation, the World Health Organization announced that "depression is the leading cause of disability worldwide, and is a major contributor to the overall global burden of disease."[8] Several other studies link depression and loneliness by showing how "depression is considered a possible pathway through which loneliness and isolation affect health. Indeed, depressed individuals are more likely to report poorer health-related

---

[6] See George E. Vaillant, "Natural History of Male Psychological Health—Effects of Mental Health on Physical Health," *New England Journal of Medicine* 301, no. 23 (1979): 1249–1254; Johanna C. Malone, Shiri Cohen, Sabrina R. Liu, George E. Vaillant, and Robert J. Waldinger, "Adaptive Midlife Defense Mechanisms and Late-Life Health," *Personality and Individual Differences* 55, no. 2 (2013): 85–89; Ye Luo, Louise C. Hawkley, Linda J. Waite, and John T. Cacioppo, "Loneliness, Health, and Mortality in Old Age: A National Longitudinal Study," *Social Science and Medicine* 74, no. 6 (2012): 907–914.

[7] Aaron Kheriaty, "Dying of Despair," *First Things* 275 (August 2017): 22.

[8] World Health Organization, January 30, 2020, www.who.int/en/news-room/factsheets/detail/depression.

behavior."[9] Dr. Lissa Rankin has confirmed and developed the connection between depression, loneliness, and their deadly side effects with her research, identifying loneliness as the number one health crisis in the modern world.[10]

There are numerous causes of loneliness. As the recent pandemic swept through the world's population, cities locked-down, people quarantined, isolation, and social separation were the mandated normal, and people sank into loneliness. A recent American Psychological Association report identified "a perfect storm" of intense stressors pounding societies, families, and individuals while separation ensued. The report explained how "millions of people have lost their jobs; some have lost their homes or businesses. Families cooped up together because of stay-at-home orders are chafing under the stress, which may increase the risk of intimate partner violence and child abuse."[11] Disrupted routines and the threat of contracting a life-threatening disease exacerbated pre-existing problems such as mental illness or substance abuse. Physical distancing endangered mental health even as it protected physical health. The viral pandemic triggered the spread of mental and spiritual pandemics.

Technological communication often seems to remedy the combination of stress factors arising from the effects of the pandemic, and it allows business and education to continue by keeping people virtually connected. However, psychological and sociological studies have been showing for decades that social relationships and conversations through technology lack necessary components of meaningful relationships. In 1997, Robert Kraut and his colleagues were granted money from Apple Computers, AT&T, Bell Atlantic, Intel, and several other major tech companies to run an experiment testing the effects of Internet use. They found, paradoxically, that "greater use of the Internet was associated with small but statistically significant declines in social involvement as measured by communication within the family and the size of people's local social networks, and with increases in loneliness, a psychological state associated with social involvement. Greater use of the Internet was

---

[9] Shankar, McMunn, Banks, and Steptoe, "Loneliness, Social Isolation, and Behavioral and Biological Health Indicators in Older Adults," 378. See also Annette Allgöwer, Jane Wardle, and Andrew Steptoe, "Depressive Symptoms, Social Support, and Personal Health Behaviors in Young Men and Women," *Health Psychology* 20, no. 3 (2001): 223–227.

[10] Lissa Rankin, "The #1 Public Health Issue Doctors Aren't Talking About," YouTube, www.youtube.com/watch?v=s2hLhWS1O10.

[11] Rebecca A. Clay, "COVID-19 and Suicide," *Monitor on Psychology* 51, no. 4 (2020), www.apa.org/monitor/2020/06/covid-suicide.

also associated with increases in depression."[12] Already in 1997, they speculated that Internet use triggered disengagement from the activities of communal life. People had become overwhelmed with information rather than communicating with others. People spent more time with weak online relationships rather than with strong, long-lasting friendships or family members.[13] How much more now is the rise of technology causing physical separation between people as well as psychological anxiety and spiritual longing?

As much as Zoom parties, synchronized Netflix viewings, e-sport games, and video-chat dance parties are used as coping mechanisms to calm the interior angst of quarantine-induced loneliness, the use of technological communication lacks physical presence and manipulates communal connections. Susan Pinker writes in her analysis of technology that by "assigning our devices supernatural powers, many of us assume we can create distance when we want it and closeness when we want it. ... [A]part is actually the new together, because alone isn't alone anymore."[14] Pinker is certainly not a luddite but strongly questions the use of technology. For example, she writes about how millions of dollars are spent by public school systems to enhance the tablet program, while skilled teachers are let go and the value of personal relationships and face-to-face interaction is lost.

Technology-induced social isolation and loneliness are not new issues rising from the present pandemic. Robert Putnam's research in the 1990s acknowledged the sociological trends of social separation starting in the 1950s as technology infiltrated homes and transformed lifestyles toward the privatization of leisure time. People disengaged from communal interaction and social development. In reflecting on this sociological phenomenon, Putnam states: "By virtually every

---

[12] Robert Kraut, Michael Patterson, Vicki Lundmark, Sara Kiesler, Tridas Mukophadhyay, and William Scherlis, "Internet Paradox: A Social Technology That Reduces Social Involvement and Psychological Well-Being?," *American Psychologist* 53, no. 9 (1998): 1028.

[13] Gentiana Sadikaj and D. S. Moskowitz, "I Hear but I Don't See You: Interacting Over Phone Reduces the Accuracy of Perceiving Affiliation in the Other," *Computers in Human Behavior* 89 (2018): 141. See also Susan Holtzman, Drew DeClerck, Kara Turcotte, Diana Lisi, and Michael Woodworth, "Emotional Support During Times of Stress: Can Text Messaging Compete with In-Person Interactions?," *Computers in Human Behavior* 71 (2017): 130–139.

[14] Pinker, *The Village Effect*, 179. See also John O'Donohue, *Eternal Echoes: Celtic Reflections on Our Yearning to Belong* (New York: HarperCollins, 1999), 228: "In post-modern culture, we tend more and more to inhabit virtual reality rather than actual reality. More and more time is spent in the shadowlands of the computer world; this is a world which is all foreground but has no background. ... Much of modern life is lived in the territory of externality; if we succumb completely to the external, we will lose all sense of inner and personal presence. We will become the ultimate harvesters of absence, namely, ghosts in our lives."

conceivable measure, social capital has eroded steadily and sometimes dramatically over the past two generations. The quantitative evidence is overwhelming. ... Americans have had a growing sense at some visceral level of disintegrating social bonds."[15] These tendencies prophesied by Putnam at the turn of the millennium are only increasing. Johann Hari's research in *Lost Connections* summarizes and updates Putnam's as he comments on the negative trends of social disengagement over the past seventy years. He writes: "The structures for looking out for each other—from the family to the neighborhood—fell apart. We disbanded our tribes. We embarked on an experiment—to see if humans can live alone."[16] The experiment is failing dramatically as Hari gives evidence of high rates of depression and correlated dependencies on drug use and abuse because of the effects of social separation. Hari links depression and drug abuse to disconnections from meaningful work, other people, values, holistic understandings of one's childhood traumas, status and respect, the natural world, a hopeful and secure future, one's genetic lineage, and proper attention to one's homeostatic needs. Neural and physiological studies as well as anthropological trends are revealing how the "Self" is in turmoil.[17] Social separation has disastrous effects on persons and communities.

The symptoms of loneliness are shown to have long-term consequences. John T. Cacioppo, a social neuroscientist at the University of Chicago, focused his research of over three decades on

---

[15] Robert Putnam, *Bowling Alone: The Collapse and Revival of American Community* (New York: Simon and Schuster, 2000), 287.

[16] Johann Hari, *Lost Connections: Uncovering the Real Causes of Depression—and the Unexpected Solutions* (New York: Bloomsbury, 2018), 80.

[17] There is a growing discussion on the moral implications of the pervasiveness of social networks and digital devices in the lives of a majority of first world populations. To appreciate this discussion, see Marcus Mescher, "The Moral Impact of Digital Devices," *Journal of Moral Theology* 9, no. 2 (2020): 65–93; Jean M. Twenge, *iGen: Why Today's Super-Connected Kids are Growing Up Less Rebellious, More Tolerant, Less Happy—and Completely Unprepared for Adulthood (and What That Means for the Rest of Us)* (New York: Atria, 2017); Adam L. Alter, *Irresistible: The Rise of Addictive Technology and the Business of Keeping Us Hooked* (New York: Penguin, 2017); Rebecca A. Clay, "Treating the Misuse of Digital Devices: Psychologists are Spearheading Efforts to Help Wean People Off Technology," *Monitor on Psychology* 49, no. 10 (2018): 76; Jonathan Haidt and Tobias Rose-Stockwell, "The Dark Psychology of Social Networks: Why it Feels Everything is Going Haywire," *The Atlantic* (December 2019), www.theatlantic.com/magazine/archive/2019/12/social-media-democracy/600763/; Tristan Harris, "Our Brains are no Match for Our Technology," *The New York Times, Turning Points* (Dec. 5, 2019), www.nytimes.com/2019/12/05/opinion/digital-technology-brain.html. Tristan Harris is also the editor of the influential documentary the detrimental uses of technology on the human person called *The Social Dilemma*. Tristan Harris also is the founder of the Center for Humane Technology (www.humantech.com).

the increasing epidemic of loneliness pervading modern culture. Cacioppo, along with his colleagues Louise Hawkley and Gary Berntson, discovered five consistent symptoms of loneliness.[18] First, a lonely person is evolutionarily less fit; because of poorer health and lower energy levels, the person is less attractive to potential partners for meaningful and reproductive relationships.[19] Second, when health care providers are forced to make decisions about the allocation of resources to suffering patients, Cacioppo and his colleagues claim that seeing an isolated person with no social connections discourages them from using the limited resources on that person so as to reserve the resources for socially-connected people.[20] Third, isolated people are less inclined to pursue healthy lifestyle choices. They receive less encouragement to take care of themselves or seek out necessary health treatments compared to those surrounded by supportive friends and family. Fourth, lonely people are found to have consistently higher levels of stress compared to people with many social connections. The effects of stress, especially chronic stress (consistently activated sympathetic nervous system "fight or flight" and hypothalamic-pituitary-adrenocortical [HPA] response mechanism) deteriorates bodily organs, especially the heart, and lowers resiliency for overcoming future stress.[21] Fifth, lonely people have a weakened ability to repair and maintain their physiology. "The restorative act of sleep," Cacioppo and his colleagues find, "is more efficient and effective—that is, salubrious—in non-lonely individuals than in lonely individuals."[22] They explain, "The research on loneliness suggests that different mechanisms operate to explain short-term and long-term effects of loneliness on health and well-being. We have further found that slowly unfolding pathophysiological processes triggered by loneliness are the consequence of multiple physiological systems."[23] Cacioppo's research reveals that lonely individuals perpetuate the physical, psychological, and neurological effects of loneliness because of the isolated and disconnected perspective in which they are trapped.

Loneliness also has societal ramifications as the productivity of whole economies can decline. Those suffering from loneliness often lack the interest, motivation, or ability to go to work. When large numbers of a society's population are suffering from loneliness, the

---

[18] See John T. Cacioppo, Louise C. Hawkley, and Gary G. Berntson, "The Anatomy of Loneliness," *Current Directions in Psychological Science* 12, no. 3 (2003): 71–74.
[19] Cacioppo, Hawkley, and Berntson, "The Anatomy of Loneliness," 71.
[20] Cacioppo, Hawkley, and Berntson, "The Anatomy of Loneliness," 71.
[21] Cacioppo, Hawkley, and Berntson, "The Anatomy of Loneliness," 72.
[22] Cacioppo, Hawkley, and Berntson, "The Anatomy of Loneliness," 73.
[23] Cacioppo, Hawkley, and Berntson, "The Anatomy of Loneliness," 74.

impact is magnified. A study done by Ozcelik and Barsade gives evidence that loneliness is a social phenomenon observable by an employee's coworkers and diminishing work performance.[24] The ripple effects of loneliness throughout a population account for the fact that the government of the United Kingdom has recently designated over twenty-million pounds toward the development of the Loneliness Commission and created a position in the national government called the Minister of Loneliness under the Secretary of State for Sport and Civil Society. The founding document of this commission states: "Government's vision is for this country to be a place where we can all have strong social relationships. Where families, friends and communities support each other, especially at vulnerable points where people are at greater risk of loneliness. Where institutions value the human element in their interactions with people. And where loneliness is recognized and acted on without stigma or shame, so that we all look out for one another."[25] The crippling effects of lonely individuals in society are gaining recognition as a major world crisis.

The feelings associated with loneliness include emptiness, anxiety, hunger for intimacy, fear, and self-loathing. These desperate feelings amplify the need for either healing remedies for relief or numbing antidotes for escape. The opioid crisis and other addictive behaviors are often linked to the deep anguish plaguing human souls.[26] Despite all of the studies on the causes and effects of loneliness and, subsequently, the millions of dollars now allocated to treatments for this pervading epidemic ravaging through populations and affecting the economic development of countries, what is the root cause of this affliction? Why are people falling into depression which then cascades into disconnection and withdrawal from social connections? Why do people not feel comfortable reaching out to one another for support when dealing with pain, stress, fear, and sadness? What kind of existential longing is causing people to turn to drugs, alcohol, the Internet, or other addictive mind-numbing activities to fulfill their

---

[24] See Hakan Ozcelik and Sigal Barsade, "Work Loneliness and Employee Performance," *Academy of Management Proceedings* 2011, no. 1 (2017): 1–6.
[25] Jeremy Wright and Tracey Crouch, eds., *A Connected Society: A Strategy for Tackling Loneliness–Laying the Foundations for Change* (London: Department for Digital, Culture, Media and Sport, 2018), 6.
[26] See Hari, *Lost Connections,* 27–38; Katie O'Connor, "Drug Overdoses Surge Due to Pandemic, Early Reports Show," *Psychiatric News* 55, no. 15 (30 July 2020): 9; William Wan and Heather Long, "'Cries for Help': Drug Overdoses Are Soaring During the Coronavirus Pandemic," *Washington Post,* July 1, 2020, www.washingtonpost.com/health/2020/07/01/coronavirus-drug-overdose: "Social distancing has also sequestered people, leaving them to take drugs alone and making it less likely that someone else will be there to call 911 or to administer the lifesaving overdose antidote naloxone, also known as Narcan."

aching hearts?

To be human requires connection, an integration with a self-transcendent mission more expansive than individual pursuits. What holds healthy communities together is a worldview allowing the members of the community to endure and make sense of the world in which they live. Philip Brownell, in his chapter "Healing Potential of Religious Community," explains: "A worldview is comprised of the cognitive beliefs and cultural feelings and values that mediate between knowledge systems within a given people group. People learn worldviews from their communities, and each community re-creates itself (and its worldview), often changing in the process through social interaction. It is the metaphors and stories in that process that provide a framework by which people make sense of their lives."[27] More than simply a collection of individuals, who may still experience loneliness even when around each other, a life-giving community will facilitate interpersonal experience as each member becomes conscious of his or her part within a unified body. Each person will have distinct and important roles to contribute to the well-being of the whole. Brownell explains: "When people are drawn into relationships through their interest in one another, the spiritual response to needs, and the depth of sanctification, gifts are set loose in the community, resulting in the observation that Paul made that there are varieties of gifts, varieties of ministries, and varieties of effects (when all this works together in a community)."[28] Religious communities, as manifest in local churches, can often become the needed refuge of connection in a fractured world.

At the same time, religious affiliation and the engagement in religious practices, including prayer, communal worship, solitary reflection, and communal service projects are not merely self-help applications. The authentic practice of a faith tradition establishes a solid foundation to one's life by providing meaning and purpose while also connecting people to each other as a unified community.[29] To fulfill the longing of the human heart requires a connection to a

---

[27] Philip Brownell, "Healing Potential of Religious Community," in *The Healing Power of Spirituality: How Faith Helps Humans Thrive*, Vol. 2, Religion, ed. J. Harold Ellens (Santa Barbara, CA: ABC-Clio, 2010), 2.

[28] Brownell, "Healing Potential of Religious Community," 16.

[29] As an example of a study that investigated the relationship between religious affiliation and practice with suicide attempts see Kanita Dervic, Maria A. Oquendo, Michael F. Grunebaum, Steve Ellis, Ainsley K. Burke, and J. John Mann, "Religious Affiliation and Suicide Attempt," *American Journal of Psychiatry* 161, no. 12 (2004): 2303–2308: "Religiously unaffiliated subjects had significantly more lifetime suicide attempts and more first degree relatives who committed suicide than subjects who endorsed a religious affiliation. Unaffiliated subjects were younger, less often married, less often had children, and had less contact with family members."

community that holds a unified vision of ultimate fulfillment for all persons together, a *supra-ecclesial community*. From a theological perspective, the deepest human desire is communal unification in fulfillment with the creator God, who is love.[30] The writings of Yves Congar develop a vision of a *supra-ecclesial community*. His work addresses the fundamental Christian belief of the Trinitarian God, who is perfect unity with diversity. He also discusses God's action within the Church in the modern world through the indwelling of the Holy Spirit (see also *Lumen Gentium*, nos. 1–8).[31] Human persons are essential components of God's diversity and unity in that each person is a unique, sacred sanctuary of the Holy Spirit. The Holy Spirit labors within creation to enliven people as citizens of the Kingdom of God. As a contrast to the coping mechanisms presently used for the aches of loneliness as outlined above, by entering the life of the Church— which includes the discipline of prayer, the worship of God, and the active life of evangelization and care for the poor, sick, or vulnerable– –people long for connection with each other and God, "the partner who is at the one and the same time infinitely beyond and more intimate than our deepest self."[32] Congar's writings delve into the mystery of God's active presence in the world through the Church and that is why they are an invaluable resource to use to think theologically about the challenge of loneliness and offer a possible answer to it.

The solution to the detrimental problems of isolation and the breakdown of community will require each person's unique perspectives and individual concerted efforts, guided by divine grace, to form and maintain a communal gathering place, like the Church. As Pinker explains in *The Village Effect*, "Social contact is like a vaccine: a little can go a long way when it comes to preventing pain and loss of opportunity, while saving billions in health and social service costs."[33] Christianity proclaims that, in the midst of the vast diversity of humanity, there is one way, one truth, one life, who is the second person of the Trinity (John 14:6). The way of the life of loving and meaningful connection, as personified by Jesus Christ, is revealed to humanity through grace. God's grace precedes any human effort and impels people toward the loving unity of the Trinitarian God. As

---

[30] See the theological research of Robert M. Doran in the three volumes of *The Trinity in History: Theology of the Divine Missions*. Doran emphasizes how the human person is drawn into the interpersonal relationship with the Trinitarian Relations of love.
[31] See Yves Congar, *I Believe in the Holy Spirit*, vol. 1 (New York: Crossroad, 1997), 65–70.
[32] Yves Congar, "The Spirit Is the Source of Life in Us Personally and in the Church," in *The Spirit of God: Short Writings on the Holy Spirit*, ed. and trans. Susan Mader Brown, Mark E. Ginter, Joseph G. Mueller, and Catherine E. Clifford (Washington, DC: Catholic University of America Press, 2018), 39.
[33] Pinker, *The Village Effect*, 275.

people of faith are driven by grace and love to gather together to worship the one God of love, they form a unified body, the Church (*Gaudium et Spes*, nos. 39–40). The gathering of people united by grace and impelled by love can then become a refuge for the lonely and despairing. Pope Francis commented that the Church is a field hospital having "the ability to heal wounds and to warm the hearts of the faithful."[34] If the Church can become a healing sanctuary for the fractured society and lonely individuals, the sinful separation from God and one another is minimized. Individuals who have a sense of belonging can heal the brokenness within and restore relationships. The unification as the Body of Christ in an ecclesial community provides glimpses of divine life, which is why the Church is more than a therapeutic mechanism. On the contrary, when persons are flooded with God's grace they become instruments of God's love by their compassionate acts of care for the wounded and despairing.

THE FULLNESS OF LIFE IN AND AS THE CHURCH

This second section discusses Congar's writings that emphasize the communal nature of humanity. Much of Congar's scholarship revolves around historical divisions of the Church, from the rift between the Eastern Orthodox and the Western Roman Church, to the Reformation's divisions. Congar's work addresses how diversity and differences of religious expression can coexist along with unity in the one, holy, catholic, and apostolic Church. Congar's strategies for building stronger unity as a human community are foundational, wide-ranging, and methodological, extending their applicability to other human divisions, especially the recent issues of loneliness, individualism, and community disintegration, as discussed. Congar's wisdom from the mid-twentieth century remains relevant for issues of the twenty-first century because it is rooted in the conviction that the Holy Spirit radically transforms human life. He writes: "The Holy Spirit is that active presence in us of the Absolute who, at one and the same time, deepens our interior life by making it vibrant and welcoming and puts us in communion with others: the Spirit is what requires and is the means of communion."[35] In this second section I highlight three aspects of Congar's work: first, the process required to deepen one's interior life; second, the unifying force of the life of the Church; and third, the eschatological implications of the Body of Christ.

---

[34] Antonio Spadaro, SJ, "A Big Heart Open to God: An Interview with Pope Francis," *America*, September 30, 2013, www.americamagazine.org/pope-interview.
[35] Congar, *The Spirit of God*, 38.

The Grace and Power of Sacred Solitude

According to Congar, human persons are freed from their existential angst and fundamental brokenness by developing an interior life of prayer. In a short writing entitled "The Spirit Is the Source of Life in Us Personally and in the Church," he emphasizes humanity's hunger for the Holy Spirit. He explains: "This thirst for the Trinity and the Holy Spirit coincides with—and this is no accident—an agonizing search for identity on the part of humanity."[36] After this, Congar references W. H. Auden's *Christmas Oratorio*. This contemplation considers the motivation of the three magi for following the star. Congar retells the story of the magi through Auden's creative interpretation. To the question addressed to the three magi of why they are following the star, "The first says 'to discover how to be truthful today,' the second one says 'to discover how to be alive today,' the third says, 'to discover how to love today.' Then all say together: 'To discover how to be human today is why we follow the star!'"[37] Humans seek to discover the originating font of their nature enabling flourishing and fulfillment. Loneliness and the propensity for addictive behaviors are the consequences of persons thirsting for fulfillment but grasping for the unsatisfying, that which does not reveal the essence of human life, that which is not God.

Instead of seeing quarantine and isolation as a mandated punishment, can the quiet solitude take on a sanctity? Congar advocates for disciplined prayer practice to develop an interior disposition of freedom and a vision of the unifying love of God. Strong communities are the result of individuals prayerfully freed from selfish or isolating attachments and actions. Congar explains: "Interiority bespeaks liberty. ... The Spirit does not liberate from the content of the Law, that is, from the good, but it removes the constraint of obligations because, by grace and love, the Spirit interiorizes what they command. Henceforth my conformity to the Law comes from me; it is my spontaneous movement. I act freely."[38] Receiving the grace of freedom requires discipline, asceticism, and vulnerable receptivity. Grace establishes trust in God's freeing law of love and removes disordered attachments to the finite aspects of the physical world. Growth toward freedom is an interior journey toward love, as the magi's voyage was guided by the star, symbolic of their steadfast faith. The Holy Spirit leads people along the path of holiness and truth, which is manifested as communion with God and love of neighbors. Congar asserts: "Immersed in a world of concrete, of technology, of programmed life, and of merciless competition, a person today

---

[36] Congar, *The Spirit of God*, 37.
[37] Congar, *The Spirit of God*, 37.
[38] Congar, *The Spirit of God*, 41.

experiences the need to have an interior life ('un dedans'), some sacred personal space and, at the same time, a connection with other human beings."[39] Interior life develops in solitude.[40] It necessitates renouncing aspects of the present society contributing to loneliness so as to receive the Holy Spirit. The Holy Spirit provides the desire for community and connection. The irony of the interior life is that when persons open themselves to receive the flood of God's love (Romans 5:5) through prayerful solitude, they are impelled to love fellow human persons (John 13:34–35) in community.

Congar explains that the law of freedom requires growth at two levels, personal and communal. He wrote: "Conversion is personal, but it is not sufficient. The content of the Law, which Love makes concrete (Romans 13:8–12), has to do with one's neighbor."[41] In saying this, a clear distinction exists between loneliness and solitude. Prayerful solitude allows for conversion from despair to hope, wickedness to virtue, ignorance to knowledge.[42] When a person intentionally prays by contemplating God's self-emptying love, she is motivated to transcend personal struggles to join a community and contribute to the flourishing of others.[43] Loneliness, as discussed, causes mental and physical afflictions. Congar articulates how the benefits of the grace of liberty can radiate from the peace of interior life out to the activities of life and the physical body.[44] He writes: "The

---

[39] Congar, *The Spirit of God*, 38.

[40] See Robert Cardinal Sarah with Nicolas Diat, *The Power of Silence: Against the Dictatorship of Noise*, trans. Michael J. Miller (San Francisco: Ignatius, 2017), 23: "It is necessary to leave our interior turmoil in order to find God. Despite the agitations, the busyness, the easy pleasures, God remains silently present. He is in us like a thought, a word, and a presence whose secret sources are buried in God himself, inaccessible to human inspection. Solitude is the best state in which to hear God's silence."

[41] Congar, *The Spirit of God*, 42.

[42] Bernard Lonergan, SJ, another twentieth-century Catholic theologian, discussed the religious, moral, and intellectual conversions of self-appropriation. See Bernard Lonergan, *Method in Theology*, Collected Works, vol. 14, 2nd edition, revised and augmented (Toronto: University of Toronto Press, 2017), 238–247.

[43] Bernard Lonergan explained how conversion leads to self-transcendence: "As intellectual and moral conversion, so also religious conversion is a modality of self-transcendence. Moral conversion is to values apprehended, affirmed, and realized by a real self-transcendence. Religious conversion is to a total being-in-love as the efficacious ground of all self-transcendence, whether in the pursuit of truth, or in the realization of human values, or in the orientation man adopts to the universe, its ground, and its goal" (Lonergan, *Method in Theology*, 241).

[44] Hannah Arendt, the Jewish German refugee who sought refuge in the United States, compared and contrasted the *vita activa*, involved in the dealings of the *polis*, with the *vita contemplativa*. See Hannah Arendt, *The Life of the Mind; The Groundbreaking Investigation on How We Think*, one-volume edition (New York: Harcourt, 1978), 27: "Before the modern age, there had existed—not many but a few—well trodden escape routes, at least for philosophers. In antiquity, there was the *bios theōrētikos*: the

liberty that the Spirit brings goes beyond the purely private spiritual realm of the personal interior life. This is so, first of all, because liberty is intended for our body too."[45] As loneliness has many physical manifestations and causes harmful effects to the body, the peace and liberty of divine grace has physical manifestations and allows for healing and flourishing.[46] Congar writes: "Through our bodies, we are a piece of the world. We may be a very small piece in terms of mass but we are a decisive one because the world's evolution has culminated in us and, thus, we draw the world into our own destiny."[47] Solitude allows a person to recognize the importance and blessing of his or her existence and the talents and strengths he or she has to contribute to the benefit of humanity.

Time in prayerful solitude impels a person toward the love of community. Jesus sought out deserts and mountains for aloneness in prayer and communion with his Father. The time of solitude with God the Father empowered Jesus to immerse himself in the life of the community and form his disciples (Matthew 14:22–23; Luke 6:12). Following times of prayerful solitude, Jesus returned to the cities and called forth his disciples to form a community of zealous faithful proclaiming the good news of the Kingdom of God. He also sought out and healed the sick and exorcized demons. Prayer in holy solitude can empower each person to fulfill his or her mission within the human community. Congar discusses how the Holy Spirit imparts "charisms" to each member of the Mystical Body of Christ, the Church. He explains that "charism" means gift or talent and "does not necessarily mean extraordinary gifts such as miracles, healings, or speaking in tongues. These gifts have been present in the past and still exist. ... [they are] the plan of God's grace."[48] Too often, lonely people shamefully think that they have nothing to contribute to the

---

thinker dwelt in the neighborhood of things necessary and everlasting, partaking in their Being to the extent that this is possible for mortals. In the era of Christian philosophy, there was the *vita contemplativa* of the monasteries and the universities, but also the consoling thought of divine Providence, joined to the expectation of an after-life when what had seemed contingent and meaningless in this world would become crystal clear."

[45] Congar, *The Spirit of God*, 42.
[46] The author of this article is currently a member of a team working on a grant-funded research project entitled "The Marquette Irenaeus Project." The research team is studying the transformational effects of Christian prayer practices by identifying biomarkers of healing and self-regulation, qualitative psychological patterns of spiritual growth, and maturation of one's image of God. The project hopes to revive and teach ancient Christian prayer practices and virtuous habits that foster resiliency, community, human flourishing, and movement toward the fullness of life (www.marquette.edu/innovation/documents/ec-19-krall.pdf).
[47] Congar, *The Spirit of God*, 43.
[48] Congar, *The Spirit of God*, 49–50.

community and that they cannot perform helpful deeds for others. Because of self-doubt, they are swept into the depression of dejection.[49] In his letter to the Ephesians, St. Paul explained how each person is given charisms that build up the full stature of Christ. When each person contributes to the formation of the community of the Church by developing and using their charisms, St. Paul taught, "We may no longer be infants, tossed by waves and swept along by every wind of teaching arising from human trickery, from their cunning in the interests of deceitful scheming. Rather, living the truth in love, we should grow in every way into him who is the head, Christ" (Ephesians 4:14–15). Prayerful solitude provides space for the Spirit to work within a person and stir up the charisms residing in the person's heart and mind.

Prayer includes acts of penance, contemplation and meditation, intentional awareness of one's words, thoughts, and actions, fasting, and praise and worship of God. Christianity taught a variety of prayer methods for the last two millennia. Congar describes: "The deep dimension of our being becomes real in prayer, that admirable activity that is proper to the human being and qualifies one as human. We can experience an I-Thou relationship not only horizontally, with a human partner, but also vertically, with that partner who is at one and the same time infinitely beyond and more intimate than our deepest self."[50] The act of prayer is very personal. As Jesus taught his disciples, "When you pray, go to your inner room, close the door, and pray to your Father in secret. And your Father who sees in secret will repay you" (Matthew 6:6). Christianity's sacred traditions advocate for the importance of developing the interior, personal, individual life of the soul. When the soul is cultivated, trained, and nurtured, Congar explains that each person becomes like a finely tuned instrument in the orchestra of the living Church. He writes: "The Spirit is inciting revivals of the Gospel everywhere. This happens through persons. Consequently, this involves a certain precariousness, a fragmentary character, even an appearance of disorganization. But, as it is the same Spirit in all, both in Jesus and in us, a hidden but sovereign orchestra conductor will make the diversity converge in a unified work which is all his own!"[51] Consisting of living persons, the Church is united through the active presence of the Holy Spirit who encourages the

---

[49] See Mary Margaret Funk, OSB, *Thoughts Matter: The Practice of Spiritual Life* (New York: Continuum, 1998), 89: "The dejected one shows signs of being rough, through displays of rancor and impatience. Each day the dejected monk grows more hard-hearted toward others who need care and compassion. He displays useless grief and is caught in suicidal despair. This unwholesome sorrow draws out the energy from him and breaks down the one on whom it has fastened."

[50] Congar, *The Spirit of God*, 39.

[51] Congar, *The Spirit of God*, 50.

mutual sharing of personal gifts. This integration of charisms possessed within the great diversity of human persons is the building of the one, holy, Catholic Church, the living Mystical Body of Christ.

Involvement in the building of the Mystical Body of Christ requires the theological virtue of faith. For Congar, faith is linked closely to the communally cherished lineage of tradition. Faith and tradition together allow for personal interior spiritual growth so that the community as a whole can grow stronger. He writes: "[Faith] is a conviction to which we commit ourselves, but its content is not given us by ourselves. It is a sharing with a number of others and, in a line of historical succession, with Christ's apostles. That is why it is shared out and transmitted beginning with them. Möhler expresses this well: 'Without tradition there would be no Christian doctrine, no Church, only isolated Christians; no community, only individuals; no certitude, only doubt and opinion.'"[52] The living reality of faith, that deep interior conviction arrived at only through profound personal prayer, is rooted and grounded in the living out and passing on of tradition, which connects all people and generations to one common vision.

Through tradition, the individual becomes connected to the body of the Church but does not lose individuality. With the notion of consciousness, Congar explains his point by writing: "Consciousness belongs to persons, who cannot merge into a higher unity. The unity of persons in the Church is not a 'fusion,' but a 'communion': a large number of persons possess in common the same realities … as the content of their inner life, their memory, and thus of their consciousness. Thus, they are conscious not of their *personal* opinions but of the teachings *of the Church* that derives from the apostles."[53] People of faith become conscious of their interdependence with each other and God. The "supra" consciousness of Christians emerges as each individual is able to rise above particular differences and recognize the shared unity activated when loving and praising God together. In the Church, the "supra" consciousness *is* love and is expressed when individuals conform their wills to God's. Christians who conform their wills to God satisfy the longing of their hearts. Communion with each other in God is the means by which the disabling effects of loneliness are potentially overcome. As people cultivate their interior lives through prayer in solitude, refine their unique charisms, and participate in the great symphony of the proclamation of the Gospel, they can recognize the interconnection of a *supra-ecclesial community*. Christianity emphasizes the importance

---

[52] Yves Congar, *Tradition and Traditions: An Historical and a Theological Essay*, trans. Michael Naseby and Thomas Rainborough (London: Burns and Oates, 1966), 315.
[53] Congar, *Tradition and Traditions*, 320.

of each individual encountering the Lord in the quiet of his or her own heart. The fulfillment of this personal process of struggle and growth is the unification of one's self to God, which includes loving and communing with other people. Joining together with a shared consciousness strengthens the whole community. No longer are individuals "the aggregate of a number of particular voices but a summing up achieved by a sharing of consciousness, in which the memory of the gifts made by the Lord to his Bride is personified."[54] The human-divine communion is manifested in this world most powerfully in the life of the Church.

The Unifying Grace of the Life of the Church

Congar's writings explore the life of the Church as one body composed of many parts. The gathering and unifying of the diversity of peoples under one common belief and engaged in one shared mission is precisely what allows the collective whole to grow stronger. The individual person is who Congar held up as the great wealth of the Church. He explained how "each one is an original and autonomous principle of sensitivity, experience, relationships, and initiatives."[55] However, humanity's tendency toward sin means that the strength of the Church comes not from individual persons, but the power of God's grace that draws individuals together by wiping away division and discord. Congar explains that "the church here below is like a net full of fishes of all sorts, good and bad, like a field where weeds are mixed with wheat; both Cain and Abel can belong to it. The church's proper work is precisely to ceaselessly purify sinners from their sin."[56] As people gather as the living Church and form the supra-collective consciousness by putting aside individual opinions and selfish desires, then the Church can become, as Congar articulates, "the place and the instrument for the application of Christ's redemption."[57] Christ's redeeming act is the unification of all people, saints and sinners, drawn together as a whole and complete body acting as one to praise God.

Despite the weakness and sinfulness of humanity, the Holy Spirit draws out the best of each person receptive to God's grace. The power of grace enhances each part of the total body to strengthen the Catholic whole. Congar recognizes the dynamic universality in the great diversity of peoples coming together to praise God as the one, holy, Catholic Church. He explains: "The whole Church—its people, its

---

[54] Congar, *Tradition and Traditions*, 321.
[55] Yves Congar, *I Believe in the Holy Spirit*, vol. 2 (New York: Crossroad, 1997), 16.
[56] Yves Congar, *True and False Reform of the Church*, trans. Paul J. Philibert (Collegeville, MN: Liturgical Press, 2011), 99.
[57] Congar, *True and False Reform*, 99.

ministers, its treasure of the means of grace and its institution—is that sacrament of salvation. ... The Church is, after all, an institution of a very special kind. It acts in the present on the basis of past events and in the prospect of a future which is nothing less than the kingdom of God."[58] The charisms and values that the Church holds as sacred and which are fulfilled in Christ, are manifested through the concrete actions of each person in his or her particular time and place. Each person is integral to the life of the Church.[59] Each person has a unique role to fulfill. As people allow the Holy Spirit into their lives to magnify their actions with grace, the fullness of the diversity and catholicity or universality of God is made manifest.

Liturgy is the clearest and most dynamic demonstration of the life of the Body of Christ. Congar explains: "It was in the liturgy that believing Christians professed their faith as a community in words and gestures and the grace that God had given to men in the economy of revelation and above all in Jesus Christ and his Passover was made present in the lives of men."[60] The Church alive through the liturgy brings about the powerful movement of God towards humanity and humanity towards God. "This movement passes from the Father through the Son in the Spirit and returns in the Spirit through the Son to the glory of the Father, who takes us, as his children, into communion with him."[61] When people can experience it, communion is what satisfies the deepest longing of the human soul and what soothes the pain of loneliness and fear. When each person, blessed with unique, individualized charisms, contributes his or her loving presence in the orchestra of the Church, as manifested most poignantly in the liturgy, there is divine communion.

The Church can bring healing to the brokenness and loneliness of humanity through her sacraments and liturgies. Congar explains that the Church's "whole ministry consists, whether in the celebration of the Eucharist or in exercising functions that spring therefrom and are preparatory to it, in applying to each soul, across the centuries, the universal cause of salvation and of life found and given by Christ in His Passion."[62] Congar's vision of the Church is that of an institution which conveys divine grace. The Church is "the sacrament, the effective sign and giver of the gift of new life and of union of men

---

[58] Congar, *I Believe in the Holy Spirit*, vol. 3 (New York: Crossroad, 1997), 271.
[59] Henri De Lubac, another twentieth century Catholic theologian, also emphasized the importance of the person as integral to the life of the whole Church. See Henri de Lubac, *Catholicism: Christ and the Common Destiny of Man*, trans. Lancelot C. Sheppard and Sr. Elizabeth Englund, OCD (San Francisco: Ignatius, 1950), 326–350.
[60] Congar, *I Believe in the Holy Spirit*, vol. 1, 104.
[61] Congar, *I Believe in the Holy Spirit*, vol. 1, 104.
[62] Yves Congar, *The Mystery of the Church*, trans. A. V. Littledale (Baltimore: Helicon, 1960), 115.

[*sic*] in Christ their Saviour."⁶³ By conveying grace, however, the Church is not just another attempt to address depression, loneliness, and suicide crises that plague the human race. It does not offer another therapeutic technique to help remedy the symptoms of the pains of humanity. Becoming an active member of the Church is motivated by more than obtaining physical health benefits. Rather, the Church is the refuge for lonely, weak, and isolated sinners which then vivifies humanity by joining persons together as one Body, the foretaste of the Kingdom of God.⁶⁴ With pastoral care, Congar explains how Christ asks us "to open our souls to him, to deliver our lives up to him and to put ourselves entirely at his disposition, so that we no longer live our own life on our own account exclusively but that, by his grace, we live his own life and on his account."⁶⁵ Rather than seeking individualistic gains, personal health benefits, and self-promoting pursuits, the ironic message of Christianity is that the more each person adheres to the will of Christ, the more free and fulfilled the person will be (James 1:25). The life of the Church, and thus the healing and enlivening of the Church's members, consists of each person glorifying the Lord by contributing to the building of the Body of Christ.

The Church Drawn by the Holy Spirit to Fulfillment

The third aspect of Congar's thought acknowledges the eschatological dimension of the unified Church. The Catholic Church, as manifest in the life of local parish congregations scattered throughout the world, may appear as a feeble, sinful, political, and human institution. Due to the global pandemic, many churches halted public masses for several months. The universal Church became privatized. The living pulse of the Church as manifested through communal liturgy continued but was spread out to virtual communities. Participation in the celebration of the Mass was performed by watching it on a personal computer alone, in quarantine, at home.⁶⁶ Nevertheless, Christianity proclaims the eschatological vision of all creation uniting in a new heaven and a new earth. Keeping hold of this ultimate vision is a source of strength and hope for humanity caught in the trials of a pandemic-riddled and divisive world. Loneliness or quarantine cannot crush a person who perseveres in eschatological hope. Jesus proclaimed the fulfillment of the

---

⁶³ Congar, *The Mystery of the Church*, 115.
⁶⁴ See Yves Congar, *The Mystery of the Church*, 120.
⁶⁵ Congar, *The Mystery of the Church*, 119.
⁶⁶ For a balanced reflection about the needed careful discernment between the public performance of liturgies in the midst of a global pandemic and the preservation of all human life through quarantine, see Thomas Joseph White, OP, "Epidemic Danger and Catholic Sacraments," *First Things* (April 9, 2020), www.firstthings.com/web-exclusives/2020/04/epidemic-danger-and-catholic-sacraments.

covenant of God the Father to the world through his passion, death, and resurrection. His mission is the centrality of the Christian faith and the basis of eschatological hope. Congar poetically describes how in Christ, "the true relation [is] established between God and man, all the prophetical writings are clarified and blended together in harmony. As at Cana, tasteless water becomes a full-flavored, inspiring wine, the veil is lifted and things that before seemed meaningless take on their meaning."[67] God's eschatological promise is that the glory of each individual will be revealed in the Body of Christ. The veil of the sin-riddled, selfish, and individualistic earthbound mind is lifted so that humanity can rejoice in the glory of God flowing through the communion of saints abiding within the beatific vision. Pentecost, depicted in Acts, provides a glimpse into this glorious Spirit-driven communion (Acts 2:42–47). Amidst great diversity, each person experiences the fullness of life as they are guided by apostolic teaching announcing the transformative revelation of Jesus Christ.

PRACTICAL PASTORAL HEALING REMEDIES

Finally, this paper's third component applies Congar's teachings as practical pastoral healing remedies for the individualistic tendencies of the present age. In 2018, a study conducted at the University of California San Diego monitored 340 participants whose ages ranged from 27 to 101. The researchers found that the severity of loneliness and age had a complex relationship, with increased loneliness reports especially from the participants in their late 20s, mid 50s, and late 80s. Multiple types of surveys were used to gather this data.[68] An important outcome of this study was that participants who indicated that they sought out pursuits of wisdom, such as study, hobbies, volunteer positions, as well as actions of compassion and other prosocial behaviors, reported less loneliness. Even if people were within the specified age ranges of higher prevalence of loneliness and lived alone, when intellectually stimulated and engaged in self-transcendent pursuits, feelings of loneliness diminished.

From the neurobiological perspective, pursuing wisdom is categorized into six general categories. These include: 1) prosocial attitudes and behaviors, such as seeking to contribute to a common good or having positive emotions and behaviors toward others; 2) social decision-making and the ability to deal with life's problems; 3)

---

[67] Congar, *Tradition and Traditions*, 390.
[68] Ellen E. Lee, Colin Depp, Barton W. Palmer, Danielle Glorioso, Rebecca Daly, Jinyuan Liu, Xin M. Tu, Ho-Cheol Kim, Peri Tarr, Yasunori Yamada, and Dilip V. Jeste, "High Prevalence and Adverse Health Effects of Loneliness in Community-Dwelling Adults Across the Lifespan: Role of Wisdom as a Protective Factor," *International Psychogeriatrics* 31, no. 10 (2019): 1447–1462.

emotional homeostasis and the ability to regulate one's reaction to adversity; 4) reflection and self-understanding including reflection on the transcendent; 5) tolerance when evaluating phenomena from multiple perspectives; 6) adaptability to ambiguity.[69] Putting these wisdom categories into practical practices, Cacioppo gives advice to combat loneliness. He says: "The simplest moments of connection, especially when they involve 'feeding others,' carry an emotional uplift that does not require taking a pill, working up a sweat, or eating truckloads of cruciferous vegetables."[70] From the neuro-psychological perspective, simple but intentional behaviors of wisdom, which necessarily involve self-transcendence, allow body chemistry to change, behavioral patterns to shift, neuro-plasticity to adjust from negative feedback loops to positive ones, new habits of compassion to take effect, negative and self-defeating perspectives to be replaced with positive ones, and loneliness to be transformed into wisdom, care, compassion, social engagement, and hope.[71]

Congar writes about the transformational actions in which Christians engage when participating in the sacraments of the Church: "Baptism makes us be conceived and born as sons of God within the Church," which emphasized the importance of unity, social engagement, and connection to a greater whole, a *supra-ecclesial community*. Congar continues: "Confirmation enables us to participate in Christ's messianic anointing." This missioning is the powerful healing remedy to disengagement and isolation. Each Christian is entrusted with the duty to serve Christ and His Church. Confirmation imparts the Holy Spirit, whose grace transforms individuals, encouraging each person to participate in tasks far bigger than self-absorbed concerns or self-immanence.[72] Congar explains: "God created a body, then gave it breath. Christ means 'anointed.' In the writings of the Fathers and in the liturgy, we cannot be fulfilled as 'Christians' unless our spiritual anointing is expressed visibly and tangibly."[73] Finally, when participating in the Eucharist, individuals

---

[69] Thomas W. Meeks and Dilip V. Jeste, "Neurobiology of Wisdom: A Literature Overview," *Archives of General Psychiatry* 66, no. 4 (2009): 356.
[70] Cacioppo and Patrick, *Loneliness*, 237.
[71] See Monika Ardelt and Dilip V. Jeste, "Wisdom and Hard Times: The Ameliorating Effect of Wisdom on the Negative Association between Adverse Life Events and Wellbeing," *Journal of Gerontology: Series B: Psychological Sciences and Social Sciences* 73, no. 8 (2018): 1374–1383.
[72] For a source of Congar's thought on the transformative action of the Holy Spirit, see Gregory the Great, *In librum primum Regum expositio* 4.4 (PL 79, 267b): "Habent ergo electi praedicatores experientiam Spiritus in se loquentis in repentina revelatione veritatis, habent in subito ardore caritatis, habent in plenitudine scientiae, habent facundissima verbi praedicatione: nam et subito instruuntur et repente fervescunt et in momento replentur et mirabili eloquii potestate ditantur."
[73] Congar, *I Believe in the Holy Spirit*, vol. 3, 219.

form communion by putting aside tendencies for isolation. A communal bond is formed as individuals come together, share their vast array of charisms, and participate in an enterprise far greater than individual tasks.[74] Each person grows toward authenticity and holiness by participating in the shared rituals and embodying the living traditions of the Body of Christ. Congar writes: "It is a common saying of the Fathers that men are begotten in belief, and that they themselves in turn beget, by speaking or teaching; in other words, in establishing through the unity of the community the spiritual or moral milieu in which we are formed according to faith."[75] In the communion between God and humanity present in the life of the Church—which is participation in the sacraments as well as service of neighbors—relationships are forged, social-engagement is enlivened, and the healing of loneliness can begin.

In conclusion, the modern crisis of social isolation is a devastating and lethal phenomenon encompassing many dimensions of human life: sociological, psychological, neuro-psychological, and spiritual. Loneliness and disengagement leave existential longings within the hearts and minds of persons, causing depression, anxiety, and the fragmentation of community. Yves Congar's ecclesiological and pneumatological theology explicates the fulfillment of humanity's deepest longings when individuals gather as a communal body realized in the ideal form of the Church. When people share their unique charisms gained through the grace of the Holy Spirit for the good of the community, a healing grace permeates into individual hearts and restores communal relationships. Congar's vision of communion and life in the Church may have idealistic notions, yet he also admits that the Church is fractured and composed of sinners. Driven by faith, Congar teaches that the grace of the Holy Spirit perfects human life, in its communal and individual dimensions. The unified life of love within the Trinity is perceivable when individuals participate together in liturgies and the sacraments and engage in compassionate service to fellow persons. These are the activities of the Church that manifest the embodiment of the Holy Spirit, the source of divine unity. When each person becomes receptive to the action of the Holy Spirit and is vivified through love as a *supra-ecclesial community*, then the Kingdom of God, the unified Body of Christ in the fullness of human life, is at hand.

---

[74] Alasdair MacIntyre discusses a very similar vision of human community and uses the term "reciprocal indebtedness." See Alasdair MacIntyre, *Dependent Rational Animals: Why Human Beings Need the Virtues* (Peru, IL: Carus, 2001), 99–146.
[75] Congar, *Tradition and Traditions*, 328.

Christopher Krall, SJ, is priest of the Society of Jesus and assistant professor in systematic theology and neuroscience at Creighton University.

Looking for Good Work: From Matthew Crawford to Pope Francis via Wittgenstein

Mark R. Ryan

EACH SEMESTER, I TEACH third year business students a course in theological ethics. Since my students' choices of majors (e.g., "accounting," "marketing," etc.) directly reference the jobs they hope to have after graduating, it has seemed fitting to make 'work' one of our topics of study. I am an Aristotelian, which means that my goal ought to be to teach about the manner in which my students' work is part of their ongoing formation with the ultimate goal, one hopes, of becoming successful moral agents—or, in Aristotelian terms, achieving excellence in goodness. However, I have often been tempted to teach work's moral significance by drawing on the studies of empirical psychology and social science. Indeed, the fact that these studies adopt and adapt concepts from Aristotelianism makes the temptation greater. For instance, a body of empirical research aims at scientifically identifying the constituent parts of "happiness." The studies in "positive psychology" typically identify "meaningful work" as a feature of the lives of those research subjects who report a higher than average (subjective) experience of well-being. The studies define "meaningful work" by such characteristics as believing one's job has "room for growth." The characteristics for study are drawn up to be explicit and quantifiable criteria so that their presence could be measured. One might imagine that becoming familiar with these studies would arm students with a set of criteria enabling them to choose among alternative employment options more likely to be satisfactory; perhaps even, using the studies' other features of happiness, help students find their way to a happier life. For instance, a job advertised as having opportunities for advancement within the firm would seem more likely to fulfill the "presence of challenge and room for growth" characteristic than another job lacking a clear path of promotion. Alternatively, a job at a company whose representatives make clear that the management style is "employee-centered" would seem promising for another characteristic of meaningful work identified by positive psychology, namely, the employee's sense of being recognized by her supervisors for her accomplishments.

So, a set of categories with a family resemblance to the Aristotelian ones of flourishing, formation, and growth are transposed into terms with which social psychologists can run their experiments. Yet I suspect this approach misleads as much as it sheds light on how to understand the moral significance of work and what students might expect from a job. It imagines the student/employee as standing outside the activity of work, coordinating features of a job that suit her preferences. The study of work in an ethics class should not leave the student with an orientation wherein work is seen as one more of life's contingent constraints through which she must find a way to maximize her own preferences. In a class such as mine, students should be pushed to see work as a potential domain for discovering and exercising distinctively human capacities. Work can involve growth that occasions joy.

The search for meaningful work faces many obstacles in the contemporary world. One set of obstacles derives from what Pope Francis calls "the technocratic paradigm." The technocratic paradigm is an important source of widespread fantasies regarding work and its meaning. It seems to account, at least in part, for the authority enjoyed by empirical studies in the academy today, for it exalts the same "outside," or technique-privileging, point of view. Pope Francis affirms work's potential to contribute to human development. He continues a tradition of Catholic reflection on work in affirming that work answers a profound human need. In chapter 3 of *Laudato Si'*, titled "The Human Roots of the Ecological Crisis," Pope Francis invokes the tradition of Catholic social thought where work is related to a theologically shaped vision of human flourishing. He begins his treatment by reminding us that "meaningful work" was a revolutionary discovery within monastic life, where Benedict of Nursia saw fit to combine prayer and spiritual reading with manual labor in community life. Thus "we need to remember," writes Francis, "that men and women have the capacity to improve their lot, to further their moral growth, and to develop their spiritual endowments. Work should be the setting for this rich personal growth, where many aspects of life enter into play: creativity, planning for the future, developing our talents, living out our values, relating to others, giving glory to God." He goes on to say, "Work is a necessity, part of the meaning of life on this earth, a path to growth, human development and personal fulfillment" (no. 128).

Pope Francis also alerts us to the widespread currency of the technocratic paradigm as a social imaginary, especially in North Atlantic societies. An "epistemology" that grows out of our increasing dependence upon, and indeed worship of, technology, the technocratic paradigm shapes not only our dealings with matter but also human beings and their social lives. Reducing intelligent activity to techniques of manipulation, the technocratic paradigm presents human life as fundamentally consisting in the manipulation of inert matter (nos. 106–109). What is more, because of its ubiquity, we can expect this paradigm to have a profound impact both on contemporary understandings and organization of work and upon the self-conceptions that drive programs of pre-professional education whereby universities prepare their students to succeed in the "work world."[1]

Again, the pressure on students to think of work as a technically manipulable constraint on their efforts to maximize personal preferences is formidable. To get them beyond this sticking point, I propose to illustrate how versions of the technocratic paradigm generate fantasies about what work is like that frustrate the potential of work to be meaningful. In this paper, therefore, my approach consists in focusing attention on our captivity to the technocratic paradigm and the confusions that arise from it. These muddles lead to our finding ourselves caught up in moral fantasy with respect to the contribution of work to the moral life. Put another way, this alternative approach would concern itself with tracing the gap that opens up between the anthropology standing behind Pope Francis' affirmation of the human value of work and the organization of work in contemporary corporate culture.

This approach of identifying the fantasies that hold us captive as regards the human meaning of work informs a teaching method and can be articulated in the following two questions. First, "How does the technocratic paradigm show up within the modern design of work and the formation to which such work necessarily subjects workers?" Second, "what connections pertain between the technocratic paradigm as an 'epistemology' and the organization of modern work?"

This fantasy involves sidestepping the centrality of Aristotelian

---

[1] Stanley Hauerwas describes the impact of this model on universities. "The incoherence of university curriculums," he writes, "reflects the university's commitment to legitimate the abstraction effected by money. For example, it is crucial that the university insure that learning be organized not to be a conversation between disciplines, but rather that disciplines be representatives of competing opposites. ... Education is now job preparation for a career in a profession. But work, whether it is done in the academy, a profession, or industry, is now designed so that the workers are separated from the effects of their work. The workers are permitted 'to think that they are working nowhere or anywhere—in their careers, or specialties, or perhaps in 'cyberspace'" (Stanley Hauerwas, "What Would a Christian University Look Like? Some Tentative Answers Inspired by Wendell Berry," in *The State of the University* [Malden, MA: Blackwell, 2007], 98–99). The quotation is from Wendell Berry, *Another Turn of the Crank* (Washington, DC: Counterpoint, 1995), 13–14.

phronesis or practical reasoning via the exaltation of a technical style of thinking which tends to strike us as more universal because more transparent. Indeed, one of my worries about the empirical approach to work is its own capacity to make such technical reason appear sufficient for the clairvoyant pursuit of good work. That is, it projects an image of good work as something already identifiable by the student, without the transformation in character that moral goods require. Thus, my treatment will keep an eye on the distinction between knowledge understood as *techne* and *phronesis*.

MATTHEW CRAWFORD ON WORK

To display the connections I seek to make visible, clarifying the role of work in the moral life, I turn to a narrative of one person's experience as an employee. This employee, whose name is Matthew Crawford, describes one miserable experience in a job as a stage in his own journey to find work that is meaningful. Crawford is a writer and mechanic specializing in vintage motorcycles, living in Richmond, Virginia. Having worked with his hands in various trades throughout high school, he went on to gain college as well as advanced degrees. These led him to the kinds of jobs often referred to as "knowledge work," such as writing position papers at a think tank in Washington, DC. In time Crawford grew more skeptical about the correlation between such jobs and the exercise of human intelligence.

Before launching into this narrative, it is important to note that running through Crawford's book-length exploration of the moral significance of work, *Shop Class as Soulcraft*, is the assumption that good work answers to a profound human aspiration.[2] In other words, he shares Pope Francis's vision of work as "a path to growth, human development and personal fulfillment" (no. 128). Indeed, Crawford's story of miserable work makes sense only when seen against the background of deep personal longing for work that fulfills.

Crawford had high hopes when he was hired to write abstracts for Information Access Company in Silicon Valley, yet those hopes were soon deflated by his experience on the job. The character of the fantasy gripping the executives who first envisioned this futile and demeaning form of work is well disclosed by Crawford himself. So, one might ask, what further value could my analysis have to contribute? My modest hope is that by re-examining Crawford's account in terms at home in the work of Wittgenstein—terms Crawford does not use in his own analysis—some fresh light will be thrown on the example. In other words, what I offer is a Wittgensteinian reading of Crawford's experience, using concepts borrowed from the great philosopher such

---

[2] Matthew Crawford, *Shop Class as Soulcraft: An Inquiry into the Value of Work* (New York: Penguin, 2009).

as "language game," "method of projection," and "form of life."[3] Concepts such as these, forming part of Wittgenstein's method of doing philosophy, enable us to see and name fantasies that confuse our thinking about work and ultimately frustrate our practical pursuit of it. By so doing, these concepts automatically place us back on "the rough ground" of *phronesis*, or the discernment of "how to go on" satisfactorily in the circumstances of life as well as work.[4]

At the same time, Crawford's experience analyzed through Wittgenstein provides a specific illustration of Pope Francis's technocratic paradigm which I believe adds clarity to his claim that it operates as an "epistemology." Again, the technocratic paradigm has become the implicit horizon for our engagement not only with the material world but also the social one. Crawford's story, read through Wittgenstein, helps us spot how such a background gives rise to actions that reflect the blindness in the paradigm of which Francis warns.

WITTGENSTEIN AND LANGUAGE GAMES: "I'LL TEACH YOU DIFFERENCES"

A few years ago, I wrote an article included in an issue of an established journal of business ethics published by the international group Springer. In the last stages of its preparation, I left the final editing to Springer's team, telling myself they knew best how citations and so forth were to look to meet their standards. When I saw the text in print, I was unhappily surprised to see that the editors had made changes to the structure of certain sentences. For instance, they had inserted commas in a few places where I had opted not to use commas. While their choice to insert these commas made sense in light of a rudimentary understanding of general grammatical rules (or, how these are typically taught), these specific applications overruled deliberate choices on my part to forgo the use of commas. In trying to improve the copy through the application of grammatical rules, the editors had instead introduced imprecision in the phrasing, so that the reader would have to push through to get the point. What is more, the decision not to place commas in these places could be called a product of my aesthetic judgment as a writer trying to express a point in fitting form. The editors, for whom English may not even have been a first

---

[3] Regarding Wittgenstein's use of the term "language game," see Ludwig Wittgenstein, *Philosophical Investigations*, trans. G. E. M. Anscombe (New York: Macmillan, 1953), no. 23. Discussions of a "method of projection" can be found in Ludwig Wittgenstein, *Tractatus Logico-Philosophicus*, trans. C. K. Ogden (London: Routledge, [1921] 1992), 3.11–3.12, 4.0141. For "form of life" (German, *Lebensform*), see Wittgenstein, *Philosophical Investigations* nos. 19, 23, 241.
[4] Wittgenstein, *Philosophical Investigations*, no. 107.

language, were engaged in a process of rule-following much like following a set of assembly instructions, trying to make sentences as one might put together a piece of IKEA furniture. To use Wittgenstein's terms, two distinct language games had collided.

Wittgenstein told associates that among the titles he considered for *Philosophical Investigations*, the great work of his later period, was "I'll teach you differences."[5] Wittgenstein developed the notion of language games in his later period as a means of drawing his readers' attention back to the most fundamental character of our life with language. In his earlier masterpiece, the *Tractatus Logico-Philosophicus*, Wittgenstein had endeavored to lay out *the* structure of logical form, such that language and reality can hang together.[6] In the process, he laid down—or thought he had—the rules to which all sentences *must* conform if they are to succeed in making sense; all other constructions he dubbed "nonsense." For the early Wittgenstein, logical "form" names the intermediary that relates language to the world, a kind of condition of possibility for language to make meaningful reference to things, thus making it possible for us to share a common reality.[7]

The concept of logical form in the *Tractatus* is accompanied by that of "method of projection,"[8] according to which a form of words can be meaningfully joined to its bit of reality.[9] In his later work, Wittgenstein shows us how signs function in human life, tying together words/signs and behavior by exploring "language games." The basic structure of language games is that of representing one object (or "fact") in another form (description), or recognizing *this* as *that*. In its simplest form, one may think of language making a drawing ("picture") of an object. This picture might be found in the service of two agents engaged in some activity together, part of which involves using the picture in place of the object with the aim of getting each other to do something with the object in question (e.g., hand it back and forth). Ostensive definition, the teaching of words by pointing at the object to which they are meant to refer, is both a language game itself and preparation for participation in further games.[10]

---

[5] Ray Monk, *Ludwig Wittgenstein: The Duty of Genius* (New York: Free Press, 1990), 536–537.

[6] For a detailed and clear account of the transformation of Wittgenstein's use of the word "form" from the earlier to the later period, see Brad Kallenberg, *Ethics as Grammar: Changing the Postmodern Subject (*Notre Dame, IN: University of Notre Dame Press, 2001*)*, 83–112.

[7] Kallenberg, *Ethics as Grammar*, 84–87.

[8] See note 6 above.

[9] Ludwig Wittgenstein, *Notebooks 1914–1916*, 2nd ed. (Chicago: University of Chicago Press, 1984), 30(e).

[10] Wittgenstein, *Philosophical Investigations*, nos. 1–8, 23.

Similarly, writing an abstract of an academic journal article is a language game (*this* is *that*). The abstract is to be a representation (portrait) of the original. The writer is to model the original article in the form of a short precis of, say, 200 words. *This* (i.e., the 200-word summary) is to stand in for *that* (i.e., the 12,000-word article). One may think here of the relationship of a trail map to a long hike to be taken. The similarity (or shared "form") between the two lies in the fact that the map intends to offer the hiker an overview of the terrain (its difficulty, etc.) that she will come to know in detail when she sets off on the hike. In the same way, the abstract is to be used by the reader as though offering a faithful "map" of what she would survey in detail were she to read the entire article.

While the *Tractatus* implied that the form shared between linguistic description and "fact," between language and world, was something unitary—and thus, that the capacity to use language was one-dimensional—the later Wittgenstein comes to see "form" differently. Wittgenstein came to see that "methods of projection," the joining of language to the world of facts, is carried out in innumerable ways in human life. The whole point of the turn to language games as a method was to help students attend to such variety, or learn to see differences.

Writing an abstract for an academic article may be viewed as a "language game." In the early 1990s, shortly after being awarded an MA in Philosophy from the University of Chicago, Crawford landed his first job as a "knowledge worker."[11] During his teens and early adulthood, much of his work experience had been in manual trades such as electric and mechanics. He was now given articles published in scholarly journals to read for which he had to write abstracts. These abstracts were to be included in the company's indexing services and marketed to libraries with the idea that they would be used by students and scholars for their own research projects.

Crawford's abstracting writing work at Information Access Company (IAC) is a kind of parable of the failure to attend to differences of language games, as well as the consequences of such failure. The company began as an indexer of popular magazines, before branching out to the arena of management journals and ultimately to a variety of academic journals. Somewhere along the line it was determined that including abstracts was necessary to secure the "value-added" nature of its product. The procedure for writing an abstract seems to have been minted in the stage of management journals. Writing an adequate abstract for the typical management journal article turns out to conform to a predictable, even

---

[11] Crawford, *Shop Class as Soulcraft*, 126–128.

"mechanical," procedure. Such articles, structured by bullet points, tend to introduce a new idea every fifth bullet point. To write an abstract one need only string together every fifth bullet point. Yet the company was still evolving. As Crawford writes, "through a series of mergers and acquisitions, it now found itself offering not just indexes but also abstracts (that is, summaries), and of a very different kind of material: scholarly works in the physical and biological sciences, humanities, social sciences, and law."[12]

The problem is that the step from management journals to scholarly works in these other disciplines did not imply a superficial change for the work of the abstractor (i.e., a change in style, quantity), but a radical one, shifting the very character of the task of producing an abstract. Those calling the shots at the company were unable to detect the nature of these new demands placed on those producing their product.[13]

Techne

Wittgenstein believed that many of the (unnecessary) problems that preoccupied his fellow philosophers stemmed from being duped by appearances of similarity in our language. We fail to notice the diversity of the ways we join word and world (*this* is *that*) in our language, because the deep "grammar" of our language games does not readily show itself to us. Wittgenstein's method of language games, beginning with the most basic or primitive kinds of communication, was a means of training our attention on this grammar where we discover that meaning is bound up with use. In this mode of attentiveness, he is able to teach us differences, that is, show us the dissimilarities of language games we tacitly acknowledge in everyday life but find hard to see when we think theoretically.

In our times, the tendency to assimilate our uses of words to just one pattern takes a particular shape. If one picture is to serve for all linguistic practices, that picture is of language as a quasi-scientific "technique," a process in which explicit rules do the guiding as one works step by step toward the desired outcome (i.e., communicating a piece of information, building pre-fab furniture, or writing an

---

[12] Matthew Crawford, "The Case for Working with Your Hands," *New York Times*, May 21, 2009, www.nytimes.com/2009/05/24/magazine/24labor-t.html.

[13] Although it is not an insight for which I am beholden to Wittgenstein, but rather Alasdair MacIntyre, I further note how this short narrative history of IAC's evolution as a company also serves to make visible the key differences to which IAC's chiefs seem to have been blind. Narrative is also a form capable of helping us to see differences, then. Perhaps, if those calling the shots at IAC had made a habit of rehearsing their history, some of the complications to arise might have been foreseen. See Alasdair MacIntyre, *After Virtue: A Study in Moral Theory* (Notre Dame, IN: University of Notre Dame Press, 1984).

abstract). Wittgenstein would say that we are "captivated by [this] picture."[14]

At IAC, Crawford began his abstract writing with a quota of 15 articles a day. Among the articles he was given to read he notes one written by a classical philologist wherein "practically every other word was Greek."[15] Another, written by an evolutionary biologist, was in English of so rare a form it may as well have been a foreign tongue. About the experience, he remarks: "I was always sleepy while at work, and I think this exhaustion was because I felt trapped in a contradiction: the fast pace demanded complete focus on the task, yet that pace also made any real concentration impossible."[16]

Whether or not his supervisors fully appreciated the contradiction here described, they were clearly confident it would be resolved by the training they offered to abstract writers in which they would be given a *method* for writing abstracts. As the brief company history in the previous section pointed out, the method in question seems to have been the very one laid down in the management journal stage of the company, which by this time has become a paradigm for articles in any and all disciplines. It is modeled on the kind of syntactical procedure we might associate with computer programming. We might imagine it thus: "Identify each new idea, typically separated by five paragraphs from the previous one; String resultant sentences together in paragraph form; Revise each of the author's sentences by changing active voice to passive; Add required punctuation...." Thus, this "solution" shows that those responsible for the design of Crawford's job were captivated by the picture of language as technique.[17]

The paradigm status of this picture is strongly affirmed in Pope Francis' encyclical *Laudato Si'*. There the pope describes the morphing of technology into an "epistemological paradigm" that elevates as ideal a popular image of scientific technique. He writes: "This paradigm exalts the concept of a subject who, using logical and rational procedures, progressively approaches and gains control over an external object. This subject makes every effort to establish the scientific and experimental method, which in itself is already a technique of possession, mastery, and transformation" (no. 106). Furthermore, as a "technocratic *paradigm*," this picture has insinuated itself into several dimensions of human life. "The technocratic

---

[14] Wittgenstein, *Philosophical Investigations*, no. 115.
[15] Crawford, "The Case for Working with Your Hands."
[16] Crawford, "The Case for Working with Your Hands."
[17] Naturally, as Matthew Whelan has pointed out to me, the path that led to this so-called solution began with a business model that demands the maximization of profits. The demand for speed that such a model requires makes the reduction of complex tasks to a method very attractive.

paradigm," he continues, "also tends to dominate economic and political life." What is more, we have become highly dependent on it. According to Francis, "The technological paradigm has become so dominant that it would be difficult to do without its resources and even more difficult to utilize them without being dominated by their internal logic" (no. 108). As the pope here suggests, technology as a conceptual framework has become so ubiquitous in our times that we have come to think of having a self as consisting in the exercise of control over an inert, formless world of matter.[18]

Phronesis

Taking us back to language games, beginning with the most elementary or "primitive," Wittgenstein also drew our attention to how language is learned, namely, at the level of bodily habit.[19] To learn a language is to be initiated into a form of behavior that predates one's own entry on the scene; it is to enter into a particular, socially established way of life. For instance, a child learns the meaning of the word "chair" by climbing into one as he strives to conquer the heights of the living room. To have learned a language amounts to a kind of mastery of these particular ways of negotiating the world into which one was born. One can be called fluent in the language insofar as one is able to continue navigating one's life, that is, with no more than the usual physical and social scrapes characteristic of human life. Indeed, to be able, through one's words and actions, to make oneself intelligible to others—and avoid debilitating collisions with reality—requires both careful observation and imitation of those around you and creative application of past lessons to new circumstances. In ethics, we might follow Aristotle in designating the result of this inculcation of tacit knowledge for managing one's world with the term *phronesis*.[20]

Above I described the activity of abstract writing as an example of a language game, the term is used by Wittgenstein to point out the different patterns of use characteristic of our life with words. In Wittgenstein's language games, we may glimpse the key role of *phronesis* in human forms of life. To have mastered a language game is to have learned how to go on within one of these patterns of communicative behavior. The proof of learning is the ability not

---

[18] For a complementary account of the modern identity, see Charles Taylor, *Sources of the Self: The Making of the Modern Identity* (Cambridge: Cambridge University Press, 1989), especially 143–176.
[19] Ludwig Wittgenstein, *On Certainty*, trans. Denis Paul and G. E. M. Anscombe (New York: Harper and Row, [1969] 1972), no. 476.
[20] Aristotle, *Nichomachean Ethics*, trans. Martin Ostwald (London: Pearson, 1999), Book VI.

merely to imitate, but to extend the rules of the game into new contexts. Having seen and comprehended how the game is played, one is able to follow the directive: "Now, do the same!" It is, if I may return to a phrase from the *Tractatus*, to have acquired skill in a particular "method of projection."[21] To have mastered that skill is to be capable of seeing the kinds of connections assumed in the language game ("this" is "that") and of making similar connections on one's own.

Writing an abstract can rightfully be called a language game insofar as it involves a method of projection from the original article to a neat summary thereof—*this* is *that*. The question is whether the same language game is being played when one is writing an abstract for a) a management journal article, b) an article in classical philology, and c) an article in genetics. To see whether these language games involve the same method of projection, one simply asks whether the skill required to "go on" or "do the same" is the same in each case. We might imagine that during Crawford's training he successfully abstracted several management articles. Did this achievement enable him to go on, "do the same," when given an article in classical philology? As it turned out, he was not. He lacked the skill or fluency needed to play *this* language game (i.e., the one required to write an abstract of the article in classical philology). In this case the missing skill seems easy to identify. If you do not read Greek, you will have little comprehension of an article in which every other word is Greek! To illustrate the incommensurability, even when the language remains English, Crawford offers a further example, this one from Nature Genetics, another source of articles he was asked to work on. The following example comes from the Letters section of that journal, at the time of his writing about his experience at IAC (2007):

> We show that miR-214 is expressed during early segmentation stages in somites in that varying its expression alters the expressions of genes regulated by Hedgehog signaling. Inhibition of MAR-214 results in reduction or loss of slow-muscle cell types. We show that su(fu) mRNA, encoding a negative regulator of Hedgehog signaling, is targeted by miR-214.[22]

As this example shows, fluency in a language game is not reducible to knowing what a word means in the sense of a dictionary definition. Fluency in a discipline like genetics can only be gained through long years of practice under the bodily presence of a mentor. Just like, we may say, when a child first enters into language through being in a

---

[21] See note 5 above.
[22] Crawford, *Shop Class as Soulcraft*, 132.

home with older persons present. Earlier we approached the problem by asking whether writing an abstract for the three articles involved playing the same language game—whether, that is, it involved the same skill. Now we are in a position to see that this question is equivalent to the question of whether the fluency required for handling each of the articles is found in the same person, where "person" names the experience and training unique to each human being's biography.[23] In the design of this job, what the company leaders believed could be bypassed was precisely the mastery in a language game of the seasoned practitioner. The later Wittgenstein saw language less and less as something to be studied apart from language users. Ultimately, the skills of language use are inseparable from the people who deploy them.[24]

While Wittgenstein's language games reveal *phronesis* to be at the heart of our way of life, the technocratic paradigm shoulders out *phronesis* in favor of its own, purportedly supreme, language game. At IAC, once trained in their abstract writing "method," it is assumed that Crawford and his coworkers will be able to go on doing the same for the various examples of writing they are given. Of course this assumes that as the abstract writer plows forward, she will simply flatten the landscape before her, reducing all articles to some fundamental commonalities. As Crawford saw, this method presupposed that to write an abstract of an article does not require that one understand it. That is, one does not need to enter into the thought-world of the author in order to represent her reasoning. Ironically, it is supposed that close attention to the article itself would distract one from the method, which is presumed to be the important thing. Thus the fluency characteristic of the writer of the article, and expressed *in* the article, does not touch the abstract writer as she carries out her task. *Techne* is said to be a method of a different order from such skill. In the Pope's words, it stands apart from the world, and dominates it. In Wittgenstein's terms, this language game sits enthroned above all subcultural fluencies and is able to dominate them. So elevated, *techne* appears universal.

---

[23] For a deeper treatment of the role of "biography" as part of the human form of life, see Herbert McCabe, *Law, Love, and Language* (New York: Continuum, 2003).
[24] Kallenberg, *Ethics as Grammar*, 104–107. We may think here of how the very body of a professional pianist differs from that of a professional gymnast, their training over time having inculcated different habits into them. This is not to say there will not be overlap in these habits, or that their lives as human beings do not need certain virtues if they are to flourish.

FORM OF LIFE

A final Wittgensteinian term of art that can be usefully brought to bear on Crawford's experience at IAC is "form of life," a phrase we have already seen. The failures mentioned above culminate in the failure to design work in sync with the human form of life. The human form of life belongs to our nature as embodied reasoners, or linguistic animals if you prefer. We are inescapably bodies living together in a shared world determined by our language, when "language" is conceived broadly as Wittgenstein does to encompass non-verbal forms of communication such as gesture, painting, music, etc. As theologian Brad Kallenberg has shown, the word "form" undergoes a transformation from the early to the later Wittgenstein.[25] In the *Tractatus*, form signified the logical space in which objects, considered as simple entities, existed. This implied that language must somehow picture an object in its relation to a surrounding world. Form thus makes possible a world of "facts," understood as logically possible combinations of objects representable by language.[26] By the time of the *Philosophical Investigations*, form had come to refer to the myriad ways we communicate or live together or our "form of life." Wittgenstein's adoption of the term form of life in his later work thus shows his increasing acceptance of the richly varied social life of human beings.[27]

Put differently, in retrospect, Wittgenstein's adoption of the notion of form of life can be seen as his moving past a problematic outgrowth of his approach in the *Tractatus*: the bifurcation of language (i.e., what he would come to see as skill in speech, learned through the body, but once focused on "propositions") and world (i.e., what he formerly envisioned as real or imagined "states of affairs" and would eventually become for him the social form of life we inhabit).[28] The way of seeing that arises from such habitual bifurcation, where the technician or philosopher stands in the gap devising means for fitting language to world, also captivates the designers of Crawford's work at IAC.

---

[25] Kallenberg, *Ethics as Grammar*, 83–112.
[26] Kallenberg sums up that, for the Wittgenstein of the *Tractatus*, "form is the a priori structure of the world" (Kallenberg, *Ethics as Grammar*, 85). See Wittgenstein, *Tractatus Logico-Philosophicus*, 2.014, 2.0141.
[27] Kallenberg shows the gradual nature of the change in Wittgenstein's understanding of form, pointing to a middle period characterized by Wittgenstein's critical encounter with Sir James George Frazer's *The Golden Bough*, and the positive influences of Johann W. von Goethe and Oswald Spengler (Kallenberg, *Ethics as Grammar*, 96–100). For a helpful description of Wittgenstein's mature period, see Kallenberg, *Ethics as Grammar*, 101–112.
[28] For example, Kallenberg points out: "Once Wittgenstein undertook to explain the mechanism of language by means of the picture theory, he had trouble preventing himself from speaking about language as one thing and the world as another" (Kallenberg, *Ethics as Grammar*, 89).

Crawford's work had been designed according to a kind of ideal language, one first abstracted from the form of life that was its natural surroundings and then by an act of will transported elsewhere. This process, we may say, exemplifies Pope Francis's technocratic paradigm as it begins in economics and gradually usurps politics and other institutions of human life (*Laudato Si'*, no. 108).

We noted above in our discussion of the language game we play with the word "chair" that such games involve bodily engagement with our environments. We first learn what chairs are by climbing into them. Through climbing, the one-year-old hopes to overcome the obstacle called "up," or perhaps intends nearness to the adults. Having surmounted the prior physical challenges, an older child might climb a chair as a means of getting a glimpse of a card game, yet another world to be conquered. When in high school one presumably learns the importance of sitting erect—one's own back flush against the back of one's chair—throughout dinner with one's new girlfriend's parents, who are deciding whether you are a trustworthy date for their daughter. These examples show that language games are interwoven with ways of communicating bodily with other human bodies in a shared world.

Arguably, the early Wittgenstein held a "picture theory" of language, claiming that language was a means of representing objects which existed, in some sense, "over there," that is, outside of language itself.[29] This framework, according to which a gap separates language from the world, naturally gave rise to the question of just how language does this. That is, how can we be sure that this bit of language really does correspond to that bit of reality? As the term was applied in the early work, the question concerned how language and world shared a "form."

One unhappy consequence of this way of framing the problem is that it tempts philosophers to re-make spoken language into something ideal so that it fits the abstract logic that is meant to guarantee the fit between language and world. Rather than attending to our actual linguistic behavior, the philosopher strains to make practice conform to the ideal. But if language and world are not separable, the need to account for how language fits the world evaporates. Where does this leave the philosopher?

In his later work, as previously noted, Wittgenstein acknowledges that the ways our language construes the world are multiple and irreducible, and gives up on the *Tractatus*'s aspiration to present *the* way in which language and world must correlate. Language and world are internally related, and so there is no need for attempts to explain

---

[29] Kallenberg, *Ethics as Grammar*, 88; Ludwig Wittgenstein, *Tractatus Logico-Philosophicus*, 2.223.

how they fit together.[30] Following from this, Wittgenstein turns from "language" *per se* to language as used by a community of speakers.[31] "Form" for him ceases to refer to a logical structure supposedly underlying both language and world and comes to signify "forms of life" found in human communities.[32] He therefore turns his attention away from the effort to construct a new, ideal language—now seen as the philosopher's peculiar "temptation"—and turns toward the language we already have. Ordinary language, words in their customary uses, become both the object and the instrument within Wittgenstein's method of doing philosophy. The philosopher, moreover, steps out of the gap supposed to have existed between language and world and into the "hurly burly" of our everyday life with words.[33]

For our purposes, in what follows, there are two crucial characteristics of what Wittgenstein calls our form of life. First this form of life is social, meaning that we flourish or wilt depending on the quality of the relationships within which we subsist. Second, our linguistic skill—that by which we accomplish the tasks necessary to sustain those relationships that are a given within our form of life—involves our brains and bodies being in tune with each other. In other words, linguistic fluency is largely a matter of tacit knowledge; it is a kind of knowing-how that rarely reaches the heights of explicit formulation.[34]

The human form of life makes relationships, and their good order, primary. One theologian has called justice "the virtue of togetherness."[35] Yet Crawford recounts how the key relationships were corrupted as a consequence of the organization of his job at IAC. These relationships were constitutive of the business as a network of persons. They include: 1) the relationship between the laborer (i.e., the

---

[30] Kallenberg, *Ethics as Grammar*, 189–90.
[31] Kallenberg takes on the question of discovering a unity underlying Wittgenstein's earlier and later writing by proposing that such unity has a narrative form. He traces this story like thread by detailing how the human subject "migrates" from the periphery to the center of Wittgenstein's focus as he arrives at his later philosophy (Kallenberg, *Ethics as Grammar*, 11–47).
[32] Kallenberg, *Ethics as Grammar*, 103.
[33] Ludwig Wittgenstein, *Philosophical Grammar*, trans. Anthony Kenny (Berkeley: University of California Press, 1974), no. 29.
[34] Brad Kallenberg, *By Design: Ethics, Theology, and the Practice of Engineering* (Eugene, OR: Cascade, 2013), 150–158. Kallenberg there discusses the work of neuroscientist Antonio Damasio. See Antonio Damasio, *Descartes' Error: Emotion, Reason, and the Human Brain* (New York: Penguin, 1994).
[35] John R. Donahue, SJ, "Biblical Perspectives on Justice," in *The Faith That Does Justice: Examining the Christian Sources of Social Change*, ed. John C. Haughey (New York: Paulist, 1977). Quoted in Paul Wadell, *Happiness and the Christian Moral Life* (New York: Rowman and Littlefield, 2008), 222.

abstract writer) and the customer or end user of the abstract, such as a scholar pursuing her own research in a related field; (2) the relationship between the abstract writer and the original authors; and (3) the laborer's relationship with himself, or the laborer's sense of dignity, which is impacted by her awareness of the quality of work she performs. What is more, collateral damage ensues upon the quality of relationships within the organization, such as those among the abstract writers and between them and their supervisors.[36]

First, in a healthy economic arrangement the supplier of a good or service and his customer share a common interest in a quality product.[37] From the supplier's side, this helps ensure a satisfied customer, more likely to return in the future. The customer desires something truly helpful for her own needs or projects. Digging deeper, Crawford notes that his own desire for knowledge, which might have been fulfilled in the work of reading and writing abstracts, aligns with the customer's presumed desire for knowledge which animates her own research activities. Both of these shared goods are undermined when poor workmanship issues in a product of poor quality. Just as Crawford's abstract writing failed to engage him in the author's thought world, so the shoddy abstract provides no genuine glimpse of this world to the end user.

Turning to the abstract writer's relationship with the author, Crawford again observes that his own desire to know might have found its mirror image in the author's desire to be known, or to share what she has learned.[38] Yet the circumstance of a quota of 28 articles per day made it impossible for Crawford to expend the time and energy necessary to read comprehendingly. He was therefore plagued by the feeling he was not doing justice to the authors.[39]

Finally, Crawford's work was so structured that he was incapable of taking pride in it, making it hard to be within his own skin at work. His relationship with himself was fractured because he could not observe in his performance an authentic exercise of his own skill. As noted above, Crawford recalled the soporific effect of his work:

> This exhaustion is surely tied to the fact that I felt trapped in a contradiction. The fast pace demanded absorption in the task, but that pace also precluded absorption, and had the effect of estranging me from my own doings. Or rather, I *tried* to absent myself, the better to meet my quota, but the writing of an abstract, unlike pulling of levers on an assembly line, cannot be done mindlessly. The material I was

---

[36] Crawford notes for example that because of the futility they perceived in their work, the social life of fellow workers tilted toward fantasy and escapism.
[37] Crawford, *Shop Class as Soulcraft*, 136.
[38] Crawford, *Shop Class as Soulcraft*, 136.
[39] Crawford, *Shop Class as Soulcraft*, 134.

given was too demanding, and what it demanded was to be given its due ... my efforts to read, comprehend, and write abstracts of 28 academic journal articles per day required me to actively suppress my own ability to think.[40]

Sadly, as he recounts, this alienation from himself gradually eats away at his attunement to the needs of the customer and the author. It is difficult to remain committed to one's customer as worthy of honor while serving them up a piece of junk.

That *phronesis* or knowing-how is characteristic of our form of life is a theme that runs throughout Crawford's book. Throughout *Shop Class as Soulcraft*, Crawford elucidates the claim that manual work satisfies a deep human need. It does so in part because it involves the mind's focused engagement with the messy, often recalcitrant material world. The objective standards discovered in such work provides a basis for just human relationships.[41] He finds that so-called "knowledge work" often ironically lacks the same requirement for concentrated intelligence. Indeed, the very labeling of certain jobs "knowledge work" involves mistaking (mis-taking) a certain technical or abstract sort of cognition for the whole of human intelligence.[42]

It is then no accident that this mentality issues in designing work in which human intelligence is neither challenged nor developed. In the case of Crawford's abstract writing, the opportunities for *phronesis* would have run parallel to the mental activity of the authors in creating the articles. The world of thought found in the article is a language game whose mastery stems from the author's many years of bodily training in field, lab, and lecture hall, under the supervision of

---

[40] Crawford, *Shop Class as Soulcraft*, 133–134.
[41] Crawford, *Shop Class as Soulcraft*, 65–68.
[42] Crawford, "The Case for Working with Your Hands." Furthermore, Wendell Berry has written about intelligence in a way reminiscent of both Crawford and Pope Francis. For Berry, the grand story of technology, what he in one place calls "technological determinism," leads to the separation of human intelligence from place. This results in human disorientation or confusion, reflected in our language. A natural consequence is tyranny over places and the world as such. "The technological determinists have tyrannical attitudes, and speak tyrannese, at least partly because their assumptions cannot produce a moral or a responsible definition of the human place in creation. Because they assume that the human place is any place, they are necessarily confused about where they belong. Lacking a place that would provide an intimate field of action, intelligence becomes tyrannical. It fails to perform the attention to local differences required for intelligent action. In contrast, in any culture that could be called healthy or sane we find a much richer, larger concept of intelligence. ... And we find that the human mind, in such a culture, is invariably strongly *placed*, in reference to other minds in the community and in cultural memory and tradition, and in reference to earthly localities and landmarks" (Wendell Berry, "Standing by Words," in *Standing by Words* [Berkeley, CA: Counterpoint, 1983], 57–58).

a past mentor. Similarly, for Crawford to enter into this thought world even as an informed spectator would require time, effort, and imagination. Yet the technocratic paradigm employed in designing Crawford's job suppresses the reality of training. In allowing a simple procedure to take the place of attention and imagination, it creates deadening forms of work. In short, a distorted vision of our form of life is created as the role of *phronesis* is displaced by overreaching *techne*.

CONCLUSION

A reasonable aim of a course on the ethics of work might be to identify and explore the chasm between the claim of Catholic tradition that work has human value and the deformed (and deforming) jobs too often encountered in the contemporary work world. This will require of the teacher some awareness of how academic knowledges fund a degraded and degrading work world.[43]

I have argued that Pope Francis's "technocratic paradigm" helps us understand the nature of the intrinsically frustrating, if not morally injurious, kinds of jobs on offer in today's work world. Furthermore, Francis's reiteration of the meaningfulness of work presumes the principle of the common good and its assumption that human beings subsist within social relations upon whose good ordering each member's happiness depends. Crawford's experience illustrates that poorly conceived work entails degradation of human relationships.

Moreover, I have used Wittgenstein to spell out just how the technocratic paradigm operates in the deformation of the work world. Crawford's experience at IAC, elucidated using Wittgenstein, allows us to see how being beholden to the technocratic paradigm occludes precisely those differences constituted by skilled, tacit knowing. Correlatively, Wittgenstein and Crawford show us that resisting the technocratic paradigm requires learning to see differences. Crawford

---

[43] In a complementary discussion, Wendell Berry points out the tendency of the disciplines of the modern university toward greater and greater abstraction of knowledge from local communities. Another name for this abstraction is "specialization." The specialist's abstract knowledge serves states and large corporations through its pretensions to universality. Knowledges fitting for "anywhere" accompany organizations understanding themselves to be from "nowhere," that is as having no local place of residence. As Berry puts it, correlative to the trajectory of abstraction, such knowledge progressively prescinds from its own accountability to the human localities that spawned them. In a way highly reminiscent of Wittgenstein's comment that the speech of academic philosophy often represents "words on holiday," Berry points out that these sciences generate habits of speech wherein words are severed from communities of speakers or, in Wittgenstein's terms, "forms of life" (Berry, "Standing by Words," 24–63). For a helpful account of how Berry's insights might be applied to the project of envisioning an authentically Christian university, see Hauerwas, *The State of the University*, 92–107.

himself relied upon his upbringing in the trades, a training based on responsive engagement to material realities independent of one's will, to name the "contradictions of the cubicle."[44] He returns to the shop as a motorcycle repairman, and finds there a community of practitioners with shared moral standards. Furthermore, I suggest seeing Pope Francis's own alternative to the technocratic paradigm, namely "integral ecology" as his way of "seeing differences" and thus showing a way forward to a more human way of life. Integral ecology in *Laudato Si'* is in part a way of seeing the world. Rooted in the "gaze of Jesus" (II.VII), this vision presumes the doctrine of the Trinity (no. 240), and is expressed in the phrase repeated throughout the document, "everything is connected." The vision of integral ecology, moreover, becomes a moral principle as the awareness of solidarity between human societies and nature generates a new frame for human responsibility.[45]

Finally, preparing students for the ethical task of discovering meaningful work will not likely be served very far by providing them a set of empirically verifiable criteria ("opportunities for advancement," etc.). Students simply will not know what to do with such a list, though they may deceive themselves into thinking the procedure for its use is obvious. The deception is in the idea that meaning will be discovered if we simply get the criteria to line up within our jobs. Indeed, if we want to help our students name the kind of technocratic fantasy behind Crawford's work at IAC, our best resource may be narratives like his, taught with some Wittgensteinian prodding. Ⓜ

Mark Ryan received his PhD in Religious Ethics at the University of Virginia (2006). He has been nurtured in his work by the thought of Alasdair MacIntyre, Stanley Hauerwas, and Ludwig Wittgenstein. He has been teaching moral theology and business ethics as a Lecturer at the University of Dayton since 2014 and serves as a member of the Catholic and Marianist Identity Committee of the School of Business Administration at the University of Dayton.

---

[44] Crawford, *Shop Class as Soulcraft*, 126 (chapter title).
[45] Vincent J. Miller, "Integral Ecology: Francis's Spiritual and Moral Vision of Interconnectedness," in *The Theological and Ecological Vision of Laudato Si': Everything Is Connected*, ed. Vincent J. Miller (London: Bloomsbury, 2017).

www.ingramcontent.com/pod-product-compliance
Lightning Source LLC
Chambersburg PA
CBHW06202522042
43662CB00010B/1481